my
JOY COMES
— *in the* —
MORNING

Finding Hope and Spiritual Healing
from Sexual Assault and Child Sexual Abuse

CHANTEL D. PLAUTZ

Publishing Services provided by Paper Raven Books
Printed in the United States of America
First Printing, 2020

Paperback ISBN = 978-1-7356209-0-9
Hardback ISBN = 978-1-7356209-1-6

DEDICATION

To the voiceless: I hear you.

TABLE OF CONTENTS

ACKNOWLEDGMENTS

I believe, by the grace of God, this book was in existence before I physically came into being. Just as God was, and I was—it was. I also believe that God has a bigger plan, and that none of this really has anything to do with me. If you can follow that divine logic, you can also understand what I mean when I say that I have always felt something "BIG" was coming. I just did not always know what "it" was exactly. But, one thing I do know is that when the difficulties of life find us and send us reeling, the Lord always makes a way forward, and He reminds us that we are not alone in our suffering.

God's Word tells us that we are to "[16] Rejoice always, [17] pray continually, [18] give thanks in all circumstances; for this is God's will for [us] in Christ Jesus." (1 Thessalonians 5:16–18) Well, I do. Today, I am able to rejoice, pray, and give thanks and praise to God from whom all blessings flow.

———·————●————·———

To my Triune God—Father, Son, Holy Spirit—all of whom is One God, and all of whom have walked with me on this journey, collectively and individually:

I am thankful for the entire journey—that which has passed and that which is yet to come. I count it all joy! I rejoice in the magnificent work You have done in and through me, Lord. I treasure my prayer time with You, each day.

Father God, I know You created me with and for a purpose; You know the plans You have for me. You are love, and You love me. You have taught me how to love myself. You are my Abba Father. I thank You.

Jesus, You are my Lord and Savior. Thank You for the many blessings I have because of Your sacrifice on the cross. Because of You, I am holy, righteous, and redeemed. You have made it possible for me to heal, overcome, and receive deliverance from the past. I thank You, Lord Jesus.

Holy Spirit, Your Presence fills my body, soul, and spirit. You offer counsel, grant wisdom and discernment, and fill me with Father's gifts, fruit, and Spirit. You guide my steps and show me the way in which I am to go. You are my Comforter. And, I thank You, Holy Spirit.

LORD God, thank You for the blessing it is to serve You, each and every day. You are my God, and I praise You.

To the members of my Trusted Care Circle:

Each of you walked with me during a very dark and difficult time in my life, offering support, guidance, and loving care. It gives me great joy to know you. You spoke truth into me when I needed to hear it: I am treasured and loved—deeply; I am not alone in my suffering—ever; I am worthy of healing—always. You held my hand and hugged me when I needed reassurance. Thank you for your prayers, for standing with and for me throughout, for your "silent wisdom," and for taking this healing journey with me. I appreciate and love all of you beyond measure. "I thank my God every time I remember you." (Philippians 1:3)

To my Dream Mother:

God certainly knew what He was doing when He purposed for our paths to cross those many years ago. We have shared laughter and tears, good times and trials. When I needed you, you took me in—into your life, into your home, into your heart. I can't imagine my life without you in it, and I'm thankful to the Lord for creating you. Through you, I have seen and received selfless love, unconditional acceptance, and a lifetime of blessings. I only wish Pops could be here to see this. I know he would be so proud! I love you more than all of the stars in the sky—loads and bunches. Thank you for loving me.

To my Stephen Minister, Donna:

The Lord brought you across my path about four months following the completion of my formal therapy. However, you came into my life at the just-right time—God's timing is always perfect! You have stood with and for me in prayer, spoken truth into me and my life, and sat with me in silence while I cried.

Sometimes, you shared my tears. You continue to walk with me, faithfully, to this very day, and you give all of the glory to God throughout—you are truly His servant. I am blessed and so very thankful to the Lord for the gift that is you. I love you, my dear sister in Christ. Thank you kindly for walking with me on my spiritual journey. "I have not stopped giving thanks for you, remembering you in my prayers." (Ephesians 1:16)

To my parents, Denny and Sherry:

Thank you for giving me life. My dad has gone on to be with the Lord, but following his passing, I was led of the Lord to use a portion of the financial inheritance I received from his estate to fund the cost of publishing my first book. Thank you, dad, for all of the sacrifices that you made and for providing so well for our family. I love you and I miss you, but I know I will see you again in heaven.

———·———————●———————·———

To the many ministry supporters, prayer partners, and spiritual mentors:

I am humbled and blessed to see how the Lord has placed each of you in and on my path, for both similar and different reasons. God's ways are not my ways, and I am thankful and overjoyed to see how God is using each of you on my spiritual journey and in the ministry that He has created. God's Word implores us to "seek first his kingdom and his righteousness, and all these things will be given to [us] as well." (Matthew 6:33) As I continue to serve the Lord in ministry and missions, I thank you for sharing God's abundant gifts with me—in the kingdom there is always enough. Each one of you has made a difference in my life— thank you. I love and appreciate you beyond measure. Together, we are making a difference in the lives of women and children around the world. Thank you for your godly witness, support, guidance, partnership, and love. It is a blessing to serve the Lord alongside you, especially knowing that it is all for the Kingdom of God. Onward and upward!

———•————————•————————•———

To the counselees and mentees I have been blessed to help (past and present):

Thank you for trusting me to walk with you through the darkness of the past (and present) and into the glorious light of the Lord. You all inspire me beyond measure! I am in awe of your strength and resilience. Keep. Moving. Forward.

———•————————•————————•———

To my elementary school guidance counselor:

Thank you kindly for your care and compassion, those many years ago. You could not have known, at the time, how God was using you in my life—but He did, mightily! Your time and counsel gave me the strength to endure. I am better off because you were in my life.

———•————————•————————•———

To my Beta Readers:

What amazing faithfulness and support you have shown to me, in taking time out of your already-full schedule to read my edited rough draft manuscript. I value your input, expertise, and insight—thank you for helping to shape the end product of this book. Your support and love encourage me. Thank you for your friendship and partnership in ministry, and for helping me to "birth" this book into reality. You. Are. Loved.

To my Publishing Team:

When I initially embarked on the journey of book writing, and I was searching for the right publisher, the Lord repeatedly led me to Paper Raven Books. There were many signs along the way. As we have worked through each step of the editing and publishing process, I have been amazed by the grace, compassion, and enthusiasm your team has exhibited. I have enjoyed working with each of you on my book project—Morgan, Darcy, Joy, Jesus, Joe, Shena, Karen, Claudia, Amanda, and Victoria—and I am so thankful for your invaluable input and innumerous contributions to this project. Each contribution has served to make my book more meaningful. I mean, when I learned that JOY and JESUS were assigned to the project, I knew that God's hand was on it. Wow! Just wow! Thank you all kindly for taking this amazing journey with me.

PREFACE

Throughout my lifetime, and especially in my adulthood, I could see that the Lord was slowly and purposefully preparing me for what was to come. Initially, He placed the desire in my heart to pursue some type of occupation that would allow me to help others. While I did not have a clear vision for what the destination would be (would I become a lawyer, a teacher, a counselor?), I learned as much as I could about anything that would serve to help people. The thousands of hours of college courses, conferences, specialized training, seminars, and continuing education classes provided me with invaluable knowledge across a range of subjects including: developmental psychology, human trafficking, sexual assault, child sexual abuse, satanic ritual abuse, domestic violence, intimate partner violence, and a number of other topics related to sexual violence and violence against women. Over time, the path became clearer and eventually led to the ministry work I do now.

I have witnessed firsthand the effects of trauma on sexual violence survivors. I am a survivor. I have also observed, ministered to, counseled with, and mentored countless women and children, a majority of whom have a history of sexual violence. This ministry has taken me across continents, countries, states, cities, towns, townships, and villages, both urban and rural areas. I have traveled by plane, train, subway, bus, and even elephants in the jungle to minister to people in bus stations, homeless shelters, churches, and homes. I have sat next to survivors while they've cried, reminding them that they are not alone in their suffering.

I began writing this book in May 2012, but my story has been unfolding over 40 years. A majority of this book was written in the first few months, while the remainder of it had to be lived out and written about over time. What began as an idea soon formulated into chapters, which were then expounded upon and edited, rewritten and reedited, all through lived experiences.

Throughout the writing process, I utilized my own experience in healing from sexual violence as well as the sacred journeys that I have been blessed to walk on with fellow survivors.

While writing this book, I have encountered spiritual warfare, have been on the receiving end of an abundance of betrayal and an overall lack of support by people who should have been there to support me, and had to learn the hard way who is for me and who is not. I knew that the resistance was a sign of something that the Lord was trying to accomplish, so I pressed onward. I was inspired by a deep-seated passion to be a voice to the voiceless, as I saw the need for a tangible expression of the hope and healing that can only come from a loving Father, through His Son Jesus Christ. It is my fervent hope and prayer that readers will come away with a better understanding of how to not just survive but to thrive, whether you are a survivor of sexual violence or are supporting someone in your life who is. Together, we will keep moving forward.

INTRODUCTION

For many years, the events of my life robbed me of my joy. I did not understand why so many terribly tragic things had happened to me. I longed for the kind of joy only the Lord can bring about, that comes seemingly out of nowhere and brings about internal peace and contentment regardless of circumstances. I had to learn to open my heart to the joy that comes in the morning after a night of weeping.

In the United States, one in six women and millions of men have been victims of sexual assault. Child Protective Services estimates that 63,000 children are sexually abused each year, and 93% of the child victims know their abuser.[1] Sexual violence, in

---

1 "RAINN Statistics," 2020, RAINN, accessed Sept 25, 2020, https://www.rainn.org/statistics.

its many forms, has been in existence for a very long time. We can find examples of it throughout history and even in stories recounted in the Bible, and we know that it can affect anyone, regardless of age or gender. In light of these facts, we are all faced with profound questions. Why is sexual violence *still* occurring? What should we, as a society, do about it? How do we deal with it in a way that brings about a deep level of healing and a significant, lasting change to a person's life? These are important questions, and we need to be asking them.

For those of us who have personal experience with the issue, having survived sexual assault or child sexual abuse in our lifetime, we are faced with even more complex and difficult questions. Why did the sexual assault or abuse happen to me? How will I overcome the sexual violence that someone perpetrated against me? Will I ever be able to trust anyone again? How do I make sense of and heal from past hurt and pain? Is there any hope for me? How do I combat my enemy, the devil? To whom do I turn when I feel as though I am lost and all alone on such a painful and arduous journey? Throughout the course of this book, we will answer these questions and more. You will learn to love yourself, God, and others. You will develop an ability to surround yourself with trusted and caring people. You will find better ways to care for yourself while you heal. You will discover your real identity. You will better understand how imperative it is to reach a place of forgiveness and reconciliation in all areas of your life.

We will explore how the application of God's Word enhances our healing journey.[2] I will chronicle the instances of sexual assault and child sexual abuse that occurred over the course of more than 20 years of my life starting early in my youth, sharing my own arduous journey toward healing, with the hope of leading you to the cross and to the One who holds my healing and yours—Jesus Christ. At the end of each chapter, you will find a list of Questions for Reflection and a healing prayer entitled Come into the Light. These sections will help you process each aspect of your healing journey. You are encouraged to purchase a journal and recount any related thoughts and feelings, documenting your own healing journey as well as those things about which God may be speaking to you.

I wrote this book because I wanted to speak the truth in Christian love about my own healing journey through years of

---

2 Please note: All Scripture will be in the New International Version, unless otherwise noted.

sexual assault and child sexual abuse. There is something inside of me, which is spurring me forward, giving me the courage and the strength to step out and share my story. I believe this book will make a significant difference in the lives of countless survivors. I want to help those of you who are trying to deal with past sexual assault and abuse to develop a better understanding of your own spiritual journey as well as provide practical tools and resources to those of you taking a similar healing journey in your own life or supporting a loved one who is a survivor. Moreover, I want to encourage you to keep moving forward, especially those of you who may be in need of receiving the hope and healing that can only come from a saving relationship with the Lord Jesus Christ. You can do it, and you do not have to do it alone.

I encourage you to read this book as many times as you need to. There is no specific timeline for getting through it. Just take your time. Breathe. Find your rest in the Lord. God knows the plans He has for you, and He will lead you forward, if you allow Him to do so. I also invite you to be gentle with yourself as you heal. It is a profoundly painful and intensely intimate journey toward healing from sexual assault and child sexual abuse. I know this because I have lived it. However, it is certainly a journey worth taking. And this journey, just like any other, is meant to be taken one step at a time. Jesus Christ is our hope and the strength we need to endure and rise above. We are never alone because He is with us always, and He will be with us each step of the way. Be encouraged, dear friends. What He has done for me, He can also do for you. You need only to believe!

—Chantel D. Plautz

Chapter 1

SPEAKING THE TRUTH IN LOVE

"Do not be afraid; you will not be put to shame. Do not fear disgrace; you will not be humiliated. You will forget the shame of your youth...." (Isaiah 54:4)

The sun shone through the clouds like the first light that wakes a darkened room. And as the sun's rays gently permeated the vibrant sky, they spoke to me as if to say, "finally, I have arrived." It was a Sunday morning in early 2011, and I had begun to come out of a deep, dark spiritual bondage after enduring years of sexual violence. But from somewhere way down in the depths of my spirit, I had faith that a *complete* spiritual healing and divine deliverance would, in fact, come. I had faith in God to do the miraculous. I knew Him to be a healer. And I believed.

———————•———————

I was born in Denver, Colorado, but I grew up in rural Nebraska, the middle child of three siblings. I had what I remember to be a rather normal early childhood. I had a mom and a dad, two siblings—one older and one younger—an extended family, friends, and pets, all of whom I knew loved me. I went to school every day and attended church worship on a somewhat regular basis with my family, grandmother, or neighbors. I spent my free time with siblings and friends, playing in the woods near our house, collecting tadpoles and gigantic worms as fish bait in the summers, and riding snowmobiles in the winters. We had a family farm close by, and we would gather mulberries to top our ice cream or build tree houses in the huge cottonwoods on our home property. The cotton from trees was so thick that you could gather up bunches of it and make a fluff ball in your hands. I would often look at the tall trees, lined up like toy soldiers, and think that they were waving at me when the wind would move their branches back and forth. The vivid imagination and the uncompromised eyes of an innocent child can see and appreciate things that others often cannot. Those were simpler times. To a certain extent, I had lived a rather carefree life growing up in the country.

I really do not recall when the sexual abuse began. Throughout my journey, there are small periods of time wherein some of the memories are lost or not as easily recalled, which is common for sexual assault and child sexual abuse survivors. I may remember something very specific about a certain experience, while other memories are more general. And some other details are just gone or tucked away as a means of self-preservation, a gift from God, designed to help me continue living and functioning each day. For the purpose of this book and in sharing about my journey through sexual assault and child sexual abuse, I will be utilizing the term *instance* to describe each period of assault or abuse. To that end, I believe the first instance of abuse began when I was approximately 6 years old. Over the course of the following years, until I was about 12 years old, the sexual assault and abuse continued. This perpetrator was someone known to me and to some of the members of my family. This individual exposed me to pornographic magazines and movies. They placed me in sexually compromising situations. They did sexual things to me and had me do sexual things to them. I remember not understanding what was happening and escaping in my thoughts to somewhere else above myself—to another place in my mind—until the assault or abuse was over. Every. Single. Time. I was a child. I coped in the best way I knew how, at the time.

Although some of the same fun activities from my childhood continued during this time, the carefree part of me was no longer there. The activities I once enjoyed with ease became coping mechanisms, something I now used to escape, to find refuge in the midst of the storm. I started to look at these activities and locations as safe places in my life. I was not the same anymore; the sexual assault and child sexual abuse had changed me. Just like a damaged plane, making a nosedive toward the ground below, it felt like my life was suddenly out of control. It was. I would have called for help as I was spiraling downward, but my communication system was not functioning properly, and as a child I did not know how to repair it. "MAY DAY! MAY DAY!" was not a part of my child-like vocabulary. I didn't know how to put a voice to my feelings and experiences. Nothing made sense anymore. Everyday life was a struggle. I reasoned as a child, because I *was* a child. As I look back now, I realize that I just did the best that I possibly could.

I remember, at some point during the fourth grade, asking my teacher if I could go and visit with the school counselor. But when I would talk with the counselor, we worked on other things going on in my life at the time. I did not have the vocabulary or the knowledge to speak about the sexual abuse that I was enduring, let alone how I felt about it. What I do remember, however, is how the counselor helped me to feel loved, accepted, and no longer alone in my suffering. It is quite strange, really. How was it possible to feel all of these positive things and not tell anyone about the sexual abuse? How could talking about other things going on in my life (outside of the sexual abuse) still bring in some element of healing? I guess it is just an example of how compassion goes a long way, and how love covers a multitude of sins.

In the summer of 1984, the first instance of sexual assault and abuse ended when my family and I moved to another state. For this, I was extremely thankful. But the related memories and the internal pain and suffering traveled with me.

The second instance of sexual assault and abuse took place in the summer of 1988, between 10th and 11th grade in high school when I was 16 years old. I knew this perpetrator, and some of my family members knew this person as well. I trusted this person. I looked up to this person. But looking back, I also know that this person groomed me through compliments, spending time with me, and buying me things. I mistook this attention as genuine love and affection, something I was greatly in need of at the time. They knew this, as all individuals who are grooming children know it. They rely on it. Rather than being genuine love and affection, it was a ploy by the perpetrator to get my defenses down, to ingratiate me to them in some way. It created a false sense of security and an environment wherein I did not feel like I could tell anyone about what had happened to me. It was almost like, if I did, I would be betraying them in some way, which shows you how twisted thinking becomes in those situations. I was repeatedly shamed and made to feel as though the abuse was my fault, both immediately after the abuse had ended and for several years afterwards. This *false* shame came from people I was supposed to be able to trust and who should have believed and supported me from the beginning. There are no words to describe the level of pain associated with this type of betrayal.

Following this instance of abuse, I found it increasingly difficult to lead a "normal" life. But as I had done with the initial instance of sexual assault and child sexual abuse, I also pushed these related memories and feelings deep down inside. Surely, if I did not think about them, they would go away, right? Wrong. I developed a series of coping mechanisms, including taking care of everyone else around me, becoming involved in activities to occupy my time, and trying really hard to please the people in my life from whom I desired so desperately to receive love and affection. In many ways, this approach worked. If I was busy taking care of others, doing activities, and pleasing others, I did not have to face the evil things of the past. However, avoiding this evil only allowed it to fester under the surface. It would come out, eventually, and I would have to deal with it at some point.

The third instance of sexual assault and child sexual abuse involved a longer duration of time and multiple perpetrators, both male and female. All of these situations occurred between 1988 and 2000, between the ages of 16 and 28. It is much easier for me to think of and refer to this group of people collectively, even though the sexual assault and abuse were perpetrated by different individuals over a long period and many different locations. Just as with the first two instances of sexual assault and abuse, I knew and trusted all of the perpetrators. In the early years of this span of time, some of the perpetrators exposed me to strip clubs, not with the purpose of me dancing but to expose me to a world that, as a child and a young adult, I should not have witnessed. Then, some of these perpetrators exposed me to pornography and placed me in sexually compromising situations. I overheard sexual situations as they were going on. And I was placed in numerous situations wherein I was made to do sexual things and to have sexual things done to me. Some of these perpetrators groomed and manipulated me, as well.

During the first few years of this time, I managed to excel in a variety of activities in high school, which was my primary coping mechanism. I was a varsity cheerleader, vice president of my senior class, Sweetheart Queen at winter homecoming my senior year, and honor roll throughout high school, in addition to the community service work I did. All of these activities were enjoyable, and I did a good job in each of these roles. I was a leader and someone whom many people admired and trusted. To everyone around me, I am sure it looked like I had it all together, as if life could not get any better. But outward appearances can be deceiving sometimes, as inwardly I was dying a slow and painful death in my soul.

After high school, I went on to college, first in Florida and then in Kansas. I was working full-time and going to school full-time, majoring in developmental psychology. However, as certain elements of sexual assault and child sexual abuse continued, I could not handle everything that was going on in my life. I dropped out of college after completing two years of classes, stopping just shy of receiving my associate's degree. The past was catching up to me. Something had to give, or I was going to break. Many people in my life at the time saw this as giving up. To me, though, it was necessary for my very survival.

A couple years after this, I received a promotion at work as the new Regional Corporate Training Director for a rental car company, which required me to move to a new city. It would be a fresh start. I was going to be okay. In a new place with new surroundings, I would enjoy the challenges and travel that my new job would provide and would make new friends. I appreciated and looked forward to the adventures. But something was desperately missing from my life. I continued to go to church on occasion, but I was still looking for love in all the wrong places. I was seeking to fill up the pit in my soul and heart with something. My faith was there, but something was still missing. Could it be that there was too much in the way of reaching my heart? As my travel schedule would allow, I found times to be in worship, which helped a lot. But I was still hurting inside. I didn't think I could handle digging up the past in order to start dealing with the related pain, so I did what I knew how to do, what I had learned to do as a young child. I buried the pain deep inside, thinking that the further down that I buried it, the longer it would take for it to surface next time.

The fourth instance of sexual assault occurred sometime in 1996, I think. I cannot really be sure. I was around 24 or 25 years old. I can remember that it was cooler outside, and it had been raining that night. I know that I had driven myself in my own car to meet some of my friends for a small gathering after work, and I had ordered a Sprite to drink. This was a place we had gone often. I remember laughter and visiting. Then, everything went black.

The next memory I have was of waking up on a sleeper sofa, in the midst of being sexually assaulted by two people, a husband and wife. Both perpetrators were people I knew. As one of the perpetrators was raping me, I remember seeing a sliver of light coming through the vertical blinds on the sliding door, into the apartment in which the assault was taking place. I remember how the light pierced the carpet, as the sexual assault was piercing my physical body. I heard laughter and intimate discussions. I felt pain and pressure. I could smell and taste things that were very foreign to me. I could also identify body odors and strong cologne. The surface of the furniture was rough. I could feel my tears as they escaped from my eyes and slid down my cheeks onto the pillow beneath me. I was both hot and cold throughout the night. I felt dirty and shameful, as I was forced into various physical positions. I was not a person; I was an object of someone's twisted sexual desires. I blacked out often.

At some point, I remember getting physically sick in the kitchen sink. In the process, I had knocked over a drinking glass, and it shattered into a million pieces in the sink. This is literally how my heart felt. Shattered. Into a million pieces. A long stem and leaves from an ivy plant were cascading down into the sink beside me. It is so strange the things that you can remember during a time of trauma and crisis. But what really stands out are the things that you can't forget, no matter how hard you try. The assault went on throughout the night, as I went in and out of consciousness.

I woke up the next day in this same place. I was naked, lying on the sleeper sofa, and I was looking around, trying to figure out where I was and what had gone on. As things became clearer, I knew where I was and some of what had occurred. I soon learned that I had no way home. My car was still located at the gathering place from the night before. I was unsteady and confused, but somehow, I managed to get myself dressed. Then, one of the perpetrators drove me to where I had left my car the night before, and they just dropped me off and drove away. I am not really even sure how I made it home that day, but I did. I remember thinking that if I just went to sleep, perhaps I would wake up and it would all have been a bad dream. I did manage to rest. When I woke up, though, I knew it was clearly a nightmare, one that I had lived through.

I continued to go to work as if nothing had happened, which was very awkward, since one of the perpetrators also worked there. I was coping in the only way I knew how, which was to bury the pain and hurt deep inside and pretend that it did not exist. For a while, this means of coping served me well. I continued to stay busy with work, travel, and various activities with friends and family. In time, I moved from this city and back into an area where I had lived previously. While doing this created a somewhat new environment for me, almost like another fresh start, it actually placed me back into a circle of people that I had been assaulted and abused by in the past (the third instance) so that sexual abuse continued, on occasion, for the next few years.

Eventually, you come to a point where you just do not feel like you can absorb any more pain or hurt. I would wonder to myself, "What more could anyone do to me? How can I possibly feel any worse than I do right now?" And that is about the point when you figure out that you are completely numb to the pain and hurt. It was all too much to bear or process. You cannot possibly feel anything else, so how do you go about processing it?

———————•———————

The final instance of sexual assault occurred in the fall of 2000 when I was 28 years old. Someone I was dating at the time exposed me to pornography in the midst of sexual assault. It all happened so quickly that I did not really have time to process it, let alone stop it. As with each instance of assault and abuse to this point, I just went to a place inside of myself—and then *above* myself—until it was over, a survival response known as collapsed immobility. I went through the motions because that was a "normal" response for me to have, for most any survivor to have. Just lie there and take it, unable to move or speak, hoping it will all be over soon.

In 2011, I experienced a series of traumatic events that shook me to my core and unearthed the memories of sexual assault and child sexual abuse from my past. I could no longer run away from the pain, push the feelings away, or pretend they did not exist. It was time to stop running. All of this led me to seek professional help. About a year or so prior to this time, I had seen an advertisement on TV for a local sexual assault center; while I was not ready to seek help at that time, I made a note of the number for the day when I would be ready for help. That day finally came. I made up my mind that I was going to get help. And I knew the Lord had provided it free of charge through this local sexual assault center. But the enemy—the devil—was trying very hard to keep me from getting to the assault center on that first day. My car broke down, and my head was full of doubts and thoughts meant to distract me. Certain people in my life also thought they knew best how I should handle the situation. I made a very important decision that day: I would shut out all of the voices that were not of God or did not align with His will. When I did that, it all became very clear to me. So, I arranged for someone to pick me up from the shop where I had taken my car for repairs and to drop me off at my new therapist's office. There was no turning back now.

———·——————●——————·———

On July 19, 2011, my life changed forever when I met Catharine, a therapist at the local sexual assault center. I was broken wide open from the tragic and traumatic events of my past. But I experienced speaking the truth in love, for the first time, when I met with and began to share my truth with her. As I have now shared with you, I had endured repeated sexual assault and child sexual abuse over the span of more than 20 years of my life and at the hands of more than one perpetrator. I had lost my innocence. I had experienced profound betrayal—deep, painful betrayal—related to the sexual assault and child sexual abuse, among other challenges I had faced. I did not know if I would be able to trust again. Ever. I was broken, filled with shame, blame, guilt, and self-doubt. And I was in desperate need of being able to share my story with someone who would not judge me for the evil acts that others had perpetrated against me in my childhood and young adulthood.

At first, I did not know that feelings could be false and that the shame, blame, guilt, and self-doubt I was experiencing were false. I would learn and come to understand this much better over time. We can have a feeling that is both good (justified) and false, at the same time. Fear is one example of this. In its good form, it represents a reverence for God; it can also represent something we should be afraid of and provides protection from it (e.g., a poisonous snake). In its false form, however, it is a fear instilled in us through some manipulative or other negative means, like force, fraud, or coercion. All I knew was that I was suffering and that I needed to express my feelings to someone. I needed someone to listen. I needed someone to hear me. Up to that point, I had shared some of the general details with a small group of people, but I was usually met with silence, a rather immediate dismissal of the severity of the experiences, various and often-empty spiritual platitudes, and an underlying message that sexual abuse happens to a lot of people. The point was not that it happens to many people; the point was that it had happened to me. I imagine many of you can relate to the experience of being met with responses like this.

From the moment I walked into her therapy office, Catharine made me feel safe. How did she do this? She gave me my space. She honored my personal boundaries. She allowed me to just breathe, she encouraged me to take my time, and she gave me permission to answer when I was ready. She allowed me to cry. She sat with me in silence while I processed deeply painful things. She reminded me that I was not alone. She understood me and my journey. She knew exactly what I needed to hear, and what I didn't need to hear—her words were not "empty" platitudes. She had compassion. She cared. And I knew this from everything she did and said. She kept her word to me; she modeled stability; she was reliable. She was gentle and understanding. She also spoke truth to me, which I needed to hear. She was in God's perfect place, doing exactly what she was called to do—help people.

Finding "safe" people is not always an easy task. As survivors, we desire this, but we don't always know how to go about doing it. Later in this book, we will look more deeply at the subjects of finding safe people and being safe people, and we will talk about why this is especially important for survivors.

———•——————•——————•———

Beginning the day following my first day of formal therapy, I began keeping a personal journal. Initially, I wrote in it several times a week. Eventually, I started writing in my journal on a daily basis and continued that practice for years to come. While the healing process looks a little bit different for each person, I know it was (and is) a very useful tool for me. Throughout the course of this book, I will be sharing many of my personal journal entries with you to give you some deeper insight into my related feelings and struggles, the grief I was processing, and the beautiful healing journey the Lord took me on. These entries will be in *italics*, so as to set them apart from the main text in this book. You will see these journal entries shared throughout this book, beginning in Chapter 2.

———•——————•——————•———

During my own healing process from sexual assault and child sexual abuse, I learned from my therapist that sexual assault affects approximately one in three women and one in six men. Although this is true, the saddest thing is that it is probably even more prevalent, because many girls and women—and, yes, even boys and men—are afraid to speak up about the sexual violence perpetrated against them. These reasons may include feeling ashamed, being truly afraid for one's life, or just not knowing where to turn and who to trust with such personal, private, and deeply devastating information. Talking about the assault means admitting it actually happened, which for many survivors is a scary thought. It is like exposing an open wound. However, not talking about sexual assault and child sexual abuse is like putting a small Band-Aid on that gaping wound; over time, it will fester and will never heal correctly. If we do not talk about the damage, how can we undo and heal the damage sexual violence has caused?

For the purposes of shared understanding, it is important that we take a step back to define terms. *Consent* means that a person has as much right to say "yes" as they have to say "no." Sexual violence changes a child's development and can alter their understanding of what people want; when adults place the burden and blame on children in the cases of child sexual abuse (e.g., asking why they didn't stop the abuse, why they allowed it to happen, or why they kept going back to that place or person), they are ignoring basic facts about development and consent.

When an individual engages in any kind of sexual activity with an adult who has not given their permission or with a child, who inherently does not have the developmental capacity to give consent, that person is committing sexual assault. Sexual assault and abuse include but are not limited to inappropriate touching, rape, attempted rape, and child molestation. These acts can be verbal, visual, or anything that forces a person to join in unwanted sexual contact or attention, and it can happen in and under many different situations or circumstances.

I was not aware of all the parameters that sexual violence encompasses until I learned of them from my therapist and during the course of my healing process, which helped me to identify, uncover, and connect to nearly all of the instances of sexual assault and child sexual abuse in my past. I say nearly because there are some "unknowns"—instances of sexual violence that are not as easily recalled—that often occur in the life of a survivor. We will dig more deeply into these unknowns in a future chapter. The trauma associated with sexual violence leaves scars that take time to heal fully, many of which may remain unseen to the naked eye. The negative effects of sexual assault can last for months or even years following the abuse, and some related health problems can last for a longer period. But there is healing for all of us.

If you or someone you know has experienced and endured sexual assault or child sexual abuse, in any way, tell someone you can trust. Do it today. Do not continue to suffer in silence, scared and alone. There is help available and people who care. You only need to avail yourself to this help and care in order to move forward on your own healing journey. God's Word encourages us to speak out: "Let the redeemed of the LORD tell their story—those he redeemed from the hand of the foe." (Psalm 107:2) For those of us who have experienced sexual victimization in any way, it is not an option to remain silent forever. We could...but why? The events of each instance of sexual assault and child sexual abuse eat away at us over time, and it affects virtually every area of our life. Standing in our truth and getting help is our right as survivors. We deserve the chance for someone to hear us, and we deserve the chance to heal. We have a voice, and we should use it for that purpose. Speaking the truth in love is God's best for us; it frees us from the chains of the past and makes healing possible. Difficult truths often need to be conveyed, and speaking the truth in love is the need to share these truths in a kind, gentle, inoffensive manner. The enemy and evil things live in the dark. Talking about the abuse we have endured brings them into the light, and this is where our true healing can begin to take place.

Imagine hundreds of sunflowers in a large field. Have you ever noticed how all of the sunflowers turn towards the light? They do that because the sun is their source of strength and allows them to grow and to come into full maturation. The same is true for us as it pertains to the Son. When we turn toward the Light of Christ, we, too, can grow and come into full maturation, being raised up into who and what the Lord has called us to be. Come into the Light. This is speaking of coming into the deeper understanding of who Jesus is—our salvation in Him. Jesus is the Light of the world. He is The Way, The Truth, and The Life. He is the Savior of the world. When you come into the Light, Jesus will comfort you and feed your soul and spirit. Come into the Light, dear friends. Jesus is there. I know Him to be faithful. He will meet you right where you are.

Today, I am choosing to stand in my own truth and share my story of survival from sexual violence. My hope is that someone reading this book will be compelled to reach out and ask for the help you so desperately need, or if you are already on the road toward healing, to find the encouragement needed to continue to move forward. It is easy to lose your voice and feel as though you do not matter. You DO matter. It is easy to feel like you want to give up when the grief work gets too hard. Do NOT give up. Keep. Moving. Forward.

I affirm you, as a person. I affirm you, in and on your healing journey. And my promise to you is that I will speak the truth in love to you for the remainder of this book. I pray that you will find your voice and use it to heal and to help others. You are not alone in your suffering. Ever. You can (and you will) learn to love again, and I hope that will include loving yourself. I pray that you would also find your real identity—your identity in Christ—and a deeper and even more precious relationship with Jesus, in and through your healing and spiritual journey. As we move forward together through this book—you, me, and the Lord—we will discuss these topics and more.

I am so thankful for the Lord's hand upon me and for the help that I have received through Catharine, the sexual assault center, and my trusted care circle members. As the Lord has continued to provide healing—body, soul, and spirit—I have also continued to make the choice to put on my new garment of praise every day. You can make this same choice, too.

———————•———————•———

Questions for Reflection

1. What is my truth? What is my survivor story from sexual violence?

2. Do I have a correct understanding of all of the sexual assault and child sexual abuse that others perpetrated against me? Is there anything about which I may be in denial?

3. Is it possible that there are memories I cannot recall? If so, can I be okay with that?

4. What is the truth about my family of origin, the family I was born into and grew up with? Did they love and care for me? Did they abandon me? Did they protect me? Did they harm me?

5. Where does God fit into my life? Where does He fit into my healing journey?

Come into the Light

Gracious Lord and Heavenly Father, I certainly do not know everything there is to know about You or about Your ability to heal me. I want to. I have a desire to move past the pain and hurt that others have caused me, and I recognize that I need Your help to do that. I want to know You more. I want and need to be whole and healed. I want all that You have for me—I know that starts with letting You in where the pain is. This is so hard for me to do, but I am asking You to come into my heart and heal me. I cannot do this alone. I need You, God. Will You walk with me on this healing journey? In Jesus's name, I pray. Amen.

Before we move any further into this book, it's imperative that we come to an understanding. We all must work out our own salvation; each of us must know Christ Jesus for ourselves. It must be genuine and from the heart. Salvation (being "saved") is God's atoning sacrifice on the cross, achieved through only one means—through only one man—Jesus Christ and His shed blood on the cross at Calvary. We are all sinners in need of a Savior. "For the wages of sin is death, but the gift of God is eternal life in Christ Jesus our Lord." (Romans 6:23) Jesus paid a price that we could not pay—He gave His life, so we could live with Him for eternity. I made this personal and public choice (to trust Jesus as my own personal Savior) when I was nearing the end of my eighth-grade year in junior high, upon completion of confirmation classes at my (then) home church. As a survivor, many years later, this decision would only serve to help me on my healing journey. My faith in Jesus is the main reason I am excelling in life today—it was a real life-changer for me. If you do not know Jesus as your Lord and Savior, and if this is your desire, I invite you to pray the following prayer.

PRAYER OF SALVATION:

Lord Jesus, I do not want to just know about You; I want to know You. I want a relationship with You, Lord, a personal experience with the Son of the Living God. Jesus, come into my life. Wash all of my sins away and cleanse me with the life-giving blood of the Lamb. I receive You and I trust You. My hope is in You and in You, alone. I am not talking about a religion, not fabricated and manufactured stuff, but You, Jesus; I receive You into my life and into my heart. I believe in You, above all. I want to know, as Peter declared it, "Thou art the Christ, the Son of the Living God!" Renew my mind and bring about a true heart change in me. Empty me of myself, as well as anything that is not of You, Lord. I renounce all other gods; I want You to be my Lord and my Savior. I want You to rule over my life. Set me aflame with Holy Spirit; live and breathe in me, as only You can. Fill me to the point of overflowing with the power and Presence of Holy Spirit, the gifts of the Spirit, and the fruit of the Spirit. Thank You for saving me. I want to serve You, and only You, for the rest of my life. Show me how to walk in Your will and walk in Your ways, to the glory of Your Holy Name. In Jesus's name, I pray. Amen.

———·———————●———————·———

Dear friends, if you prayed this prayer, I believe that you have been born again and are now saved. Jesus knows the content and intent of your heart. God doesn't look on the outward appearance. He looks at your heart. It's not the words you say, but it's the intent of your heart—it truly is a heart matter.

Welcome to the family of God!

Chapter 2

HOW TO CARE FOR OURSELVES WHILE WE HEAL

*"Be strong and courageous. Do not be afraid or
terrified because of them, for the* LORD *your God goes
with you; he will never leave you nor forsake you."*
(Deuteronomy 31:6)

We all have a basic desire, somewhere deep inside, for someone else to care for us. As infants, we rely on our parents or other caregivers to provide for our needs. I once saw a scene in a documentary that beautifully expressed this need. A baby elephant had become stuck in a large crack, and while its mother desperately tried to help the baby escape, she also signaled to the other females in the herd that their aid was needed. The herd of elephants worked together and finally freed the baby, who ran to its mother's side and clung to her. It is fundamental to our nature to want to be cared for like this, to know that we can trust someone to be there for us and to help us when we need it.

During childhood, and especially in the formidable years, each person should go through certain developmental milestones. This could (and should) include several aspects of healthy attachment to the caregiver(s) in the child's life. In part, this is developed and achieved when the parent or primary caregiver is appropriately attentive and especially sensitive to the overall, everyday needs of the child, as shown to them through consistent, prompt, and caring responses.

For some survivors, however, this desire is more of a dream than a reality. You may have grown up in foster care, with an absentee parent, or in a broken home. Perhaps you were abused by one or both of your parents, the very people who were supposed to care for you. God's Word speaks to that: "Even though your father or mother may have abandoned or forsaken you, I will care for you and take you in." (Proverbs 10:27) God knows, dear friends. God surely knows. He realizes that the very people in our life who were meant to help us are sometimes the very people who hurt us. You cannot go back to the very people who hurt you and expect them to, all of a sudden, start helping you. If this is your truth, it is even more reason why you need to know how to care for yourself while you heal. After I began to share about the sexual assault and child sexual abuse I had endured, some people told me to "get over it." Others told me to "cheer up." Still others told me that "it happens to a lot of people." While some people are well meaning, not everyone is for you. But God is for you. "And if God is for you, who can be against you?" (Romans 8:31)

Even before I began to share about my experiences, I had developed an abundance of coping mechanisms. You will hear about coping mechanisms several times throughout this book. Oftentimes, coping mechanisms are not necessarily positive. Many can be negative, while some can be both positive and negative. Some of my mechanisms included: gravitating towards busyness, being overly organized, being obsessive in my thoughts and compulsive in my actions, drinking alcohol, turning to food for comfort, isolating myself, shopping, and wanting to control everyone and everything around me. You see, while being organized is a positive characteristic (and for a period in time, I used this skill set successfully to help others organize their homes and offices), I sometimes took it to an extreme in my own life. And anything we do to an extreme should be reevaluated in the light of Christ so we can find a healthy balance. Over time, I was able to find that balance with the help of the Lord. Coping mechanisms are necessary, but they should be helpful and not hurtful.

As a survivor, you may believe that you are responsible for holding it all together. However, I have news for you: You are not responsible for holding it all together. "So, this is what the Sovereign LORD says: 'See, I lay a stone in Zion, a tested stone, a precious cornerstone for a sure foundation; the one who relies on it will never be stricken with panic.'" (Isaiah 28:16) This is God's assurance that we will never walk alone and that we will not need to shoulder the load all by ourselves, especially in healing from sexual assault and child sexual abuse. You do not need to walk alone. You are not walking alone. In fact, Jesus tells us in the Gospel of Matthew that His yoke is easy and His burden is light, and in Him, we will find rest for our souls (see Matthew 11:28–30). Go to Him. He's waiting with open arms. As you heal, it is important to be gentle with yourself. What does that mean, specifically? Pace yourself. Give yourself the benefit of the doubt. Do not take on more than you can adequately handle. Healing, in and of itself, is an arduous journey. You may often feel tired, grow to be easily agitated, and become emotionally vulnerable. Just be gentle with yourself, dear friends. You want this healing journey to be fruitful and lasting.

I have found the small-step approach to be invaluable in the healing process. It's a strategy I learned in my ministry training and essentially means not biting off more than you can chew. In other words, do what you need to do, but do not overwhelm yourself or your schedule. Give yourself space to decompress. Do a little bit at a time and then take a break. Eat well and get lots of physical exercise. Take care of yourself. "[19] Do you not know that your bodies are temples of the Holy Spirit, who is in you, whom you have received from God? You are not your own; [20] you were bought at a price. Therefore, honor God with your bodies." (1 Corinthians 6:19–20)

Share only what you are able to share, when you are able to share it. Put your name on the list; do not just focus on taking care of others or drowning yourself in work or activities so you can "forget" the pain. It does not work that way. You need to take time for yourself. Get some rest. Then, do more grief work, but only as you are able. We must go through it in order to move past it. However, healing is a journey. The sexual assault or child sexual abuse you have suffered through will take some time to be uncovered. So be gentle with yourself while you heal.

When you accomplish a task or share deeply personal things, do something special for yourself to celebrate. Take a walk in nature, go out for a meal, get a pedicure, plan a "me" day, read a new book, have a picnic, go see a movie, take a bubble bath, listen to music, or share your successes with someone you love and trust. You can make your own list of ideas and write it down in your journal. I invite you to do that now. Also be mindful that not everything on your list has to cost money. When you make your list, follow through on doing something from that list after you have accomplished something. Do not just write it down and forget about it. You have taken a big step in your healing process by opening up and sharing about what has happened, and you should take time to celebrate that, however it is most feasible for you. Give yourself permission to cry. It is cleansing, and it frees you from holding everything inside. Contrary to popular belief, crying is not a sign of weakness: "Jesus wept." (John 11:35) He did that openly and honestly. "Those who sow with tears will reap with songs of joy." (Psalm 126:5) In time, your heart will learn to open up to receiving the joy that comes in the morning.

It is also important to create "safe places" for yourself while you heal. For me, in my childhood, this consisted of going down to the crick or spending time at my grandma's house. In my adulthood, this consisted of my apartment home, my church, and a place deep in the woods where I would go and commune with the Lord and just "be" amongst His creation. Each survivor has to find places that help him or her to feel safe. Once you have found those places, it's important to maintain healthy boundaries for yourself. For many survivors, boundaries are nonexistent. A majority of the time our boundaries were not honored. We never had a chance to set them, and we never knew how. Setting and maintaining healthy boundaries is imperative to successfully caring for yourself while you heal. Perhaps it is necessary to develop a new group of friends, to cut off communication with friends or family members. Maybe, for you, that looks like not allowing people to take advantage of you anymore. Or it might possibly involve putting yourself and your needs "on the list." Whatever it looks like for you, you will want to develop boundaries that are healthier than they ever were before. Sometimes we also must set boundaries for others in our life who do not know how to set them on their own.

I encourage you to keep a journal. I did this during the course of my own healing journey, and I still do it to this day. I believe that you will find it to be cathartic to purge your thoughts and feelings onto paper, and even more helpful to go back occasionally and read what you have written. You may be surprised to see and read the progress in your own healing journey through the spiritual discipline of journaling. You can write about how you feel, what you did that day, or what someone said to you that made a difference. You can spend time in prayer and then journal what the Lord speaks into your spirit. You can also write about something you read in God's Word that really spoke to you on that particular day. Throughout this book, I will be sharing some of my personal journal entries with you (again, these will appear in *italics*, so as to set them apart from the original text of the book). The purpose of sharing these journal entries is to help you better understand the actual grief and healing journey of a sexual violence survivor. I will share my ups and downs, disappointments and successes. I will start by sharing with you my very first few journal entries.

———•———

July 20, 2011

Yesterday, I had my first counseling session with my new therapist, Catharine. We briefly discussed some of my areas of grief and pain, and I cried a lot. It felt good to cry. I was comfortable just being myself with her. It was comforting to share openly and without judgment. I felt sad and hurt as I recalled past experiences in my life. She reminded me that I am not a victim, that the things that happened to me were not my fault, and that there is hope. I knew most of these things, but it sure was comforting to hear them. This was a really good place to start.

I find that trying to process so much at one time is a bit overwhelming right now. I am trying to recall the small-step approach from my ministry training and just take it all one small step at a time; but, sometimes, it is very hard to do.

All of the sharing from yesterday has left me completely exhausted, and today I am feeling drained, angry, and sad. Memories are creeping back, often. I am having trouble speaking about it, as all of the feelings related to the memories only heighten my emotions. I am also having difficulty sleeping. I feel depressed and lethargic. I just want to curl up in a little ball, roll under and into a dark place somewhere, and sleep. I just want people to leave me alone. I do not feel like being touched. I am easily agitated. I am having trouble finding the joy in life right now. I see others being happy and smiling, and I want that for myself again.

I am staying connected, as best I can, to my core support system—my trusted care circle. This is a small group of people, though, as I find that I can only share with those I can trust 100%... and, well, that is a very small group of people. I have had to put this to the test over time. I just cannot risk it right now. I am emotionally vulnerable and fragile, and I know this about myself. I must take care of me. I need to continue to be gentle with myself as I heal. My faith in the Lord has always been and will continue to be at the top of my list, in terms of where I glean my comfort and the strength needed to endure and rise above. The Lord is with me, and I find immense solace in knowing this truth.

I will meet with one of my pastors tomorrow to discuss all of the things going on in my life right now. I know it will be painful, but it will also be healing and free me from more of the pain and hurt that is buried deep inside of me. I need to keep moving forward in my sharing and healing from the past and present hurts and trauma. I know that I am a survivor, and I will get through and past all of this in time. I pray that God will use it all for good—I know that He will, all in His perfect timing.

July 21, 2011

Today was a rough day. I have been thinking a lot about the assault and abuse I endured, and trying to leave myself open to feel and release emotions. I met with one of my pastors tonight; he is one of my trusted care circle members. Our visit was intense. We talked about my first appointment with my therapist and about how challenging the grief work is going to be for me. We discussed some of the people who have betrayed me by sharing certain details of the abuse without my permission for them to do so—it is so incredibly painful... completely re-traumatizing, in a way.

To a certain extent, trust is a big opportunity area in all of my relationships. But I want to be able to trust again. I want to be stronger emotionally, to be able to react to all things appropriately. I have given myself permission to feel the deep and intense pain and just "be," to deal with things at a pace that works best for me. I feel really good about that decision.

My pastor told me that he hoped God would help me to erase and re-record over the negative tapes that often play in my mind. I want that for myself, too. Some of those negative tapes are that I am not lovable; I am wrong or at fault; I am not good enough; people use, abuse, or leave me because I deserve it or have done something to cause it. I desire for all of the negative tapes to stop playing in my mind, but I need some help to do that. Lord, I need You to help me find my way.

I need to develop a better, healthier self-worth and self-esteem—I know the abusers (and others in my life) have completely shattered this area of my life. I also know that God loves me, and He will help me heal and rebuild. And, I want to love myself as He does—all of me. I want the little girl inside of me to heal and to be free.

———————————•———————————•———————

July 25, 2011

I am so angry and emotional this morning. I am having great difficulty thinking a good thought about certain people in my life.

Why is life so hard sometimes? I really do not know if I have the energy to deal with everything that I need to deal with so I can work through things and move forward in my life. I feel so depleted— completely drained. I am so tired. I need a break. What about me... does anyone even see me? Does anyone SEE me? Does anyone see ME? I have felt invisible for the past 30 years of my life. It seems that everyone else needs care. They need attention; they need, need, need. Do MY needs even matter? I have so many pent-up emotions! I feel as though I may just explode as I try to uncover the events of the past and work through them. It all hurts me so deeply.

Sometimes I question if I can actually do this—talk about all of the sexual assault and abuse, pain, and hurt from the past— because I am just so tired. I want to close out the entire world and just sleep. I need a lifeline...I need someone to rescue me. I have told a few people, and now I just need to keep moving forward and trust that God will provide to me everything that I need, when I need it. Surely, He knows.

July 26, 2011

I met with my therapist again today—this was our second session. It was emotionally intense. We discussed many of the things going on in my life presently, and we talked about the first instance of sexual abuse (6 years old to 12 years old). We talked about most of the experiences and all of the related feelings. My therapist reminded me that at that age there was nothing I could have done to stop the abuse—I needed to hear this truth.

We also talked about several other things going on in my life during that time, as well as since then, and we made a connection to the negative self-worth, self-image, and self-esteem that I already struggled with due to feeling forgotten and unloved, and because of the sexual assault and child sexual abuse that was repeatedly perpetrated against me. It was a nightmare—all of it—but it did help to talk about it. I am thankful.

It's important to understand that journaling is just one of many spiritual disciplines. Let us look at a list of additional spiritual disciplines that you might also enjoy and benefit from practicing while you heal. We will view them in correlation to the fruit of the Spirit (see Galatians 5:22–23) and place them into three separate categories: (1) your relationship with God, (2) your relationship with others, and (3) your relationship with yourself.

───────────●───────────

SPIRITUAL DISCIPLINES

Your relationship with God (in conjunction with the first three virtues of the fruit of the Spirit: love, joy, peace)

- silence
- prayer
- listening to God (the voice of God will never contradict His Word)
- spending time in God's creation (walking, sitting in the park or the woods, etc.)
- counting your blessings
- praying Psalm 23
- reading the gospels (not for purpose of study, but for the purpose of being fed spiritually)

- solitude

- praise

- spiritual fasting

- reading a daily devotional

- Bible study

- worshiping the Lord

- listening to praise and worship music

- spiritual journaling

Your relationship with others (in conjunction with the second set of three virtues of the fruit of the Spirit: patience, kindness, goodness)

- showing hospitality (inviting someone over to your house, when it is safe)

- getting rid of the things you no longer need

- no gossiping

- serving others

- sharing your faith

- loving those with whom you disagree (blessing those who curse you)

- being a good steward of your resources

- praying for others (intercessory prayer)

- treasuring God's gifts (God, people, family, faith, etc.)

Your relationship with yourself (in conjunction with the third set of three virtues of the fruit of the Spirit: faithfulness, gentleness, self-control)

- sleeping (at least seven to eight hours per night and getting extra sleep when you feel as though your body needs it for renewal on all levels)

- silence

- building margin into your life and schedule so you have something left to give (time, energy, finances, etc.)

- slowing down (reassessing priorities and schedule, finding balance)

- saying no/yes where it is appropriate and displays healthy boundaries

- playing (activities of personal interest and with children, if possible, on occasion)

- media fast (taking a break from electronics for a period of time)

- forgiving others and seeking forgiveness where needed

- humility
- taking care of your body
- physical exercise

———•——————•——————•———

Over the years, I have practiced all of these spiritual disciplines at least once, and many of these disciplines are a part of my daily walk with the Lord. In some cases, I have been practicing them for many years. However, some of them I now just do only occasionally or as the Lord leads me. It is all about finding the right balance of some in each category that speak to you and your walk with God. Everyone's combination of spiritual disciplines is different, because we are all unique and we all have different seasons of life; therefore, it may be necessary to change your list a few times a year or at various times throughout your life. Additionally, it is important not to become overly rigid about practicing these disciplines. Seek to find a good balance, as observing spiritual disciplines should not overwhelm you. It is not meant to be a "box" that you check off each day. It is also not intended to be something you dread doing. Instead, these spiritual disciplines should add, in a positive manner, to your life and your faith walk with the Lord, and that goodness should spill over into all areas of your life. Overall, I pray that sharing the above list of spiritual disciplines with you will be a blessing to you on your healing journey. Trying something new can be daunting, but do not be afraid. Practicing spiritual disciplines is a very positive and enriching experience. I encourage you to give it a try.

———·————●————·———

During our healing journey, we need someone to encourage us. However, at times it may feel as though there is no one around. Sometimes there actually will be no one else around, physically. Sometimes, we will need to be an encouragement to ourselves. It is in these times that God can and will encourage us through His Word. On a regular basis, and in a different combination, I read or recite from memory the following proclamations found in God's Word. I encourage you to mark these Scripture in your Bible so you can more easily find them when you are reading God's Word. I have found that highlighting or underlining Scripture helps it to stand out on the page. I've even written the date upon which a certain Scripture was brought to my attention by God, the Holy Spirit, or through Bible study. Another wonderful suggestion is to insert your name into or speak in first person when proclaiming a Scripture—this will make it more personal and allow you to hear that the Scripture is actually truth for you. For example, you can say, "…The joy of the Lord is MY strength" or "…I, (insert name), have the mind of Christ." You might try some of these notation methods for yourself as well.

SPIRITUAL PROCLAMATIONS

I encourage you to pray and meditate on these spiritual proclamations daily:

- "…the joy of the Lord is your strength." (Nehemiah 8:10)
- "The LORD has done it this very day; let us rejoice today and be glad." (Psalm 118:24)
- "…the one who is in you is greater than the one who is in the world." (1 John 4:4)
- "…the God we serve is able to deliver us from it…" (Daniel 3:17)

- "…we have the mind of Christ." (1 Corinthians 2:16)

- "The LORD reigns…" (Psalm 93:1)

- "I will extol the LORD at all times; his praise will always be on my lips." (Psalm 34:1)

- "If God is for us, who can be against us?" (Romans 8:31)

- "37 No, in all these things we are more than conquerors through him who loved us. 38 For I am convinced that neither death nor life, neither angels nor demons, neither the present nor the future, nor any powers, 39 neither height nor depth, nor anything else in all creation, will be able to separate us from the love of God that is in Christ Jesus our Lord." (Romans 8:37–39)

- "I can do all this through him who gives me strength." (Philippians 4:13)

- "For the battle is not yours, but God's." (2 Chronicles 20:15)

- "Be strong and courageous. Do not be afraid or terrified because of them, for the LORD your God goes with you; he will never leave you nor forsake you." (Deuteronomy 31:6)

- "[16] This is what the LORD says—he who made a way through the sea, a path through the mighty waters, [17] who drew out the chariots and horses, the army and reinforcements together, and they lay there, never to rise again, extinguished, snuffed out like a wick: [18] 'Forget the former things; do not dwell on the past. [19] See, I am doing a new thing! Now it springs up; do you not perceive it? I am making a way in the wilderness and streams in the wasteland.'" (Isaiah 43:16–19)

- "Your word is a lamp for my feet, a light on my path." (Psalm 119:105)

- "[3] I will proclaim the name of the LORD. Oh, praise the greatness of our God! [4] He is the Rock, his works are perfect, and all his ways are just. A faithful God who does no wrong, upright and just is he." (Deuteronomy 32:3–4)

- "The Spirit of the Sovereign LORD is on me, because the LORD has anointed me to proclaim good news to the poor. He has sent me to bind up the brokenhearted, to proclaim freedom for the captives and release from darkness for the prisoners, [2] to proclaim the year of the LORD's favor and the day of vengeance of our God, to comfort all who mourn, [3] and provide for those who grieve in Zion—to bestow on them a crown of beauty instead of ashes, the oil of joy instead of mourning, and a garment of praise instead of a spirit of despair. They will be called oaks of righteousness, a planting of the LORD for the display of his splendor." **(Isaiah 61:1–3)**

- "…speaking to one another with psalms, hymns, and songs from the Spirit. Sing and make music from your heart to the Lord…" **(Ephesians 5:19) and** "Let the message of Christ dwell among you richly as you teach and admonish one another with all wisdom through psalms, hymns, and songs from the Spirit, singing to God with gratitude in your hearts." **(Colossians 3:16)**

- "[22] But God has helped me to this very day; so, I stand here and testify to small and great alike. I am saying nothing beyond what the prophets and Moses said would happen— [23] that the Messiah would suffer and, as the first to rise from the dead, would bring the message of light to his own people and to the Gentiles." (Acts 26:22–23)

- "…as for me and my household, we will serve the LORD." (Joshua 24:15)
- "…the zeal of the LORD Almighty will accomplish this." (Isaiah 9:7)

God is more than capable of caring for us, and He can teach us to care for ourselves with His help. I call this "Self-Care with God." While you may be familiar with the term "self-care," you most likely have not heard Self-Care with God. It includes many of the spiritual disciplines you already read about earlier in this chapter. At its core, however, it involves a Christ-centered approach to self-care. God wants us to take good care of ourselves. Some of my favorite go-to Self-Care with God activities include art therapy, walking, and journaling, as well as reading the Bible, listening to praise and worship music, and reading a daily devotion. The main point with self-care is that we are not just engaging in it during the course of therapy but are also adopting it as a normal part of our daily life. I believe self-care is good but "Self-Care with God" is better.

God calls us to bear one another's burdens. However, we need to maintain healthy boundaries when doing so. I cannot help you carry your load any more than I should expect you to carry mine. That is the job and responsibility of Jesus (see again, Matthew 11:28–30). But I can walk with you through a difficult time, pray with and for you, and remind you that you are not alone in your suffering. This extra care can often come in the form of a single person or through an established support group. We will talk more about this later. You will have to find what works best for you while also maintaining healthy boundaries.

Through His grace and mercy, the Lord will often place into your path the people who can walk with and help care for you, too. "He lifted me out of the slimy pit, out of the mud and mire; he set my feet on a rock and gave me a firm place to stand." (Psalm 40:2) As you move forward, it will be rewarding to develop the skills necessary to care for yourself, with the help of God. In the next chapter, we will look at the importance of creating a trusted care circle, how that sets us up for long-term healing success, and the people you should consider for this very important role in your healing journey.

Questions for Reflection

1. What were some of the things that people said to me or told me that were not helpful in my healing journey? What was helpful? What did I tell myself that was not helpful? What did I tell myself that was helpful?

2. Have I been trying to heal on my own? Have I asked anyone else to help me? Have I allowed God in? Have I given Him a chance to help and heal me? What are my coping mechanisms? Are they helpful or hurtful? Do I have established "safe places"?

3. Is the term "Spiritual Disciplines" new to me? Do I practice any of these disciplines already? Am I open to trying new things? Do I have a workable list?

4. Am I open to keeping a journal? Have I been doing that throughout the course of reading this book? How could (or has) that be helpful to me on my healing journey? Did I try to journal in the past but found that it did not work for me? What could I do

differently this time around in order to make it a more positive experience?

5. Is the term "Self-Care with God" new to me? How do I care for myself? Is God a part of that process? When I achieve a milestone in my healing journey, do I do anything special to celebrate? Do I have a workable list?

———•———————•———————•———

Come into the Light

Gracious Lord and Heavenly Father, healing is difficult. There are times that I want to give up, escape, forget about everything. Sometimes, people say the most hurtful things to me. Forgive them. Help me to forgive them. Sometimes, I say the most hurtful things to myself. Help me to find better words—fill me with Your Word—so I am speaking life, and not death, over myself. I tend to think that I have to have it all together. But You know the plans You have for me, and You desire to walk with me. Help me to let You in, more and more. I desire this. Help me to take better care of myself, with Your help, and to develop and maintain healthy boundaries. Help me to look to You for the things that only You can provide. When I feel like giving up, help me to turn to You. Help me to cast my cares upon You because You care for me. Help me to celebrate my successes. Help me, also, to develop safe places for myself. I need You, Lord. You are faithful to walk with me through the grief. Help me to find my rest in You. Help me to heal. Lead me in the way I am to go. I want to follow You. In Jesus's name, I pray. Amen.

Chapter 3

CREATING A TRUSTED CARE CIRCLE

*"Carry each other's burdens, and in this way, you will
fulfill the law of Christ." (Galatians 6:2)*

G od calls us to bear one another's burdens and to do that in Christian love. As believers, we are all one in Christ Jesus. While we all desire to be cared for in a loving manner, we must be realistic and understand that not everyone will be able to fulfill this need for us. We must find the right individuals who we can trust and who will be a part of our own trusted care circle. Before you set out to assemble your trusted care circle, it is important to acknowledge that you will be the first member of your trusted care circle. Yes, *you*. Just as we discussed in Chapter 2, there will be times that you will need to care for yourself. There are also times when you will be looking for care from others. Both are good. God did not create us to do life alone. We all need a support system. But we must do this important step with the help of the Lord.

What is a trusted care circle? In general, this is a select group of people who will walk with you throughout your healing process—whatever that looks like for you—and support you according to your needs. These are the people you can call on, even in the middle of the night. They have your best interest in mind; they are *for* you. When the whole world feels like it is against you, these people are your safe place to fall. They will help bear your burden. Ideally, they will do so without judgment. At times, they might need to tell you things you do not want to hear, but you need to let them. Be open to allowing different perspectives to shape the course of your healing process. Sometimes others can see things more clearly than we can. Our perspective only shows us what we see, while others can see a situation differently. Think of it as an extension of your own vision, seeing is magnified and sometimes even clarified. However, the best perspective is God's.

He sees everything, and you can trust Him to show you the way forward. Think of it, too, as an even greater extension of this new vision, untainted and complete. And He will always lead you on the easiest path you will go on.

There is a common saying: "Grief is a process and healing is a journey." It is also important to remember the need for pacing yourself as you heal. A solid support system is integral to the overall success of your healing journey, but you want and need to select key people to walk with you through a time of processing deep-seated grief. For me, this trusted care circle ultimately consisted of my therapist, one of my pastors, one family member, and one dearly beloved friend. It did not start out that way, though. When I began formal therapy, I had made a list of those to whom I had told bits and pieces of my experiences over time. Some were family members and others were friends. I was hopeful that my trusted care circle would include many, many people. However, within the first two weeks, nearly all of them had fallen by the wayside. At first, I didn't understand why. Those who did not make my final care circle failed to respond to me in any way, assumed that a spiritual platitude or two would make it all better, or literally avoided me whenever they saw me.

At some point, it became clear who would and who would not be a member of my trusted care circle. This was a painful, but necessary, part of my healing journey. Most likely, the same will be true for you. In these instances, it's important that we not take offense or hold on to any type of unforgiveness towards those who failed us or could not walk with us for whatever reason. Failing to do this will only hurt us, not them. We need to be willing to give grace to those who can't walk with us. Ultimately, it's the right thing to do. After all, we all have different gifts given to us by the Lord.

You need to know that not everyone will be capable of or willing to take this walk with you. Many will choose not to believe you. Some will even abandon you. Some will talk about you behind your back and share deeply personal information with others without your permission for them to do so. Moreover, some will only hinder you on your journey by holding you back from reaching your healing goals and, in some cases, make the pain and hurt you are already experiencing worse over time. Some others are not even capable of doing something as simple as listening. This was so difficult for me to understand in the beginning, but I now understand it to be an undeniable part of the process.

It is also necessary for you to develop and maintain healthy boundaries for yourself so that you are under a good level of protection while you are healing. "Do not be yoked together with unbelievers. For what do righteousness and wickedness have in common? Or what fellowship can light have with darkness?" (2 Corinthians 6:14) When you are coming out of spiritual (or any type of) bondage and entering into your healing process, you will encounter a lot of challenges. Healthy boundaries look different for each person, but they serve to ensure you are stable emotionally, mentally, psychologically, and physically. These boundaries are derived from our identity and, in some ways, actually help to form our identity. In Chapter 9, we will take a deeper look at our identity formation and how boundaries play a significant role in that formational process. A lack of healthy boundaries can create a very unstable life. However, healthy boundaries come from a good sense of our own self-worth, which we are then able to model for others.

In the end, all you need is to find one trustworthy person who will believe and support you according to your needs. If you are able to find more than one person, that is even better. But do not give up until you find that one person. Keep. Moving. Forward.

How do you create your trusted care circle? First, I encourage you to pray about it. Ask God with whom you should align on your healing journey. He knows. Second, look for trusted, caring people in your life, starting with your church, such as your pastor, a spiritual leader (same-sex), a spiritual mentor (same-sex), a friend in a Bible study group (same-sex). It is important for me to note that suggesting these caring people are same-sex individuals helps to ensure your safety and maintain your healthy boundaries. Of course, being a female and having a male pastor is a personal choice (and this is also the most common gender for a pastor) and these individuals have taken a vow before God to honor Him and others, regardless of the care receiver's gender—male or female. It is our desire that all would conduct themselves in an honorable manner. I am sharing with you my educated suggestions, but you will have to make the best decision for yourself. As the Lord leads you, ask them if they are willing to walk with you on your healing journey. Once you have an idea of whom you might ask, you can inquire as to if they are even open to the idea. Meeting with them in person to ask is generally the best approach, but you can call them if that is more your style. You can let them know that you're entering into a time in your life where you need extra support, and that you feel they would be an ideal person for the role of a trusted care circle member, and tell them why you feel the way that you do about them. Be honest. Be open. Advise them that you don't know how long the journey will take, but you do hope they will take the journey with you. Be prepared for them to say yes or no, and give them the grace to do so. I was not necessarily prepared in all instances, and some of the no responses were crushing. As I look back on it, though, I understand those were just not the right people for me—and that is okay.

If you do not already have a home church, I would recommend looking for a church that teaches the Holy Bible, not just some form of it. This church should also believe in the LORD God—Father, Son, Holy Spirit. There are many false teachers in the world today. You do not want to be involved in a church that looks and acts like the world. Pray about it. Ask God to lead you to a solid, God-fearing, Bible-believing and Bible–teaching church. He will. He is faithful to do it.

I would suggest looking into obtaining a Stephen Minister. Stephen Ministry is a Christ-centered, caregiving ministry, wherein a care receiver (you) is paired up with a caregiver (a same-sex Stephen Minister) that walks with you through a difficult time in your life, praying with and for you, listening to you unconditionally, and sharing their faith, God's Word, and Christ's love without judgment. This person can come from your own church or another church in your hometown. There are many different denominational churches offering a Stephen Ministry program (or their version of a caring ministry). Sometimes, depending on your circumstances, it can actually be ideal if they do not attend the same church as you. Pray about it. God knows. He will not lead you astray. My Stephen Minister, Donna, attends a different church than I do, and that is okay. She was not even a member of my trusted care circle (originally), as she came into my life about four months following completion of my formal therapy—I had four other individuals who served as my official trusted care circle members. And while most of them continued walking with me, even past the point of when formal therapy ended, Donna filled a role in my care team that only she could fill. God surely knows.

You can consider asking a dear friend to become a member of your trusted care circle. This should be someone who is not part of the problem areas in your life. You're looking for someone who adds to your life and the positive trajectory of your healing journey. Your desire should be to move toward the path of greater wholeness and away from the path of greater brokenness. Many people choose to continue down the path of greater brokenness because they don't feel or believe that they deserve any better. You need someone who is willing to take that walk with you, whatever that looks like for you. I hope you choose the path of greater wholeness, dear friends. I hope you choose to be healed.

You can always consider asking someone from your own family to be a trusted care circle member, but I would recommend that you ***proceed with great caution*** on this option. Many family members may be too close to you to provide the type of care you may need. Specifically, it may be difficult to maintain healthy boundaries within your family of origin— there just may be too much negative history. A pretty good indicator of future behavior is past behavior, as they say. Since you are dealing with sexual assault or child sexual abuse, it is highly likely that some level of dysfunction may be present in your family of origin, which could possibly include parents and siblings. And as I have alluded to previously, for some survivors, family members were or are the perpetrators. You can examine how each person handles themselves in their own life—do they conduct themselves in a trustworthy manner, or do they let you down repeatedly? For me, choosing my youngest sister to be a member of my trusted care circle was an easy decision because I had learned over time that she could be trusted; that she was for me; that she genuinely cared about me—I saw evidence of this, over time. Just proceed with caution as you are considering family members for your trusted care circle.

Of equal importance is the task of determining which therapist or counselor you should select to guide you through the more formal part of your healing journey. You can consider contacting a local sexual assault center, just as I did. You can get a referral to a therapist or counselor from your primary care physician. You can also contact an organization that provides services to sexual violence survivors and ask for a referral from them. I recommend a Christian counselor if you can find one in your area. Again, pray about this and all selection decisions.

Although I did not pursue this option for myself, you could also consider looking into joining a support group. There are many resources for this, but the best one would likely come from your therapist or counselor.

The Lord will order your steps if you seek Him, and He will place the correct people in your path. But you must ask for and utilize godly wisdom and discernment throughout. You can trust Him to guide your entire trusted care circle selection process. He will. He is faithful. Overall, your main goal is to avoid retraumatization, regardless of whom you select. This can be caused by consciously or unconsciously sharing traumatic details of past trauma, which causes you to feel as though you are reliving a past event in the present. The main emphasis is to avoid sharing your survivor story too many times and/or with the wrong people, to the point that it opens up so many wounds. You want to ensure you're with the right people who can help you process your thoughts and feelings in a healthy manner. This is *your* trusted care circle. Ultimately, the choice is yours.

You can meet with your trusted care circle members at your church, in a coffee shop, at your therapist or counselor's office, in a park, or at a restaurant. Perhaps you can think of even safer options on your own. If the situation is warranted, you can also consider meeting in your own home. Just remember to maintain healthy boundaries because you need to ensure that your safe places remain safe for you. The frequency of meeting with the members of your trusted care circle may be different from member to member. For example, you may prefer to talk with one member over the phone, while meeting in person with another member might be more fruitful and helpful to you. You might consider meeting with a member once a week, though it might be advisable at times to meet more often or less often, depending on where you are in your healing journey. On occasion, you may find that you need time to just breathe. This is okay. Give yourself permission to do that. I know that there were times I needed to pause and reflect, and that had to be done by myself and with the help of the Lord. Other times, I needed a sounding board or to see a friendly face. Just know that you have options when your trusted care circle is properly created.

What do you do when a member of your trusted care circle passes away, moves, or needs to be removed from your care circle for some reason? It is advisable to take a step back, reevaluate, go through the necessary grieving steps, and possibly find a new member. Maybe it's not even necessary to replace them. However, you can't allow a setback to derail you from your overall goal: moving forward in your healing process and becoming whole in Christ Jesus. Take it one step at a time. Pray about it. It will all come together. God will lead the way.

Finally, I believe that a trusted care circle is not complete without the Lord. In addition to our other trusted care circle members, we also have the Lord to provide care to us on our healing journey. His care is the best care of all. He understands our pain, because whenever an evil act such as the perpetration of sexual assault or child sexual abuse against any one of us has occurred, it directly affects Him, as Holy Spirit lives and breathes in us. When Holy Spirit is in us, anything that happens to us also happens to the Lord. He truly understands our pain and suffering. You should know that the most important relationship we have in our life is the one we have with God through Christ Jesus our Lord. I believe the most essential member of your trusted care circle is the LORD God. Why, you may ask? He will never leave you nor forsake you. He will not judge you. He will love you unconditionally. He will always be there for you. He will give you everything you need to endure and rise above. God does not set us up for failure; He always sets us up for success. We can trust Him to walk with us on our healing journey.

————•————————•————————•————

August 7, 2011

I have not written in my journal for over a week now (10 days). The main reason is that I started doing some really deep and heavy grief work following my last session with my therapist, and I was overwhelmed with intense grief, fear, and pain. I suppose this was to be expected.

I had been experiencing nightmares, feeling emotional and under a heavy, heavy shroud of grief. I talked with one of the members of my trusted care circle about this, and she helped me through this difficult time. I am thankful for her unconditional support. I think I was just not ready to go deeper into the experiences yet. And that is okay.

About a week ago, I had a spiritual breakthrough. God brought someone across my path who shared with me several words of knowledge from the Lord. He told me that God needed me to know that I am not alone in my suffering; that I am seen and remembered by the Lord; that I am God's child; that He is always with me; that

He would never forsake me. This person knew nothing about my journey. When I heard all of this, I burst into tears. It was exactly what I needed to hear in that moment. God surely knows.

This same man shared some Scripture with me that the Lord had placed on his heart for me, as well as more words of knowledge. Specifically, I had been praying for God to deliver me from the oppression I had been feeling, but what I needed to be praying for was that God would deliver me from the fear that was causing the oppression. This was a major revelation and connection! Before I went to bed that night, I prayed for God to deliver me from the fear that had held me captive for years—to take it from me, along with all of the related feelings, praying for His peace and joy and love to envelop me—and He was good to His Word. The Lord answered my prayers, as when I went to bed I slept so peacefully. The next morning when I woke up, the fear and heaviness that had been oppressing me were completely gone. Now, I will continue to focus on moving forward in my healing journey. With and through Christ, I know that will happen.

This same man confirmed God's call on my life (ministry) and told me that God would be using everything that had occurred in my life for good. I am overjoyed to have received this affirmation. Thank You, Jesus! God is so good all the time.

Over the course of a four-month period, my therapist, Catharine, listened to me unconditionally and reminded me of my truth: I am not alone in my suffering, I did not cause the abuse, it was not my fault, I deserve to heal, I am not a victim, and I have hope. It takes a very special person to sit with you and listen to the details of your suffering—yes, *all* of the details— and Catharine was a godsend to me in my time of great need. She, along with three other trusted people in my life, expressed selflessness and a willingness to take this journey toward healing with me, seeing me through all four months of the formal therapy process. They supported me according to my needs, offering prayer, a shoulder to cry on, and a hand to hold. They sat with me in silence, encouraging me when I felt down, reminding me that I was not alone. They all stood by me when so many others had abandoned and forsaken me. I am forever grateful to each of them for their compassion and loving care. Above all, we can choose to trust in God to provide the courage and strength we need to endure and rise above the circumstances of our past.

As you move forward in your healing process, a range of thoughts, feelings, and emotions will start to surface and begin to unravel before you, like an old spool of thread. In fact, I'm certain that much of what I have share with you, to this point, has stirred up a plethora of emotions in each of you. These need to be processed, and I know that this can often feel overwhelming. We will explore some of these feelings and emotions on a deeper level in upcoming chapters. Memories will be uncovered, generally at the most inopportune time. Nevertheless, I encourage you to keep pressing on: keep sharing, keep getting help, keep choosing to heal. If people do not understand, keep searching for someone who does. Sharing your deepest and most personal feelings with just anyone is never wise; you must carefully create a trusted care circle. The burdens of a survivor are massive, but God has promised the following: "to bestow on [us] a crown of beauty instead of ashes, the oil of joy instead of mourning, and a garment of praise instead of a spirit of despair." (Isaiah 61:3) We can do it, dear friends, with the help of God.

Questions for Reflection

1. Have I ever considered creating a trusted care circle for myself? Why?

2. Who could potentially be a member of my trusted care circle? Why?

3. Who should NOT be a member of my trusted care circle? Why?

4. Am I willing to include God in my trusted care circle? Why?

5. Where could I meet with my trusted care circle members? How often could/should we meet?

Come into the Light

Gracious Lord and Heavenly Father, I've been on this healing journey alone. I desire to not only create a trusted care circle, but I desire for You to be a member of it. I admit that, at times, I am lost and I don't know the way forward. But You do. Show me the way I am to go! Give me the godly wisdom and discernment I need to make the best decisions for myself, and help me to engage fully in my own healing process. If my boundaries are out of line, help me to hedge them up and secure them, in and through You. I desire to heal from the sexual violence that has occurred in my life, and I need Your help to continue to move forward. Help me, Lord. I need You. Be with me, Lord. I need You. Walk with me, Lord. I need You, and I love you. In Jesus's name, I pray. Amen.

Chapter 4

UNDERSTANDING OUR FEELINGS AND EMOTIONS

"I will give them praise and honor in every land where
they have suffered shame." (Zephaniah 3:19)

Shame. Blame. Guilt. Self-doubt. Fear. Torment. Shock. These are all such needlessly heavy burdens to bear; burdens that, as survivors of sexual assault and child sexual abuse, are not even ours to begin with. These feelings, much like our devious enemy the devil, seep into every facet of our soul. This is an enemy who is always at the ready, complete with a plan solely created to destroy us and hold us eternally captive amid the dark and painful memories related to our past. This enemy is hell-bent on tightening our already-binding chains and keeping us from living the life God has planned for us.

The feelings and emotions I have shared above are all very common, experienced by most anyone who has endured sexual violation in any way. I experienced *all* of them. I also battled with depression, sadness, and anger. These feelings, among others, can be as nebulous as the celestial sky. However, it is Father's desire to show us things that we otherwise would not have seen on our own, to reveal the trauma, the damage it has caused, and heal it. He has the ability to unearth the things that are buried deep in our heart so the Light of Christ can come in and healing can take place. You do not have to live with any of these false feelings forever. The enemy would tell you that you do, but God says otherwise. Although we have feelings and emotions, they do not control us; we can and should learn to control them instead. "For the Spirit God gave us does not make us timid (fearful), but gives us power, love, and self-discipline (a sound mind)." (2 Timothy 1:7)

Emotions and feelings, in general, often stem from unresolved trauma that is harbored within the heart and soul (mind, will, emotions) of a survivor. When a soul has unchecked and unhealed trauma, on any level, it is very common for this trauma to manifest in other ways—physically, mentally, emotionally, spiritually, and socially—some of which actually may go undetected. We need to get to the root of the trauma in order for true healing to take place. It is then that, with the help of the Lord, we are able to move away from the trauma of the past, from the fear of the future, and live fully in the present, whole and healed in Christ Jesus.

In God's Word, we read about a man named Terah. He was the father of Abram (later called Abraham), Nahor, and Haran (see Genesis 11:27–32). During his lifetime, Terah's son Haran died. This created a deep state of grief for Terah. As God called them to move on from a place called Ur of the Chaldeans and go to the land of Canaan, Terah decided to settle in a place called Haran, which bore the same name as his late son. Grief can do strange things to people when it goes unprocessed and remains unhealed. When he was supposed to keep moving on, as the Lord had instructed, Terah stayed in a perpetual and literal state of grief instead of fulfilling the call of God on his life. Grief can bring in sickness and infirmity among other spiritual afflictions and physical ailments. So, while it is important to grieve and to do that in a healthy manner, it's also important not to set up camp in a state of grief indefinitely. You can grieve, but you can also move on with the help of the Lord.

September 3, 2011

I have not written in my journal for about three weeks now, so I need to catch up...but I have been making a lot of progress in my grief work and healing journey. I'm very proud of that.

To this point, I have met with my therapist for four sessions. We have talked in detail about the first instance of sexual assault and child sexual abuse (6 years old to 12 years old), including the related feelings and how it occurred. I understand that people do not hurt other people unless they themselves are also hurting in some way—this knowledge has been very helpful to me on my own healing journey.

*The initial instance of abuse took my innocence and robbed me of my childhood. My therapist and I talked about the **how** and the **why**, including the fact that I did not do anything to cause the abuse to happen, and it was not my fault. Although I may have* *wanted to tell someone what was happening to me, I suffered in silence and shouldered the pain and hurt all alone. It is not always possible to talk to those around you, and there are many reasons for this. This "remaining-in-silence" phenomenon is very common for survivors, but I was not alone in my silence and suffering—God was with me, always. I knew that then, and I reestablished this truth in my present. My feelings do matter. My thoughts deserve to have a voice. I was thankful that my therapist listened to me when I shared with her from my heart.*

We also discussed the second instance of assault and abuse (16 years old). We discussed the specifics of what happened and how I felt about it. We also discussed the fact that I was the "bad guy" in this situation, viewed to be at fault by many, which could not have been further from the truth; and, sadly, I learned that this happens to many survivors. Why is it necessary to blame a survivor for the sexual assault and child sexual abuse that someone else has perpetrated against them? It is cruel and hurtful; it is divisive and wrong; it is retraumatizing.

There were people who were not there for me during this time in my life. As a result, I believe I began to look for this behavior in the relationships I had with men over the coming years. These men (with the exception of one or two of them) only treated me the way that I (deep down) thought I deserved to be treated. I was abused, taken advantage of; I did anything and everything I could think of to please them, even if it was at my own expense; they were often emotionally unavailable to me and often used me for their own benefit or gain. As I identify and come to terms with all of this, I am upset that I allowed myself to endure such poor treatment from them (again, with one or two exceptions). However, I know this occurred because I had such a low self-esteem and self-worth, and such a poor self-image because of the assault, abuse, and abandonment I had endured, both emotionally and physically. Now that I have been able to identify these things, I know better. Now that I know better, I can do and expect better for myself in the future. It truly is God's best for me.

We also talked a little bit about the third instance of sexual assault and child sexual abuse (16 years old to 28 years old). This perpetration involved multiple people, pornography, various sexual situations, as well as sexual assault and abuse. I feel so lethargic and depressed when I write about these experiences. While I feel like stopping, I am determined to keep moving forward! These were and are very, very dark times in my life. I often felt forgotten during this *time. I was not able to discuss with my therapist the various details of the third instance of sexual assault and abuse as I had been able to do for the first and second instances—I found that recalling the memories was and is just too painful. We will get into more of that during our next therapy session.*

We have talked a lot about grooming and about how my second- and third-instance abusers did that, specifically. They formed relationships with me, tested the boundaries, and utilized touching, intimidation, and secrets, in order to control and manipulate me. I did not necessarily realize the grooming was taking place at the time, but I now realize that it was, as I recall certain events of the assault and abuse—grooming was definitely happening.

I am working on creating healthier boundaries in my life, within all of my relationships, as I know this is God's best for me. I now am in a place where I can actually do that. Gone are the days when I met everyone else's needs and mine were placed last or not considered at all. I deserve respect. My feelings matter. I matter! I AM ALLOWING NO MORE ABUSE OF ANY KIND IN MY LIFE. NONE! I deserve much better than I have been receiving and allowing, and not just from all of the perpetrators. I deserve to surround myself with people who will love, support, and care for me.

I deserve a man who will love, treasure, and respect me; to have a life filled with love, joy, and peace. This is God's desire for me, too.

I realize that although many people let me down by their responses and behavior, others caused me to feel loved and as though I could share more when I was ready. At times, the feelings were too much, too overwhelming...so I just stopped feeling and/or acknowledging them altogether. However, I am making great progress. I am really trying to focus on sharing the details of the assault and abuse, and better understand how and why it happened. I realize that I need someone to hear me, and my therapist and the other three members of my trusted care circle allow that to be a reality. I am so very thankful.

*As I share more and more about the actual experiences, it is allowing me to be free from the shame, blame, guilt, and self-doubt. I realize that these feelings were and are **false**—they were never meant for me. I have resolved that the assault and abuse was not my fault, that I am a survivor, and that I am not alone in my suffering and pain. I continue to be open to the healing process and to sharing about my experience with sexual assault and child sexual abuse. I will continue to evaluate how I can best introduce into my life the things I needed, but did not receive, and to do so in a positive* *manner. I will continue to be gentle with myself and take this journey one small step at a time. I will be honest about my experiences and realize that I deserve healing and positive relationships in my life.*

I am concerned about getting through the sharing of the remaining instances of sexual assault and abuse because I am afraid of what I may uncover and how it will cause me to feel. I know that I need to continue to make changes so I can move forward. I want to heal and I want to help others; I want God to bring good out of all of this evil and negativity. I know God will help me to do that. I trust in Him 100%. I know that He will never forsake me!

I do have a right for others to hear about and validate my feelings. I deserve happiness, healing, and a joyous future. I deserve love, peace, and hope to be present in my life. I am worthy of being loved, by others and by myself. I am slowly rewriting the negative tapes in my mind with positive messages. I am committed to healing and moving forward in a positive manner, expecting and creating a better life for me! All glory to God!

September 5, 2011

"The LORD has done it this very day; let us rejoice today and be glad." *(Psalm 118:24) I received another breakthrough today—I was able to let go of shame, blame, guilt, and self-doubt related to the sexual assault and child sexual abuse I endured. I could finally reconcile these **false** feelings, and the Lord helped me to remove them from my heart. I understand that I no longer need to hold on to those false feelings because God has already taken on all of that through Jesus Christ on the cross. The enemy had been holding me back through these emotional strongholds for nearly 30 years. NO MORE! "May I never boast except in the cross of our Lord Jesus Christ, through which the world has been crucified to me, and I to the world." (Galatians 6:14)*

September 8, 2011

God continues to do a good work in me. I released more emotions today, from the depths, from the deep, dark crevices of my heart. They are gone! God has something amazing planned for my life and for me. I am open to it. I am ready for it, in God's perfect timing. I am thankful to God for taking me to it, according to His will. My "new normal" is beginning to come into focus. I am grieving and letting go of the past. The little girl in me is healing. The godly woman in me is loosed and free, a little more each day. The child of God in me is coming alive again in ways that I have not felt in years, maybe ever. It is the most prolific experience I have ever felt and endured, and yet I embrace it and "consider it pure joy!" (James 1:2)

A common assessment tool used in my line of work is the Adverse Childhood Experiences (ACEs), a survey that asks 10 yes-no questions pertaining to various situations a person may have faced before the age of 18.[3] The situations included in the brief questionnaire are deemed to be common for causing adverse effects in children that can persist into their adult years. These situations include types of abuse, neglect, and household dysfunction. All of these experiences would certainly pose a high risk to any child, so, the assessment clearly reveals the presence

3 "Adverse Childhood Experiences," April 3, 2020, Centers for Disease Control and Prevention, https://www.cdc.gov/violenceprevention/aces/index.html.

of the risk factors within the home. What the assessment does not look at, however, is stressors outside the home that can also contribute to the child's risk for adversity. It does not take into account the child's positive and protective factors, the people or places outside of the household that can bring a positive, healing element—the community can often assist in the healing process. There is also no emphasis given to the great differences in each individual, the risks each one faces, and the fact that nothing in life is a guarantee; things can sometimes be worse than imagined or better than once believed.

Most importantly, it does not capture resilience. A high ACE score does exhibit a predisposition to trauma and exploitation. Based on my ACE score of seven (answering "yes" equates to one point, with ten being the highest possible score), I should be at or very near the worst end of every possible outcome in virtually every area of life. But, as I am clearly revealing to the entire world through this book, I AM HEALED! How is this possible? This assessment is missing one other VERY IMPORTANT FACTOR: God and His ability to heal us. Yes, life is filled with difficult situations and adverse experiences that bring about an abundance of feelings and emotions, as well as understood risk factors. But it is also filled with hope and healing. You are not your experiences. You do not have to live the life you saw your family live. You can break the cycle, and you can have the healing and wholeness in the Lord that Jesus died to give all of us. I believe the choice is ours to make.

In the Bible, we read about someone named Elijah. At some point in his journey, he found himself depressed, sitting under a juniper tree, asking God just to let him die. Sometimes life is difficult to deal with. Sometimes, like Elijah, we feel as though we are losing our way. We feel we cannot possibly go on. I know there were instances when emotions got overwhelming for me and other times I was attacked by suicidal thoughts. However, we need to remember that it is through suffering that we can draw closer to the Lord. It is through suffering that we become more Christ-like.

- "Therefore, since we have been justified through faith, we have peace with God through our Lord Jesus

Christ, [2] through whom we have gained access by faith into this grace in which we now stand. And we boast in the hope of the glory of God. [3] Not only so, but we also glory [rejoice] in our sufferings, because we know that suffering produces perseverance; [4] perseverance, character; and character, hope. [5] And hope does not put us to shame, because God's love has been poured out into our hearts through the Holy Spirit, who has been given to us." (Romans 5:1–5)

- "[2] Consider it pure joy, my brothers and sisters, whenever you face trials of many kinds, [3] because you know that the testing of your faith produces perseverance. [4] Let perseverance finish its work so that you may be mature and complete, not lacking anything." (James 1:2–4)

Now, you may read the two passages above and ask the following questions: How is it possible to glory (rejoice) in our suffering? Why would I ever choose to "consider it [all] pure joy?" Why would God ask us to do that? Does He not know how painful sexual assault and child sexual abuse are to endure? The answers to these questions may surprise you.

God is not asking us to glory (rejoice) in our suffering because of the suffering itself; He is asking us to glory (rejoice) in our suffering because of what it can (and will) produce in us— *perseverance* (the ability to endure and rise above), *character* (a godly character), and *hope* (a hope that does not put us to shame). Dear friends, this is a beautiful thing. And this is possible to do when we realize that God's love has been poured out into our hearts through the Holy Spirit, who has been given to us. With God and His love, all things are, indeed, possible.

Similarly, God is asking us to consider it [all] pure joy, not because of the trials, but because of what the testing of our faith in trials produces in us: perseverance, making us mature and complete, not lacking anything. This is also a beautiful thing. The enemy would like nothing more than for our faith in God to suffer a death blow, rendering it useless in our life. The enemy likes to try to convince us that we are condemned and that we are supposed to live in the past. But God knows how painful sexual assault and child sexual abuse are to endure. He understands our pain, because whenever an evil act such as the perpetration of sexual assault or child sexual abuse against any one of us has occurred, it directly affects Him. He truly understands our pain, and we never walk alone.

———•———

I have very fond memories as a child of working in the garden with my paternal grandma. She and I would plant flowers and various kinds of produce in the garden at her home in Nebraska. I remember that she would spend a lot of time making sure the soil was prepared correctly so it could take the seed at the beginning of the planting season. Likewise, careful attention was given to ensuring that the garden was weeded on a regular basis so those things that my grandma wanted to grow would not be overtaken by the weeds. She showed me how to prune the plants, how to care for and water the plants while they were still growing, and how to pick the produce once it was ripe. These memories are some of my most treasured, as we always talked about life and explored the different types of birds and other elements of nature while we were out in the yard. In many ways, she was one of my rescuers, a soft place for me to fall.

Faith can be looked at much like gardening. We can even view our faith, as well as our feelings and emotions, as plants. We (our heart) should be the good soil. You could envision the plant of faith in the center of the garden and all of the feelings and emotions plants are surrounding it. Since the faith plant is in the center, and Christ is to be the center of our life, it makes sense that the faith plant should be the largest, with the largest and deepest root system. However, when the negative feelings and emotions plants are surrounding our faith, those negative plant root systems steal valuable and life-sustaining nutrients from the faith plant's root system. As a result, our faith begins to shrink to the point that it becomes strangled by the negative roots, and in some cases, it shrivels up altogether and dies.

The negative root systems—rejection, resentment, unforgiveness, bitterness, fear, doubt, and worry—take over, and before you know it, our faith is so debilitated that it feels like all hope is gone, too. Dear friends, we cannot allow this to happen. We need to allow the Lord to remove these *false* feelings and emotions, like weeds in a garden, and replace them with positive feelings and emotions, like love, joy, and peace. We need life-giving plants in our garden (our heart). We need to ensure that we not only have good soil but also that we are taking in good seeds. Seeds can be received, retained, and reproduced. Is it possible that we have received seeds into our "good soil" that are not good, that we were never meant to receive, that are producing rotten fruit and strangling our faith? We need to remove those bad seeds, and the Lord can help us with this pruning process. In a later chapter, we will do that together.

Once the bad seeds are removed, we need to view what we take in to our spiritual garden in the future through the lens of Galatians 6:14 "through the cross of Jesus Christ, I am reconciled to the world and the world is reconciled to me." In other words, Jesus is our plumb line. He is to be the center of all things. We may feel a certain way about something, but we don't have to become that feeling. I can feel sad, but I don't have to become sad. I can feel mad, but I don't have to become mad. When we feel a certain way about something, we should acknowledge and "feel" that feeling, and perhaps share about how we are feeling with someone we can trust. However, we need to complete the process by giving those feelings over to the Lord, who cares for us, because holding on to them causes us to become those feelings instead of releasing them to the Lord. We need to learn to fully process our feelings and to let them go.

Most of our feelings are connected to a memory. Even if that memory is fragmented, it is often possible to "camp out" in our feelings, to live in and out of the past. In Christ, we have the ability to take our thoughts captive. In fact, in God's Word, we read that we are to pull down all strongholds and hold all thoughts captive to the obedience of Christ Jesus (see 2 Corinthians 10:3–6). Did you know this? Yes! Another thing to consider doing is a powerful visualization exercise. Find a quiet place, close your eyes, and imagine the Lord in front of you. See the negative thought in big bold letters in front of you and watch as it is shrunken down and placed at Jesus's feet. This can be very helpful, and you should feel immediate peace when you do this exercise with the Lord. The Lord designed us such that we would have control over our feelings and emotions, not the other way around. You can have a thought, but you don't have to act on it. Wow! When the enemy tries to condemn us and convince us that false feelings are ours, we need to remind him of what God's Word says about condemnation.

• "Therefore, there is now no condemnation for those who are in Christ Jesus, [2] because through Christ Jesus the law of the Spirit who gives life has set you free from the law of sin and death. [3] For what the law was powerless to do because it was weakened by the flesh, God did by sending his own Son in the likeness of sinful flesh to be a sin offering. And so, he condemned sin in the flesh, [4] in order that the righteous requirement of the law might be fully met in us, who do not live according to the flesh but according to the Spirit." (Romans 8:1–4)

Another feeling or emotion commonly experienced by a survivor is fear. The enemy often seeks to control us through the spiritual stronghold of fear. I have not worked with a survivor who has not struggled in this area. Fear is a common tactic used by the enemy, as well as sexual violence perpetrators. We even see its prevalence in domestic violence. In a later chapter, we will discuss fear and how to overcome it with the help of the Lord. It's also important to know and be reminded that most feelings have a spiritual origin, and they need to be dealt with on that level (we will learn more about this in a later chapter, too).

Yet another feeling is bitterness rooted in anger. Holding on to the negative feelings that we, as survivors, have against those who have abused us only puts us in a spiritual prison. Without realizing it, we can become in bondage to a curse. God's Word encourages us to "bless those who seek to curse [us] and pray for those who mistreat [us]." (Luke 6:28) God has enough love and faith for both us and the offender; He has the power to redeem any and all hurtful circumstances. We need to let go and let God do what only He can do. He will take full responsibility for whatever punishment should be administered to the offenders. "Be not overcome with evil, but overcome evil with good." (Romans 12:17)

Are there other feelings and emotions present in the life and healing journey of a survivor? Most certainly. Some of them could include abandonment, grief, depression, ambivalence, helplessness, and panic. Just as there is an assortment of people in the world, there is also a wide range of feelings associated with sexual violence. God's Word tells us that "a woman giving birth to a child has pain because her time has come; but when her baby is born, she forgets the anguish because of her joy that a child is born into the world. So, with you: Now is your time of grief, but I will see you again and you will rejoice, and no one will take away your joy." (John 16:21–22) Let joy arise in the midst of your suffering, dear friends. Let joy arise! Continue to be open to allowing your heart to experience the joy that comes in the morning after a night of weeping.

God created us as human and spiritual beings; we all have feelings, which can be complex. For example, as discussed in an earlier chapter, fear can be both good (reverence and respect to and for God) and bad (being afraid of something). We are just not meant to "camp out" in our feelings. "Why, my soul, are you downcast? Why so disturbed within me? Put your hope in God, for I will yet praise him, my Savior and my God." (Psalm 43:5) While it's necessary to acknowledge what you are feeling—good, bad, or indifferent—it's also imperative to process your feelings and emotions in a healthy way with a trusted individual and to take them to the Lord in prayer. Life can bring change and times of waiting as well as times when we need to deal with difficult people. In all of these times, our feelings and emotions can try to take us to places of the past with ingrained patterns of how we usually deal with things or can move us into a new place. One is familiar, while the other is unknown. God's Word tells us that "the heart is deceitful above all things and beyond cure. Who can understand it?" (Jeremiah 17:9) In other words, don't follow your heart or be led by your feelings or emotions.

Instead, I suggest that where we are in life is not always where God intended for us to be, especially with respect to the damage that sexual violence causes. God desires to lead us out of that place, onto a new path, if we are willing to follow Him out. Are we willing to go with Him, onto this path of greater wholeness? "Be strong and courageous. Do not be frightened, and do not be dismayed, for the LORD your God is with you, wherever you go." (Joshua 1:9, ESV)

In God's Word, we read about something magnificent that Jesus did while walking with His disciples on the way to Jerusalem (see Mark 11:12–25). As He approached a fig tree— desiring to eat the fruit of it but finding none—He quickly cursed the tree and then went about His business. Why would He do this? I believe that Jesus knew, first of all, that He has authority over all of creation, including the fig tree. I believe He also knew that something about the tree was not right as it was not bearing any fruit. If it was not fig season, then He would have gone on His way without cursing the fig tree. But He cursed it, all the way down to its roots. He was making sure that the tree would not even live. He was cutting it off from its source. Something was wrong, and it needed to be addressed. Jesus could see deeper than the tree, the leaves, and the branches; the root system was bad. It was a spiritual matter, and He had to deal with it. If we have bad feelings, we need to be asking ourselves what is at the root of it. If it's not helping us to bear fruit in our life, it must be removed, root system and all, just like the fig tree that Jesus cursed all the way to the roots.

I once watched a dead tree being removed from a yard using a machine called a stump grinder, which grinds up all of the roots into mulch. As I watched through the window, I was struck by how methodical the stump grinder moved from one place to the next. It had a clear mission, but it was precise in the work it was meant to perform. You certainly would not win a race riding on it, as the grinder did not move very quickly. But it didn't need to be fast; it needed to be precise. If any part of the root system of the tree stump is left behind, it will regrow. As I watched the tree being dismantled and the stump being removed, I was reminded that this is what God does for us when we ask Him to forgive us. And, when we allow Him to do the good work of forgiveness in our heart, we can grow. Completely. When we let go and the forgiveness and healing process is complete, it removes the old, dying parts of us—roots and all—and it leaves room for new growth. How refreshing! We will further discuss this important concept of forgiveness in Chapter 10.

Remember: Your emotions are a gauge, not a guide. You may feel one way today, or in this very moment, but it won't always be that way. In Christ, you have the power to control your feelings, not the other way around. The choice is yours to make. "My flesh and my heart may fail, but God is the strength of my heart and my portion forever." (Psalm 73:26) Trust me when I tell you that choosing to live out of God's best for you is a wonderful choice. He knows. And, yet, He still continues to walk with us. How amazing. In God's Word, we also are encouraged to "be anxious about nothing, but in everything by prayer and supplication with thanksgiving, let your request be made known to God. And the peace of God, which surpasses all understanding, will guard your hearts and your minds in Christ Jesus." (Philippians 4:6–7, ESV)

———————•———————

Many survivors also experience something called triggers. I had heard this term some years ago, but I became especially familiar and acquainted with it over the course of my formal therapy with Catharine. Triggers bring a response of fight, flight, or freeze. It's quite common for someone experiencing a trigger, or an exacerbated trauma response, to become withdrawn or disengaged, daydream or skip school, act out or behave aggressively, become hyperactive or overly reactive, exhibit numbness or refuse to answer, or feel unlovable. In one way or the other, the survivor is preparing for real or perceived injury or a feeling of powerlessness. There is often a dissociation that occurs. This is a break in how your brain handles information. A person experiencing this can feel disconnected from thoughts, feelings, memories, and surroundings. The person can feel numb or detached, feel little or no pain, and become immobile (among other experiences). I learned that my triggers are plentiful, including the smell of a certain type of soap, the feel of an itchy couch or rough carpet, and the sight of white, creamy textures like shampoo, conditioner, or icing. It also bothered me when someone would tell me I am pretty, beautiful, or looking good. This extra attention just made me uncomfortable.

I needed to remind myself that it is okay for people to compliment me and to not allow that to tie in with the sexual assault and child sexual abuse of the past. I also needed to remind myself that the sexual assault and child sexual abuse was not my fault and that I am a survivor. I did nothing wrong. I did *nothing* wrong. When I came to terms with the truth—that I am more than a sexual favor or an object of someone's evil, sick, and twisted desires—God's Word and how He sees me began to take over and become the standard by which I saw myself, my real identity. I am certain that you likely have triggers, too, but please choose to believe that the Lord can and will help you to remove or manage these triggers and put things into their proper perspective, to see things through His eyes. It is from His perspective that lies turn into truth, damaged emotions are healed and restored, and victims become survivors who are also overcomers in Christ Jesus our Lord. "From the ends of the earth I call to you, I call as my heart grows faint; lead me to the rock that is higher than I." (Psalm 61:2)

It is important to understand that survivors can experience both real and perceived trauma in the present or from the past. This is because the senses are involved in the trauma: seeing, feeling, hearing, tasting, and smelling. One technique that is often helpful in these moments is to ground yourself in the present. You can do this by rubbing your hand on a solid surface, reminding yourself that you are not in the past where the trauma occurred but that you are safe in the present. Having a safe person to call in times of need is also advisable. They can help you to process the trauma in a healthy way. Developing a list of go-to coping mechanisms for times such as this will be helpful to you as you continue to move forward on your healing journey. The overall goal is to get to a point where, even when something triggers you, you are able to self-regulate and recover from the trigger safely and effectively without too much effort. Be at peace within yourself. "Let the peace of Christ rule in your hearts, since as members of one body you were called to peace. And be thankful." (Colossians 3:15)

Overall, the Lord can remove the guilt and repair the mistakes of the past. He can remove all of the false feelings and emotions, if we allow Him to do that, to strengthen our faith. The Lord does not condemn us; He loves us. He is in the restoration business and "by his wounds we are healed." (Isaiah 53:5) We need to trust in the Lord for our healing and deliverance, remove Him from our timetable, let Him do a good work in and through us according to His timetable, and just find our rest in Him. He is our hiding place. He is the One who makes joy in the morning possible.

Questions for Reflection

1. What feelings and emotions am I experiencing? Are any of these feelings *false*?

2. Do I have control over my emotions? Why? What do I need to address?

3. Tending my spiritual garden, what seeds do I need to remove? What root systems do I need to remove?

What are the feelings and emotions that I desire to address?

4. Have I been rejoicing in my suffering? What does that really mean to me?

5. Do I have any triggers? How can I overcome these triggers, with the help of the Lord?

***

Come into the Light

Gracious Lord and Heavenly Father, I recognize that my feelings and emotions have been unstable. There were times that I felt a certain way, and then I became that feeling—I now know that this is not Your best for me. I desire to receive Your help in not only better understanding my feelings and emotions, but also determining which of them are *false*. I want to have control over my emotions. I need Your help. Show me how to feel in a way that I don't become what I am feeling, unless it is a godly feeling and, then, I welcome it into my life and into my heart. If my spiritual garden needs to be weeded out, please help me to do that completely. If I have any triggers, please help me to identify them and to overcome them through Your Son Jesus. I can feel healing taking place, and I give You all of the glory. Continue to lead me in the way I am to go—I desire to follow You. In Jesus's name, I pray. Amen.

Chapter 5

LEARNING TO TRUST

"Those who know your name trust in you, for you,
Lord, have never forsaken those who seek you."
(Psalm 9:10)

I think I was about six years old when I found myself standing on the end of a diving board, looking down into the deep water below. I was frightened. I wanted to run away, to be anywhere but on the edge of that diving board. But there I was. And with a line of children behind me, all waiting to jump in, I didn't feel like I had any choice but to jump off of the board and into the water. Something was holding me back though: fear. Crippling fear. The kind of fear that paralyzes you on every single level. The only part of my body that could move was my eyes, and they were scanning the water below, looking around the indoor room where the pool was located for some kind of escape. I continually found there to be no other way out.

Eventually, I was able to focus on something that *was* comforting to me: my swimming teacher in the water below me. Her arms were raised up toward me, and she had a smile on her face. She was very encouraging. Patient. Loving. She reminded me that when I jumped into the water, I would not be by myself. She would be with me. If my head went below the water, she would be there to catch me. And soon I would rise above the surface of the water again, able to breathe. I would not drown. I would begin to swim. And she would help me. I could trust her to be there. I jumped, my body plunging beneath the water. And then I came up, filled my lungs with air, and found my way out of the water. In order to overcome my crippling fear, I had needed to know and to hear that I would not be doing it alone. I believe we can apply this same theory to the journey of life and healing from the damage that life has done to us. It is possible to heal. It is possible to trust. And God can help us to learn how to trust again.

Are we born with the ability to trust? I believe the answer to that is yes. We must have some sense of trust in those around us as we depend on our caregivers to provide for our needs. So, to a certain extent, as our needs are met and we have a history of needs being met, we come to trust those around us who are providing what we need. For a survivor, when an individual in a position of trust has violated us, a very strange dichotomy is created: I trust you because you meet my needs, but I also fear you because you hurt me. How do we reconcile that? For me, I know that I struggled for many years with understanding how to navigate this area of my own life. On many levels, we are taught from an early age to trust those around us. But as we grow older, we learn that trust is earned. Wow. That is very confusing. Trust goes right out the window.

But God has a better way. He is able to help us rebuild this area of our lives where emotional wounding and physical damage has caused a breach in our hedge of protection. Through Him, we can receive a clean heart, a clear mind, and establish a healthy relationship. We can learn to walk in His will and His ways, to the glory of His holy name. This is how we learn to develop trust.

As you move forward on your healing journey from sexual assault and child sexual abuse, understand that it is quite normal to be facing adversity and to feel constantly tested by any number of things. For many years, I not only had great difficulty trusting others but also could not fully trust myself. And spiritual attacks from the enemy were prevalent throughout. There is a battle going on between Satan and the Lord for our soul. Understand, also, that when Satan asks to sift us all like wheat (see Luke 22:31), we have a choice to succumb to the attacks of the enemy or to yield and humble ourselves to God and trust Him to see us through. When we run from the world and it's not to God, we are running from God's best for us. God is our hiding place. He preserves us from trouble. He delivers us (see Psalm 32:7). And remember, dear friends, Jesus is always praying that our faith would not fail us.

The pressure to trust can be so intense. I want to trust, but I don't know how. I want to learn how to trust, but I just need someone to show me how to do it safely. Trust requires that we move away from fear. It's not an act of our will; God's faithfulness shows us that the more we know Him, the more we can trust Him, no matter what has happened in our past.

Learning to trust is a lot like learning how to use a pressure cooker. The whole process must be handled with great care. Your goal is to cook the food in water at a very high temperature for a shorter period of time, but if any of the mechanisms fail, the pressure cooker will explode, causing serious damage to anyone and anything in its vicinity. The rubber ring under the lid ensures that the seal is tight. The valve on the top prevents the pressure inside from reaching a dangerous level. When the cooker starts to whistle, you know your food is cooked. Then it is time to release the pressure properly; a wrong move at this point could lead to disaster. Generally, you would wait for some of the steam to escape thus reducing the pressure inside of the cooker. You could also run cool water over the top of the cooker lid, which helps to slowly and safely reduce the temperature and pressure inside. Once you have reduced the pressure, it's safe to open the lid. Congratulations! You've followed the necessary steps to ensure a good end result, and you've learned how to do it safely.

Paul felt daily pressure, but he chose to see it and use it as a bridge rather than a burden. He held onto the hope of Christ; he learned that he could experience contentment in the face of adversity and experience God's strength in his own weakness.

The source for all his sufficiency and needs was definitely Jesus; he could trust the faithfulness of God. However, like us, God also knew the content of Paul's heart, and the things that God allowed him to go through helped to equip him to be an amazing and effective servant of God. Through all of the testing and the trials, God was strengthening Paul's message to his followers. Paul reminded himself that God was in control, was with him and for him, and was working everything together for his good, for the good of others, and for God's glory. When the bottom fell out and there was nowhere else to turn, when he felt abandoned or rejected, or when others had betrayed him, God showed up for Paul. He does that for us, too. He saw examples of God's faithfulness over time. This, I believe, is divine trust.

In the face of adversity, Paul was an even greater comforter because of the comfort he had received from Christ (see again, Romans 5:4—perseverance, character, hope). God was drawing Paul into an even deeper and more intimate relationship with Him. He does that with us, too, when we avail ourselves to the process. God raised him up repeatedly above his circumstances for the purpose of drawing him closer and strengthening that intimate relationship. How precious that God would love Paul and each of us so much that He would want to work in us to build a spiritual bridge rather than a spiritual divide. "The LORD has established his throne in heaven, and his kingdom rules over all." (Psalm 103:19) "And we know that in all things God works for the good of those who love him, who have been called according to his purpose." (Romans 8:28)

Just as Paul did, you can allow God to comfort you and raise you up above your circumstances and draw you into Him for the purpose of an even deeper and more intimate relationship with Him. "I have told you these things, so that in me you may have peace. In this world you will have trouble. But take heart! I have overcome the world." (John 16:33) You see, dear friends, blessings and trials can BOTH be blessings. We truly can count it all joy. We can also rise above. And we can do that because God is faithful to walk with us throughout the various afflictions in our daily lives, just as His Word says, He is truly the God of all comfort. Furthermore, strength is God's power made perfect in our weakness (see 2 Corinthians 12:9). We are those in whom Christ dwells. And it is well with us in Christ. Let us, therefore, be bridge builders with Him in the Kingdom of God. God is magnificent and faithful! Be inspired to trust in Him. He will never steer you wrong.

September 13, 2011

I met with my therapist again yesterday. We talked about the third instance of sexual assault and child sexual abuse. I am exhausted and emotionally drained. I have been working on accepting certain people in my life for who they are instead of who I want or need them to be. This is beyond challenging, but it is a necessary part of my healing journey.

September 18, 2011

I am gaining more and more clarity and insight into the plans that God has for my life and for the future of the ministry to which He has called me. He has shown me the last 30 years of my life, and I now have a better understanding as to how God will work through me and bring good to those who need help. There is so much suffering in the world and so much work to do. Praise God for His perfect ways and how He works to spread His joy, peace, and hope. I continue to do the necessary grief work. God is faithful to walk with me and work through me. I am feeling lighter and receiving more clarity, daily. God is so good all the time.

September 19, 2011

There is a lot of spiritual warfare going on behind the scenes. God is working and warring on my behalf. He is showing me how to let things go—this is a giant step forward in my healing journey. I love Jesus. I am so thankful for all He has done for me and all that He is doing in and through me. I continue to move forward, one step at a time.

September 20, 2011

I continue to work on creating safe places for myself, establish healthy boundaries and deeper levels of trust, undo the damage sexual assault and child sexual abuse have done, redefine what love really is, and understand and prepare for the changes that are presently occurring and still yet to come.

Trusting people, even members of your own family, can be difficult. I had to test my ability to trust others over time, and most of the time I was let down by someone. I realized that trust had been broken on such profound levels during all of the sexual assault and child sexual abuse. When people you trust violate you in any way, it will take time to recover and it will take time to rebuild the trust that has been broken and, in some cases, severed. This is a heart matter. We need healing to take place in our spiritual heart.

Before I entered into formal therapy, several people who were very close to me had betrayed me. This was extremely hurtful to the point that I found it difficult to even trust myself. I have learned that I can trust others and myself best by utilizing and calling on the godly discernment that the Lord has instilled in me through Holy Spirit. When we do not know what to do, God does. When we seek Him for guidance, asking Him for His wisdom and discernment, we must trust Him to do for us what only He can do. Trust is stepping out in faith and leaving the results up to God.

In the Holy Bible, one great example of this is Ruth the Moabite. In the book of Ruth in the Old Testament, we read about Ruth's struggle to find her way after the death of her husband. Ruth is encouraged to return to her family, but she insists that she will instead go with her mother-in-law, Naomi, to Bethlehem. There, through a series of divine guidance from the Lord, Ruth meets a man named Boaz, whom she eventually marries. Ruth is a symbol of loyalty and devotion, as she did not abandon her mother-in-law, and the Lord blessed her for her faithfulness. She didn't know what to do on her own, but the Lord led her steps, she placed her trust in Him, and He made her path straight. God is faithful. He can be trusted. But if we can't surrender to and trust God, then we are not completely free.

If we are to relate to God in any way, we must know who He is. Who is God to you and how do you see Jesus? Jesus is a person, He is the Word (the Bible in the flesh), and He shows us through His actions that He is the very personification of trust. While being fully man, He is also fully God. In Him is only Light and Truth; there is no sin at all. His Word tells us that He is The Way, The Truth, and The Life, and no one comes to the Father except through Him (see John 14:6). I know Jesus as faithful, reliable, and trustworthy. When I needed a friend, He was there. When I needed a Savior, He was there. When I needed reassurance, He was there. I have learned over time that I can trust Him. I've been on a journey that has led me to know and trust God. And this deep place of trust in the Lord is where the very miracles you seek will be realized. Yes, weeping may endure for a night, but joy does come in the morning.

How do you relate to God as Father? What a daughter sees in her earthly father's behavior affects her deeply. If he has affairs, uses pornography, and does not uphold the vows that he made to her mother, she will internalize those actions and her sense of self-worth will suffer. She may seek relationships with men who will undervalue her. In adulthood, a daughter can continue to try to relate to her father as a young child, but she must find a way to relate to him as an adult. This comes about through the development of trust in God and divine healing in the Lord. However, when there are compromised emotional pathways during her developmental years, it will be more difficult for her to do this, though not impossible. Remember, dear friends, all things are possible with God, but apart from Him we can do nothing (see Matthew 19:26; John 15:5).

There also may be an issue with authority or an inability to respect authority, as those who were in authority are often the perpetrators. But it's God's best for us to submit and surrender to the authority around us so that our life is in the proper godly alignment. It is, therefore, necessary to separate God from the perpetrators in your life who held positions of authority over you. God is not the same; He is different. God is love. He's not mad at you. He is for you, and He wants the best for you. When we submit to His authority, it is done out of respect and reverence to Him (healthy fear). God is not going to abuse us or take advantage of us. We can trust Him. True faith and trust are knowing that there is an authority greater than you: God.

Too often, I've counseled with women and children who have been taught that God is evil or wants to hurt them. Their perpetrators may have brainwashed them into believing that God is someone that He is really not. Sometimes, sexual violence is perpetrated in the church. Often, a spirit of religion is tied to sexual assault and abuse. The enemy uses the abuser to thwart the survivor's understanding of who Jesus really is. They make untruthful "religious" comments during the abuse to cause confusion, often making the person completely turned off from faith in Jesus Christ, which is the enemy's ultimate goal. This only serves to compound the survivor's trauma, as there is now a negative spiritual component that must be overcome. We must sort through the lies and replace them with truth. This takes time and effort, but it is possible to rebuild the trust that has been broken.

———————•———————

I was often on the receiving end of negative, unsupportive, and accusatory comments that were not in any way helpful to my overall healing journey. I did not know this at the time, but I eventually learned that these comments often came from those who had unresolved issues in their own life. As we established earlier, hurting people hurt people; this generally stems from the pain and hurt that they hold inside. The pain must come out in some way. Yes, hurting people hurt people, but sometimes they also hurt themselves. We must pray for the Lord to place a hedge of protection around us. We must put our relationship, with and to others, in the proper perspective. "May I never boast except in the cross of our Lord Jesus Christ, through which the world has been crucified to me, and I to the world." (Galatians 6:14). We can trust again. When Christ and the cross are between others and us, especially those who have abused us in any way, we can truly learn to trust again. "It is better to take refuge in the LORD than to trust in humans." (Psalm 118:8) We can trust again because we have placed everyone and everything into the proper, godly perspective. We need a renewal of our mind. We don't trust others because of them; we can trust others because of God.

God's Word tells us that we can trust in Him. "⁷ The LORD is good, a refuge in times of trouble. He cares for those who trust in him…⁹…trouble will not come a second time." (Nahum 1:7, 9) "When you pass through the waters, I will be with you. When you pass through the rivers, they will not sweep over you. When you walk through the fire, you will not be burned. The flames will not set you ablaze. Do not be afraid for I am with you." (Isaiah 43:2, 5)

God loves you, and He will rescue you. Please understand that God knows your pain and suffering. He goes back to rescue every part of you that had been in the grasp of the enemy, especially the broken parts. Jesus came to comfort the brokenhearted and to set the captives free. You can trust and believe in Him to bring you out of the darkness and put you back together again. "Indeed, we felt we had received the sentence of death. But this happened that we might not rely [trust] on ourselves but on God, who raises the dead." (2 Corinthians 1:9)

———•———————•———————•———

- "This is what the LORD says: 'As a shepherd rescues from the lion's mouth only two leg bones or a piece of an ear, so will the Israelites living in Samaria be rescued....'" (Amos 3:12)

———•———————•———————•———

We read in the gospel of Matthew about Jesus walking on water (see Matthew 14:22–33). He had asked the disciples to get in a boat and go ahead of Him because He was going up on a mountainside by Himself to pray. Meanwhile, the disciples, faced with an intense wind that buffeted the waves in the water around them, rocked back and forth in the boat. Before dawn, Jesus went out to them, walking on the water. When the disciples saw Jesus, they were terrified. Then, Jesus called Peter forth and told him not to be afraid. As Peter got out of the boat and began to walk on water toward Jesus, he became aware of the wind, which filled him with fear. Peter began to sink in the water. However, Jesus rescued him. As soon as he got back in the boat, the wind died down. Peter had shown little faith and a lot of doubt. Had he placed his trust in the Lord Jesus Christ, fear would not have overtaken him. It's great that Peter got out of the boat, but the true test came when he failed to keep his eye on Jesus. God was saying to him, and to us, in so many words, "Whatever you go through, walk with Me!"

We must trust the Lord to be with us and for us, trusting in Him for everything we need. He has not caused the pain and suffering, but He can and will help us through it. Sometimes people use their free will to harm others, and we wonder why God doesn't stop it (we will talk more about this in Chapter 10). The Lord will make it possible for us to walk through and out of the hurt and pain from sexual assault and child sexual abuse. When we keep our eye on Him, we can truly rise above the circumstances of our past. Jesus is trust made manifest in human form. Others may have broken our trust, but the Lord is worthy of our trust. And, through Him, we can learn to trust again.

Questions for Reflection

1. Was there ever a time in my life when I did trust others? When?

2. What occurred in my life that severed or negatively affected my ability to trust?

3. Are there people in my life that I can trust? Who are they?

4. How do I define trust?

5. Do I trust the Lord? Why? What steps could I take to improve this area of my life and positively impact my healing journey?

Come into the Light

Gracious Lord and Heavenly Father, I am mindful that trust has been an area of weakness for me. But I also know You to be a God of restoration. You help us to forget the former things and set our minds on the things above. You make all things new. I am asking You to go into the deep recesses of my heart and mind, and to unearth and heal the negative effects of any damage that has been done, to help me trust again. If there were people in my life who contributed to my difficulty in trusting, please heal that and help me to forgive them. Help me to redefine trust, according to Your Word and so that I may be able to walk in Your will and ways. Help me to be able to trust You, Lord. Continue to bring healing to my heart and into my life. I know that You can help me to trust again. I desire this so deeply, with everything that is in me. I want to trust and to be healed; I want to trust and to be whole. Please meet me, right where I am, and do a good work in my heart. In Jesus's name, I pray. Amen.

Chapter 6

LEARNING TO LOVE

"'Love the Lord your God with all your heart and with all your soul and with all your mind and with all your strength.'[31] The second is this: 'Love your neighbor as yourself.' There is no commandment greater than these." (Mark 12:30–31)

The fruit of the Spirit is comprised of nine virtues: love, joy, peace, patience, kindness, goodness, faithfulness, gentleness, and self-control (see Galatians 5:22–23). Since all nine of the virtues make up the fruit, if even one of the nine virtues is missing from our lives, we do not have the fruit of the Spirit working in us, at least not completely. It is fitting that love is the first in the list; everything we do must flow from and out of love. Faith begins when you know that God loves you. However, many people live from a place of approval. They try to "earn" the love of another. You must know that God loves you not because of your performance, but because love is *who* God is. God even tells us, in His Word, that before the foundations of the earth, He first loved us. Wow. God loved us first, before He did anything else? That is amazing. He is our Abba Father, and we must remember that God chose us as His children. He loves us, and He makes it possible for us to love again when the fruit of love is present in and flowing out of us.

September 22, 2011

I met with my therapist again yesterday. The session was tough and emotional. I named all of the abusers who had perpetrated sexual assault and child sexual abuse against me. I also discussed in detail the rape that occurred (25 years old) and the last instance of sexual assault that occurred (28 years old).

This weekend, I will be participating in a spiritual retreat, including listening to praise and worship music, Bible study, reading the Word of God, daily devotions, reading a new book about feelings, praying and meditating on God's Word, and resting. I also will spend my time during the spiritual retreat staying focused on moving forward, nurturing myself, growing in my faith, allowing the Lord to draw me into an even deeper relationship with Him, spending time at my special place (prayer, nature hike, etc.), and continuing to heal in body, soul, and spirit. I know God will use our time together for good.

I will continue to reevaluate relationships (past, present, future) so I can move forward in my life with those who are adding to my life in a positive manner.

I am starting to feel differently about myself, as well as about what I feel I deserve in my life. It is scary to welcome change into my life, but I am slowly allowing my "new normal" to come into an even better focus. I am learning to see myself as God sees me, to love myself fully. It feels good. I need to continue to be gentle with myself and keep my eye on God. Hope is on my side. I am a survivor. It feels good to not only know this, but to truly believe it.

September 26, 2011

My spiritual retreat this past weekend was a blessing. God revealed Himself to me. He met me right where I was and where I am. I was able to let go of more hurt, unforgiveness, bitterness, guilt, blame, and shame. All of the false feelings are leaving me. It felt so freeing. God reassured me that He saw me and knew me and my personal struggles and that He loves me anyway. He revealed truths to me as only He could. It was emotional, freeing, and glorious! I was very aware of my surroundings, and I enjoyed and appreciated God's beauty and creation., making sure to love and appreciate His creation, but to worship Him. I feel renewed and at peace. I am overjoyed to grow ever closer to the Lord, each day. I am so in love with Jesus, and I know that He loves me.

September 28, 2011

Today is a rough day. I am very emotional. I am trying to do more grief work, but I am struggling with feeling emotionally vulnerable. Hope—this was lost and damaged in my childhood. Tough.

Emotional. Painful. I am working with the Lord on regaining and renewing the hope in my life again. I am learning to love in ways that I never have before.

———•——————•—————•———

September 29, 2011

I met with my therapist again today. The session was very productive and not quite as emotional as some (or many) of the past sessions. We talked about my recent spiritual retreat, the boundaries I have made and kept, and the journaling and grief work I have been doing. We discussed some aspects of my childhood, and I concluded that I needed to grieve for the child in me that never really was able to be a child.

We also discussed the future, with the man God has chosen for me to marry, and some of the concerns I have about that— intimacy and sexual issues—and what God's design was for that, as well as for a healthy family. My therapist reminded me that God would send to me a man who was not only Christ-centered, like me, but also a man who could and would be here for me and love me just as I am, just like Jesus loves the Church. We would work through things together, with the help of the Lord. It felt good to hear this. I needed to hear this! I also believe that it can and will happen. Wow. Amazing! I can feel my heart opening up a bit to this possibility as I move forward in my healing journey. I am seeing and feeling the hope in that, and at the same time, I am feeling a bit apprehensive, too. I just need more time. I need to continue to be gentle with myself as I heal.

I have been working through a lot of emotions and feelings, and I have a better understanding of how I have reacted to circumstances out of hurt, shame, blame, guilt, and self-doubt. Again, false feelings that were not even mine to begin with. I realize now that I am healing (and have a much better perspective on things, as well as more tools and resources at my disposal), that I am reacting to situations in a much healthier manner, making decisions based upon God's will and His best for me. This is Christ's love in action.

I am also mindful of all the times that I made a decision to eat healthier, exercise more, and take better care of myself, only to do it for a short time because my emotions actually took over and I fell short of my goal. There were times that I would beat myself up for not meeting those goals, but I realize that I was not in a healthy place to be able to achieve the goals I had set for myself. In other words, my intentions were good but my ability to cope was not. Father, please give me the strength to make the decision to follow through on these goals while looking to You and Your Word to endure, rise above, and meet these goals. I have the power and the authority in Christ Jesus to choose my thoughts rather than allowing my thoughts to choose and rule over me. I will not plan for failure; I will plan for success. And I know You will help me.

Today, my therapist told me she felt like I was making great progress and was actually ahead of where most are at this point in therapy (we held session seven of twelve today, so five remain). She told me that she felt my journey would help many people to heal. Wow. I know that God has called me into full-time ministry and that an expansion of what I am already doing to serve the Lord will come in time. He will use me and my experiences with sexual assault and child sexual abuse to help others heal, to help them hold on to hope in Christ, and to lead them to a saving relationship with the Lord. May all glory be to God.

There are many different types of love, as described in the Bible (we will learn *much more* about this topic in Chapter 9). However, let us now look at some of the examples of Jesus's many expressions of love, as found in God's Word:

1. Jesus healed the sick in love (see Matthew 14:14)

2. Jesus raised the dead in love (see John 11:35, 38)

3. Jesus fed the hungry in love (see Matthew 15:32)

4. Jesus preached the Kingdom in love (see Mark 6:34)

5. Jesus cast out demons in love (see Matthew 8:16)

6. Jesus interceded for His disciples and the Church in love (see John 17:20–21)

7. Jesus gave His life for the world in love (see John 3:16)

Let us also be reminded of who Jesus really is:

JESUS is…Healer, Savior, Deliverer, Mender, Provider, Protector, Majesty, Truth, Peace, Amazing, Alpha, Omega, Beginning, End, First, Last, Light, Goodness, Mercy, Almighty, Jehovah, Graceful, Forgiving, Faithful, Awesome, Friend, Companion, Counselor, Mighty God, Everlasting, King of kings, Lord or lords, Rose of Sharon, Morning Star, Great Shepherd, Lilly of the Valley, Christ, Name above all other names, Messiah, Alive, Lamb of God, Emmanuel, The Word, Redeemer, Yahweh…LOVE.

If we, too, are to love God, others, and ourselves and live a life wherein we are displaying godly love, we must live by Jesus's example and what God's Word implores us to do. We must live in a manner worthy of being children of God. If our words and actions do not line up with and glorify God, we are not walking in the Light. Furthermore, if we cannot place the phrase "hallowed be Thy name" above anything we do and say, we should not be doing or saying it. Did I get your attention with that last comment? That's a word for all of us. "Do not repay anyone evil for evil. Be careful to do what is right in the eyes of everyone. If it is possible, as far as it depends on you, live at peace with everyone." (Romans 12:17)

So many times, the reason it's hard for us to love is because we don't know who we are. We have an orphan spirit. Someone with an orphan spirit has no place to call home. They feel unloved, undervalued, without purpose. There is a characteristic of independence and living for one's self. Most generally, this type of spirit seeks to be in control, does not feel as though they "belong" anywhere, and has no sense of security or being secure in anyone or anything (except self). You will often see someone with this spirit living in fear, repelling others, or exhibiting fits of anger and rage. They have a clear and certain mindset that says, "Everyone is lying to me and must be out to get me." Typically, their identity is gleaned through material goods, physical appearance, and various activities as well as physical stimulation. It's important to understand that pain seeks pleasure through self-gratification or self-mutilation. All too often, we find it difficult to ask God for anything more than the basics when we don't believe He loves us deeply.

In the church, this can manifest through an individual who seeks out "religion" wherein a relationship with God is based solely on performance and trying to "earn" His love and affection. This is generally based on a spirit of religious tradition that has entered that denomination and is perpetuated by individuals in that denomination. Red flags for this include hearing phrases like "you must do it this way because this is the way we've always done it." Just because that may be true, doesn't make it right in the eyes of God. It's quite possible to be in the church and still be operating in a wrong spirit. In or out of the church, this can manifest through an individual who seeks out rebellious or addictive behaviors as their means of coping. They struggle with feelings of fear and abandonment, are insecure and jealous, constantly in competition with others, driven by success, and use people as objects to fulfill a desired goal. They are also lacking in self-esteem.

Who you are makes you do what you do. When we can't accept, receive, and walk in the love of the Father, we accept counterfeit affections. To the contrary, we need to seek to live *from* God, not *for* Him (or man or self). God's Word says, "My sheep hear My voice, I know them, and they follow Me." (John 10:27). Dear friends, we need to be listening to the voice of God so we can be following after Him with our whole heart. Our act of complete surrender to God creates space for us to accept that He loves us. Because He first loved us, we can fall deeply in love with Him. True love of the Father teaches us how to let go.

I know a little bit about this orphan spirit because I've ministered to and counseled with many orphan spirit souls. Some of these orphan spirit souls are also my friends, family, and acquaintances. To a certain extent, I can personally relate to this journey. For a time, I lived it in my own life. I was a spiritual orphan, but that was before God found me in the pit and rescued me from the darkness and I found my home in Him.

———·————●————·———

If the orphan spirit resonates with you, and you are seeking after God but are also doing things as the world would do, you are playing both sides of the fence. You are operating in a spirit of harlotry. To be clear, this spirit can pervade many different churches, denominations, and individuals. In God's Word, we read about this spirit: "Adulterers and adulteresses! Do you not know that friendship with the world is enmity with God? Whoever therefore wants to be a friend of the world makes himself an enemy of God." (James 4:4) You either align yourself with the world, or you align yourself with God. It can't be both.

This is a lying spirit. It lies to people about their identity, and the goal is to take a person's life. It wants the person to believe that their life is nothing. Common things the person will hear include I'm worthless, nobody cares about me, I'm not needed or wanted, no one will miss me if I'm gone, and why am I even here? It attaches itself to the fractured soul and injured heart of a person very easily.

This spirit attempts to convince people that you can have it both ways—the world and God. It's God's Word mixed with selfishness and pride. Someone operating in this spirit quotes the Bible but simultaneously steers you toward the world with all of the rewards without doing the actual work. This is "feel good" preaching. There is no focus on a real life with Christ or His victory over sin. The harlot is Satan's answer to the bride of Christ, and he is using this spirit to draw people away from the church and away from the One True God. God's Word tells us that we cannot serve two masters (see Matthew 6:24). If any of this resonates with you, dear friends, repent and seek the Lord for spiritual healing. He loves you, and it is His desire to, one day, receive a bride (the Church) that is pure, without spot or blemish. Let us be about doing the work of the Lord.

Now, let's turn our attention to God's definition of a healthy relationship between a man and a woman. We need to know that God's will and plan is for all of us to live in sexual health. He desires for us to live in sexual purity until we are married. God forbids sexual relations of any kind outside of marriage, which is a holy covenant between a man and a woman. We are to bring honor and glory to God by the manner in which we treat our bodies and other people's bodies sexually. With a few exceptions, I entered into unhealthy relationships with men who were not God's best for me. I was looking for love in all the wrong places. I was expecting certain treatment based on how I felt about myself because of the sexual assault and child sexual abuse perpetrated against me. None of this was God's best for me. Sexual assault and abuse interrupt God's will and plan for healthy sexuality and purity. However, God can restore us as well as the damage others have done to us; He can bring about a restoration in this and in every other area of our lives. We can learn to love again. We can love ourselves. We can do this because God first loved us. He makes all things new.

God created us in relationship, for relationship, and through relationship. We are to walk with one another in Christian love. And, let's face it: Love can be intense and messy from time to time. But we can't love ourselves and others if we have not first experienced the love of God. Jesus served, loved, respected, and honored all of His relationships, regardless of those who had betrayed, abused, lied to, manipulated, and had forsaken Him. That is *agape* love. There's a greater good involved when God brings good out of suffering. That is love. There is a quality of commitment that Jesus demonstrated in His relationship to us. That is love. Become vulnerable to the love offered to you in Christ. Jesus is love. After we experience godly love, we can see the difficulties of our past through His eyes and begin to heal. We can learn to love God, others, and ourselves again. We can "…walk in the way of love, just as Christ loved us and gave himself up for us as a fragrant offering and sacrifice to God." (Ephesians 5:2) When you do this, dear friends, you will see that your heart is learning to open up to the joy that comes in the morning.

Questions for Reflection

1. How do you define love?

2. Have you ever considered Jesus as the very definition of love?

3. Do you love yourself? Why? Do you feel like God loves you?

4. Do you have an orphan spirit? Are you willing to allow God to heal that area of your heart? Do you have a spirit of harlotry? Are you willing to allow God to heal this area of your heart?

5. What is still holding you back from loving completely? How can you overcome that with the help of the Lord? Is there a particular Scripture in this chapter that speaks to you and your heart?

Come into the Light

Gracious Lord and Heavenly Father, for so many years—maybe as long as I can remember—I have felt unloved…I have felt like I didn't know how to love. But I want to know those feelings. I'm realizing that I can't love myself until I accept Your great love for me. Help me to do this. I need Your help. I don't want to go through life absent from You and Your love. I don't want to go another day without loving myself as You first loved me. Show me what it means to walk in Your love and to then extend that love to myself and others. Renew my mind and bring about a true heart change in me. If I have any evidence of an orphan spirit or a spirit of harlotry, reveal that to me, Lord. I want to be whole and healed. I need Your help. If anything is holding me back from receiving and giving love—reveal it to me and bring it out of hiding. Heal my heart. Heal me. I want to learn how to love again, with Your help. I love You, Lord. Thank You for loving me. In Jesus's name, I pray. Amen.

Chapter 7

LEARNING TO HOPE

*"We have this hope as an anchor for the soul, firm and
secure." (Hebrews 6:19)*

Just like love and trust before it, I believe hope is the absence
of fear and the presence of faith. Try telling that to a survivor
of sexual assault and child sexual abuse, though, and watch as
a look of bewilderment washes over their face and confusion
consumes their entire being. An absence of fear? The presence of
faith? How is this even possible? But, yes, learning to hope again
is very similar to learning to love and trust again.

For some of us, learning to hope again is often a contradiction. Learning to hope seems impossible—ridiculous even—when maybe you cannot remember a time in your life when hope ever existed. The "hope" that you may be most familiar with is more like being the odd-numbered child in a group of children being picked one-by-one for teams on a playground. It is this odd-numbered child who is left out of the game, because both of the teams are even-numbered. It appears as though you are not needed or wanted and made to feel as if you do not matter. You may feel like a third or fifth wheel. And that becomes your reality, your expectation for life, this desire for someone to pick you, but somewhere deep inside, you know that no one will ever pick you. Before long, you are standing there, alone, watching from the sidelines and sitting on the bench. You have no hope.

However, this is not truly hope; this is the antithesis of hope. It is a false hope, filled with the presence of fear and the absence of faith. This is often the experience and reality of a sexual violence survivor. It's what the Bible refers to as "hope deferred." "Hope deferred makes the heart sick, but a desire fulfilled is a tree of life." (Proverbs 13:12) When our hope continually eludes us, we can lose faith that it will ever come our way. This mindset is also rooted in a false sense of identity—not knowing who you are in Christ. We will look more deeply into this topic in Chapter 9.

While hope may have escaped you up to this point, the hope that God gives to us is authentic, beautiful, and a lifeline to our soul. It is an anchor, firm and secure. It is a desired outcome, an expectation, and a deep longing for something to come to pass. Hope came in the form of a man; His name is Jesus. He loves us. He wants the best for us. He is our living hope.

September 30, 2011

I had been wondering and even asking God why He was seemingly taking me to be near pieces of water so often—at a creek by my childhood home, at my special place (also by a creek), at a lake by my home, etc.—and I asked myself these questions: Was it to be a reminder of my baptismal waters? Why did I yearn to be with the Lord in these places? Why did this feel so right? This morning while I was praying to God, praising and worshiping the Lord, I asked Him to reveal Himself to me as never before. He spoke to me in the stillness of the morning: "²...he leads me beside quiet (still) waters,

³he refreshes (restores) my soul" (Psalm 23:2–3). Of course! God has been leading me to sit beside still waters because He knows I will find comfort in Him there. He restores my soul. He has been restoring my soul. Amazing! I have been praying and meditating upon the 23ʳᵈ Psalm for a long time. The joy and peace of the Lord is my strength. Oh, how I love You, Father. You do restore my soul. You are also restoring my hope—Jesus, You are my hope.

Once again, I am mindful of how innocent I was as a child. I know, without question, that I was not the cause of the sexual assault and child sexual abuse I endured. I could not have prevented it. Shame, blame, guilt, and self-doubt are no more. Praise God for this revelation.

October 6, 2011

I met with my therapist again today. We have four sessions remaining—the end of this portion of my journey is growing nearer. It is both exciting and overwhelming.

Today's sharing was painful. I read aloud about the first two instances of sexual assault and child sexual abuse (6 years old to 12 years old; 16 years old). I had written down the related experiences and thoughts in my own handwriting, and this was the first time I had heard those thoughts aloud and in my own voice. I had to stop several times to cry, but I was eventually able to start reading and sharing again. I just took my time. I gave myself permission to do this. Catharine was very patient with me. I believe there is more writing to do in relation to the first instance of sexual abuse (6 years old to 12 years old), but I feel as though what I wrote about the second instance of abuse (16 years old) is complete.

My therapist told me that I did a great job and showed a lot of courage. I felt completely exhausted, but I also was proud of myself for what I had been able to do. I shared my faith with my therapist again today, in that I knew it was not because of my own strength, but the Lord's, that I was able to speak of the sexual assault and child sexual abuse aloud. It was because Christ is the center of my life and He gave me the strength to do it, to endure. "I can do all this through him who gives me strength." (Philippians 4:13)

Over the next week, I need to continue to move forward in my healing process by writing about the other assault and abuse perpetrated against me and by being gentle with myself as I continue to heal. I give thanks to God that He has brought me this far in my healing process. I love Him so much. I know He loves me. My hope is in Him.

October 9, 2011

I wrote about the third instance of sexual assault and child sexual abuse (16 years old to 28 years old). I did that today. Ugh. I am so glad that is over. On Thursday, I will share this with my therapist. I am a little bit anxious about that.

Today, it is cold and rainy outside. I am getting ready to do my morning devotions and read my Bible. I am listening to praise and worship music—it is so comforting. I am looking forward to church worship later this morning. I am asking God to hold my thoughts captive to the obedience of Christ Jesus; I know He will. "The LORD has done it this very day; let us rejoice today and be glad." (Psalm 118:24)

I am a survivor. The sexual assault and child sexual abuse was not my fault, and I did nothing to cause it. The false feelings of shame, blame, and guilt are now on the abusers, right where they belong! The Lord is my strength in all things. I give thanks to God that I lived through the sexual assault and abuse. I lived through it. I love Jesus so much. And I can feel hope arising in me. I am going to make this a great day in the Lord.

October 10, 2011

I am doing more grief work today. It is beyond hard. I am unable to put it into words. I am writing about the fourth instance (25 years old) and the fifth instance (28 years old) of sexual assault and abuse. I am happy to see the healthy boundaries I am maintaining. "With man this is impossible, but with God all things are possible." (Matthew 19:26) Hope is definitely coming alive in me. Praise God from whom all blessings flow.

October 13, 2011

I met with my therapist again today. I read aloud about the fourth and fifth instances of sexual assault and child sexual abuse. The session was extremely emotional and hard to get through. I cried. A lot. However, I did it, with the help of God. I am so proud of myself.

My therapist told me again today that she is very proud of me, acknowledging how courageous I am in my sharing. The sharing was beyond difficult, so it felt very good to hear these words from her. It was brave to share. It would have been brave not to share, too. I'm so thankful that I was able to share.

I am celebrating what I was able to share today, as well as all of the accomplishments to this point in my healing journey. Today, I am rewarding myself by going to one of my favorite places to write, pray, and spend time alone with the Lord. I am acknowledging and lifting up thanks and praise to the Lord for how far I have come in my spiritual and healing journey, as well as in my grief work. God surely knows.

I sat and watched a mother, father, and two young girls trying to catch butterflies across the river from me. Additionally, three young children—two boys and a girl—were off from school today, so they showed up and started talking to me. They were such sweet kids. Talking to them gave me a bittersweet reminder of how childhood should be: carefree. My time here today was a blessing. It felt good to do something to reward myself for all of my hard work. I praise God for walking with me throughout this healing journey and giving me a lasting hope in Him.

In God's Word, we read about someone who experienced challenges in the area of hope. Abram (later called Abraham) wanted a child, as did his wife. However, as the years went by, they both found themselves growing older and still without a child (see Genesis 17). Abram and his wife, Sarai (later called Sarah), were in advanced age. Based on biblical accounts, he was about 100 years old and she was about 90 years old by the time the Lord purposed for them to conceive the child that the angel of the Lord had told Sarai would be coming to them. "Against all hope, Abraham in hope believed and so became the father of many nations, just as it had been said to him, 'So shall your offspring be.'" (Romans 4:18)

As survivors of sexual assault and child sexual abuse, we need to have hope. We need to know and believe that God will bring about restoration in us and in our lives. We need to run to a place of hope in Christ when we have nowhere else to go. We need to hold on to hope and never let go. "Return to your fortress, you prisoners of hope; even now I announce that I will restore twice as much to you." (Zechariah 9:12) God's assurance is that we will not be discouraged when our hope is in Him. "Those who hope in me will not be disappointed." (Isaiah 49:23)

Moving forward on our healing journey, we can find comfort and hope in God's Word:

- "But since we belong to the day, let us be sober, putting on faith and love as a breastplate, and the hope of salvation as a helmet." (1 Thessalonians 8:5)

- "¹² Not that I have already obtained all this, or have already arrived at my goal, but I press on to take hold of that for which Christ Jesus took hold of me. ¹³ Brothers and sisters, I do not consider myself yet to have taken hold of it. But one thing I do: Forgetting what is behind and straining toward what is ahead, ¹⁴ I press on toward the goal to win the prize for which God has called me heavenward in Christ Jesus." (Philippians 3:12–14)

- "[2]...And we boast in the hope of the glory of God. [3] Not only so, but we also glory in our sufferings, because we know that suffering produces perseverance; [4] perseverance, character; and character, hope. [5] And hope does not put us to shame, because God's love has been poured out into our hearts through the Holy Spirit, who has been given to us." (Romans 5:2b–5)

- "May the God of hope fill you with all joy and peace as you trust in him, so that you may overflow with hope by the power of the Holy Spirit." (Romans 15:13)

I alluded to this in an earlier chapter, but it bears repeating. At some point in my healing journey, the Lord and I had to wrestle over this whole "learning to hope" thing. Basically, He was telling me it was *possible* to hope, and I was telling Him

I thought it was *impossible*. As we wrestled over this for a time, I came to understand what He meant. The Lord helped me to understand the hope and suffering connection. He used Romans 5:2–5 (see above) as a basis for His response to me. He said, "My child, I don't want you to rejoice in your suffering *because* of the suffering itself. Rather, I want you to rejoice in your suffering because of *what I can and will produce in and through you*, as a result of the suffering you have endured. I will produce, in you, a perseverance to rise above the adversity of life, a godly character that will help you to see and live life through Me, and I will give you a hope that does not put you to shame, because My love has been poured out through My Holy Spirit, who has been given to you. *This* is why I want you to rejoice in your suffering. *This* is what I will produce in and through you."

Wow. I couldn't believe it! There was *purpose* in my pain and suffering? I would become more, not less, Christ-like through the suffering that I had endured? Yes! That was just amazing to me. And I wanted it. I connected with my purpose, and it created a new pathway for hope and healing in me. When we lift our eyes up to the hills, we see the place where our help comes from: Jesus. Hope can arise, just as we arise above the suffering of life.

There is purpose in our pain. We truly can learn to hope again.

God's Word tells us that "Christ is faithful as the Son over God's house. And we are his house, if indeed we hold firmly to our confidence and the hope in which we glory." (Hebrews 3:6) This means, dear friends, that we are going to have faith, and we are going to hold fast to our faith until the end. If we don't give up and we don't give in, we are going to cause hope to arise. Something in us is going to shift. Our faith will increase. We are in the physical, waiting for what has already been done in the Spirit (before the beginning of time) to come to full maturation, to fully manifest in the Lord. Wow. Just wow.

We will press on. We will press in. We will allow hope to arise. We will fear not. We will have faith. We will choose to have hope. It is the anchor for our soul, firm and secure. When our hope is in Christ and Christ is in us, we can rise above and move forward in and on our healing journey. The Lord is with us. We are never alone. We can learn to hope, dear friends. "For you have been my hope, O Sovereign LORD, my confidence since my youth." (Psalm 71:5) Hold on to hope, dear friends, and never let it go. And you, too, will find joy in the morning.

Questions for Reflection

1. Was there ever a time in my life when I felt hopeful? Am I beginning to feel that, now?

2. Was there a time in my life when I felt like the odd-numbered child on the playground?

3. Have I ever equated Jesus with hope?

4. How can I be more hopeful?

5. What is my suffering and hope connection? What is my purpose?

Come into the Light

Gracious Lord and Heavenly Father, I admit that there have been numerous times in my life when I have felt hopeless. I have often thought that I didn't matter, that no one cared about me. I felt like that odd-numbered child. But You tell me in Your Word that You are for me, and my hope can be in You. I want that for myself. I want that in my life. Jesus, I believe that You are my hope—You are my only hope. Help me to find my hope in You.

Help me to allow hope to rise up in my heart. Show me how my suffering has purpose, and that through You, I can truly learn to hope again. Go deep in to my heart and allow hope to arise. Yes, let hope arise! I love You, Lord, and I praise You. I ask this all in Jesus's name. Amen.

Chapter 8

BLESSING AND RELEASING:
LETTING GO AND LETTING GOD

"He brought them out of darkness, the utter darkness,
and broke away their chains." (Psalm 107:14)

When I was nearing the end of my formal therapy sessions and looking for some way to bring a sense of closure to all of the grief work that I had done to that point, I came up with the idea of creating and holding a blessing and releasing ceremony. My therapist had suggested that I should maybe mourn the past in some way, such as by naming all of the perpetrators, losses, and associated grief. This was a great thought, but God helped me to see the spiritual benefit of expanding on this initial idea. I realize that not everyone approaches things in the same way. However, being an eternal optimist and trying to see the good in things, I did not feel good or right about just mourning the experiences that I had endured in the past. To be clear, I had been unknowingly doing that for nearly 40 years. Now, I wanted to celebrate my various accomplishments and truly recognize and acknowledge how far the Lord had brought me in and on my healing journey. I also wanted to focus on what my future held in Christ Jesus. God's dreams for me were now within reach, and I wanted to put a voice to them.

I yielded to the Lord, and I subsequently wrote and organized a worship service that would encompass all of the various aspects of my healing journey, from the mourning all the way through to the celebration. I approached this service as an all-encompassing opportunity to bless and release the good and the bad in relation to *all* areas of my life, including family, relationships, losses, pain, suffering, sexual assault, and child sexual abuse. However, for the purpose of this book, I will only share those areas from the worship service that pertain to my healing journey through sexual assault and child sexual abuse as well as the future of the ministry to which the Lord has called me.

First, however, I would like to share more with you from my personal journal entries so you can better understand my healing journey—and yours.

October 25, 2011

Today, I am aware of how much progress I am making in my healing journey. I am so proud of myself. I feel good about where I am right now. I, now, have shared details surrounding all of the sexual assault and child sexual abuse, and I am focusing on writing a letter to all of the perpetrators who abused me, which I will read aloud to my therapist in our next session on Thursday of next week. Then, I will burn the letter. I am also writing a letter to myself as a little girl— this will be hard to write and read aloud, but I will borrow the Lord's strength in order to finish it.

I have completed the initial service outline for my upcoming blessing and releasing ceremony, and I need to begin to make plans for a celebration when all of my therapy is over.

I, now, have resolved all of the shame, blame, guilt, self-doubt, self-esteem, self-worth, and self-image concerns. I have learned to love myself again, just as God loves me. I have developed better and more positive coping mechanisms and a healthier set of boundaries in my life. I am excited for what the future holds.

I continue to be gentle with myself. I need to invite the little girl inside of me to come out and play and experience new joy, and help her to understand that we have healed, so it is safe now. If things get bad on occasion, we now have developed healthy ways to handle it. Overall, I am excited to embrace my "new normal," as a healthy survivor. I am anxious (in a good way!) to help others by sharing my testimony, allowing God to use my experiences for good. I knew He could and would turn all of this into good and use it for His glory. Praise God.

November 1, 2011

I am focusing on self-control and self-discipline this week, and finishing the letters to the abusers (which I will read aloud to my therapist). I feel totally angry and enraged as I read over what I have written. However, I also feel very alive and empowered at the same time. "With man this is impossible, but with God all things are possible." (Matthew 19:26) I can do this. God will make a way. A reminder to myself: Keep. Moving. Forward.

November 3, 2011

I met with my therapist again today. The session was totally empowering. Wow! I read aloud the letters I had written to the abusers—not to send to or to show them, but to read aloud to my therapist as a part of my healing journey—and my therapist listened to me without judgment. I feel liberated and alive again. Yes! I found my voice. I am taking back my power. Just wow!

November 7, 2011

I am making the final changes to my upcoming blessing and releasing ceremony, and I now have finished the letter to myself as a little girl. Neither of these things were a small task. Not at all. I am relieved, on both accounts, to have that done. I am utilizing this week for God to prepare my heart and mind for my therapy session on Wednesday and for the upcoming worship ceremony on Sunday. "I can do all this through him who gives me strength." (Philippians 4:13)

November 9, 2011

I met with my therapist again today. I shared aloud the "Blessings and Releasing Ceremony" outline I wrote, as well as the letter I wrote to myself as a little girl. I have also been thinking a lot lately about past relationships and future encounters with men, in light of the sexual assault and child sexual abuse I have endured. My therapist and I addressed this topic today in my session. I have learned a lot through my time in formal therapy, and I realize now what I want and need in my life in terms of a relationship with a man. It's so refreshing. God will provide. I have learned to trust Him, above all.

On Sunday, November 13, 2011, at 3 P.M., one of my pastors (also a member of my trusted care circle) and I met in our church sanctuary to go before the Lord in worship to Him. During this worship service, there was "blessing and releasing," pain and tears, hope and healing. We listened to and sang songs, recited Scripture, and read prayers aloud. I released a lot of emotions. Together, with the help of God, we placed everything related to the past sexual assault and child sexual abuse at the foot of the cross. And God met us right where we were.

A WORSHIP SERVICE

Celebrating Spiritual Healing in the Lord Jesus Christ

through

A Blessing and Releasing Ceremony

Pastor: We make our opening in the name of the Father and of the † Son and of the Holy Spirit.

All: Amen.

Chantel: "A Prayer of Acknowledgment and Purpose"—Inviting God's Presence and Blessings

Gracious Lord and Heavenly Father, we come before You today, our hearts filled with thanksgiving and praise, for You assure us that wherever two or more are gathered in Your name, there You are also. We welcome You into this place and are humbled to be in Your presence. We receive You, Lord. We bless Your name, God. We glorify You and give praise to You.

I acknowledge and confess that I am a poor miserable sinner in need of a Savior. I understand that it is only by Your grace and mercy, and through a saving relationship with You, my Lord and Savior Jesus Christ, that I am truly forgiven. I willingly and wholeheartedly come before You, Oh God, and repent of all my sins and receive Your forgiveness upon me. I make the same commitment to You again today, as I do every day in prayer, which is the following: I knowingly choose to die to self and rise again in You, and You in me. I choose to be a disciple of Christ who lives by principle and not by preference, choosing Spirit over flesh. I ask You to remove anything from me that is not of You, and to replace it with the presence of Holy Spirit, to the point of overflowing. Create in me a clean heart, oh God, and renew a right Spirit within me; cleanse me from all unrighteousness.

Father, I propose to focus on the following during this blessing and releasing ceremony: "Letting Go and Letting God: Leaving the Negativity of the Past Behind and Taking a Positive Step Forward into My 'New Normal'—A Happy, Healthy, God-blessed, Abundant Future in Christ Jesus." You are my rock and my salvation; I can do all things through Christ, who strengthens me.

I thank You, Lord, for the blessing of having my pastor here with me today, offering spiritual support and guiding me through this service. I acknowledge what an immense blessing he has been and how he continues to bless me, and I thank You for placing him in my path and for the blessing of his ministry. Likewise, I acknowledge that my other trusted care circle members are with us today in Spirit, offering supportive and loving thoughts and prayers in relation to this blessing and releasing ceremony. I am so very thankful to You for them and for their faithful support and care, too. I praise You, Lord.

We thank You for providing this opportunity for us to gather in Your name, God, and we pray Your blessings upon this worship service and throughout the blessing and releasing ceremony, knowing that You will bless us, in and through it. I choose to "count it all joy" and to praise and worship You always—in the storm, in the rain, and in the Son-shine. Prepare our hearts, Lord. Draw us closer unto You, Father, ever closer— we seek Your face and yearn to be in Your presence always. In You, Lord, we find our strength and comfort; in You, Lord, we find love, peace, and joy; in You, Lord, we find our purpose for life. Be with us, oh Lord. May everything we do and say bring glory to Your Holy Name. In Jesus's most precious name, we pray. Amen.

THE SONG OF PRAISE: "Welcome into This Place" by Wess Morgan

THE RELEASING OF THE PAST—"Letting Go..."

Chantel: Naming and Grieving the Losses

1. I experienced a loss of innocence and childhood, as well as young adulthood, because of the sexual assault and child sexual abuse perpetrated against me and that took place between the ages of 6 years old and 12 years old, again at 16 years old, and again between the ages of 16 years old and 28 years old.

2. I experienced a loss of adulthood because of the additional sexual assault perpetrated against me at 25 years old and again at the age of 28 years old.

3. I experienced a loss of completing my higher education—I had to quit attending college after two years due to the stress and mental/physical/emotional anguish of the sexual assault and child sexual abuse, amid deep personal turmoil.

4. I experienced a loss of attaining a degree in developmental psychology and subsequently counseling children, falling just short of obtaining this degree and graduating college because of the negative effects of the sexual assault and child sexual abuse.

5. I experienced a loss of quality of life because of the time I spent dealing with the negative ramifications of the sexual assault and child sexual abuse; crises; and trying to cope and merely make it through a day, often burying the pain in order to do so.

6. I experienced a loss of time/memories because of the negative effects of the sexual assault and child sexual abuse, and certain memories are unrecoverable at this time.

7. I experienced a loss of interest in certain hobbies, business ventures, book writing, personal interests, and the ability to see certain projects through to completion, on occasion, because of the negative effects of the sexual assault and child sexual abuse.

8. I experienced a loss of financial security because of the negative effects of the sexual assault and child sexual abuse and the evil perpetrated against me by others.

9. I experienced a loss of self-esteem, self-worth, and self-image because of the negative effects of the sexual assault and child sexual abuse.

10. I experienced a loss of support by people who were supposed to care for me and by people who were (or should have been) in my trusted care circle. They quickly or eventually abandoned me because of a lack of follow-up on their part, never making time for me, not responding to my sharing in any way, saying the wrong things, telling me that they were ill-equipped to provide care to me (even something as simple as listening), casting me aside and, in some cases, even shunning or blaming me.

11. I experienced a loss of normal/healthy coping strategies because of the development of negative coping mechanisms, which directly resulted from the sexual assault and child sexual abuse I had endured.

12. I experienced a loss of healthy and quality relationships with men because of the negative effects of the sexual assault and child sexual abuse. I developed an inability to trust others and myself, and I often felt that I did not deserve better treatment and/or did not know how to require better from others and from myself. There were also subsequent relationships with men who took advantage of and/or abused me in my adulthood.

13. I experienced a loss of calm and true enjoyment of life because I always (or often) felt as though I needed to be on guard or was in a crisis or expecting a new crisis to develop.

14. I experienced a loss of normal/healthy feelings and emotions because of the negative effects of the sexual assault and child sexual abuse.

15. I experienced a loss of the safety of sharing with my therapist, Catharine, because our weekly formal therapy sessions had ended.

Chantel: Naming the Abusers and the Abuse

- **Perpetrator #1** – sexually assaulted and abused me on repeated occasions and exposed me to pornography against my will between the ages of 6 years old and 12 years old.

- **Perpetrator #2** – sexually assaulted and abused me, on repeated occasions, at 16 years old.

- **Perpetrator #3** – sexually assaulted me, at 16 years old, and exposed me to numerous sexual situations.

- **Perpetrator #4** – sexually assaulted me, at 16 years old, and exposed me to sexual situations.

- **Perpetrator #5** – sexually assaulted me, at 16 years old, and exposed me to sexual situations.

- **Perpetrator #6** – sexually assaulted and abused me on repeated occasions, and exposed me to pornography against my will, from 16 years old to 28 years old; I am unsure when the abuse actually began and ended.

- **Perpetrator #7** – drugged me and sexually assaulted me repeatedly within a 12-hour period, at the age of 25, along with her husband.

- **Perpetrator #8** – drugged me and sexually assaulted and raped me repeatedly within a 12-hour period, at the age of 25, along with his wife.

- **Perpetrator #9** – sexually assaulted me on one occasion and exposed me to pornography at that time and against my will, at the age of 28.

Chantel: "A Prayer of Release"—Letting Go of the Negative Memories, Thoughts, and Feelings (losses, abusers, abuse; shame, blame, guilt, and self-doubt; negative self-esteem, self-worth, and self-image; abandonment; feeling unloved, forgotten, betrayed; feeling betrayed and manipulated, in and through past relationships with men)

Heavenly Father, I praise You for Your comfort and for the strength You have given to me to name my losses, the abusers who hurt me, and the abuse that was perpetrated against me on so many occasions throughout my life. You gave me the courage to face the ugliness and the truth of my past—the sexual assault and child sexual abuse, and the various disappointments of life. I willingly stand before You and speak my own truth today.

I acknowledge that because of the sexual assault and child sexual abuse that was perpetrated against me, throughout more than 20 years of my life, from the first instance of child sexual abuse to the last instance of sexual assault, I carried around a lot of shame, blame, guilt, and self-doubt; these are *false* feelings that were not even mine to begin with. As a survivor, I am reclaiming various areas of my life. I do not wish to carry around the negativity related to all of the assault and abuse any longer or in any way in my life, and I place all of the negative thoughts and feelings back onto the abusers who hurt me, which is right where it all should have been in the first place. I relinquish all of this to You, Lord.

I also seek to unburden myself from the negative self-esteem, self-worth, and self-image issues with which I have been afflicted because of the sexual assault and child sexual abuse perpetrated against me by so many abusers. I felt unloved and forgotten, used and taken advantage of, forsaken and rejected, abused and betrayed, and often overwhelmed by the sexual assault and child sexual abuse and by the immense burdens I carried. I now know I did not cause the assault and abuse. It was not my fault, and it was not in any way a sign that I was not lovable or important. However, as a child and a young adult, we don't always know these things, and so we blame ourselves unnecessarily, taking on the blame and internalizing the pain and hurt that resides deep inside of us. It feels good to know and acknowledge this truth. Yet, at the same time, it still hurts me deeply. Today, I am choosing to let go of and unburden myself from all of the negativity in my life.

I have experienced great pain and grief related to several of my past relationships with men. They had placed me in unimaginable situations, many of which I could not see coming because of the manner in which the men portrayed themselves to me. I have held on to anger related to the most recent relationship, which ended badly and revealed years of betrayal, manipulation, and lies, and which has also created immense burdens and hardships in my life since I ended the relationship. You have brought an abundance of healing into my life in the past several months, and You have shown up in my life in ways I could not have imagined by offering Your grace and mercy and by placing caring and supportive individuals in my path. I thank You for this, and I make the choice today to release myself from the associated anger, pain, grief, and hurt of these various relationships. I give it all up to You, Lord.

I have forgiven all of them at various times throughout my past, and I have chosen to do this because You freely forgive me, God. I have forgiven everyone that I have named for their wrongdoings, and I make the conscious choice to see them as the fallible human beings that they are. The fact that they are fallible does not in any way excuse their poor and sometimes sinful behavior, but it reminds me that we are all poor, miserable sinners in need of a Savior. I choose to "take refuge in [You,] Lord, [rather] than to trust in humans." (Psalm 118:8)

I freely confess, acknowledge, release, and give all of this up to You today, Lord, including my own need to be forgiven. I further acknowledge that although I have already forgiven these people, there are still things about my past that are difficult, if not next to impossible to forget. I believe that if I can forgive them, but not forget, that it only gets in the way of my ability to be faithful in service to You, and I want to serve You to the best of my ability and in relation to Your will for my life and the calling that You have placed upon it. Therefore, I ask You today, Lord, to allow me to cast my memories related to all of this negativity far away and into the depths of the sea so that they can no longer hold me back from living the life You have intended. Today, I do this freely, God, with Your help. I can do nothing apart from You, but I can do everything with You.

I acknowledge that the enemy brought all of this negativity into my life, but that You, my God, are greater than anything that may come up against me in this life! If You are for me, who can be against me (see Romans 8:31)? I rebuke the enemy and all of his strongholds against me, in Jesus's name, and I surrender all of the negative thoughts, emotions, feelings, and memories related to my past into Your capable hands. When You died on the cross for the forgiveness of my sins, You also took on anything that would come against me in this life; it was nailed to the cross along with Your bruised and battered body. You did that for me. I am in awe of such a loving and selfless sacrifice. I am covered by the blood that You shed on that very cross. "But he was pierced for our transgressions, he was crushed for our iniquities; the punishment that brought us peace was on him, and by his wounds we are healed." (Isaiah 53:5) I am not worthy, but I freely accept and am thankful for Your selfless sacrifice. I praise You, Lord.

Today, I choose to lay all of the negativity of my past at the foot of the cross. I release unto You anything that is in me, Lord, that is not of You. I ask for and openly claim and receive Your full and spiritual healing today—the healing that has already been assured to me on the cross, as a believer in You, Lord Jesus. I acknowledge that there are some things that may be in me that You are still working out, so it is possible You may not take those from me today, and that is okay. Because You, my God, are with me always, I believe that You are providing a way to make it through those challenges day by day; and, You are doing that to help me understand and see things, to know and call upon You in order to endure and rise above. I praise You and I lift up my hands in thanksgiving for Your awesome healing powers and Your amazing grace. I bow down and worship You now. You are awesome, indeed! I am unburdened from the past. I am a new creation in Christ. In Jesus's most precious name, I pray. Amen.

All: A Moment of Silence for Reflection and Release

THE SONG OF WORSHIP: "I Choose to Worship" by Wess Morgan

THE BLESSING FOR THE FUTURE—

...and Letting God"

Pastor: This marks the point in the blessing and releasing ceremony where Chantel has released all of the negativity related to her past. Now, we turn our focus towards "Letting God," beginning with the reading of the Scripture selections that have spoken to her pain, hurt, and heart the most during her healing journey these past few months.

THE OLD TESTAMENT READINGS

23rd Psalm (Chantel)

"The LORD is my shepherd; I shall not want. ² He maketh me to lie down in green pastures: he leadeth me beside the still waters. ³ He restoreth my soul: he leadeth me in the paths of righteousness for his name's sake. ⁴ Yea, though I walk through the valley of the shadow of death, I will fear no evil: for thou art with me; thy rod and thy staff they comfort me. ⁵ Thou preparest a table before me in the presence of mine enemies: thou anointest my head with oil; my cup runneth over. ⁶ Surely goodness and mercy shall follow me all the days of my life: and I will dwell in the house of the LORD for ever." (King James Version)

THIS IS THE WORD OF THE LORD.

Psalm 119:114 (Chantel)

"You are my refuge and my shield; I have put my hope in your word."

THIS IS THE WORD OF THE LORD.

Isaiah 54:4 (Pastor)

"Do not be afraid; you will not be put to shame. Do not fear disgrace; you will not be humiliated. You will forget the shame of your youth...."

THIS IS THE WORD OF THE LORD.

Jeremiah 29:11 (Pastor)

"For I know the plans I have for you," declares the LORD, "plans to prosper you and not to harm you, plans to give you hope and a future."

THIS IS THE WORD OF THE LORD.

THE EPISTLE READINGS

2 Corinthians 5:16–19 (Pastor)

"[16] So from now on we regard no one from a worldly point of view. Though we once regarded Christ in this way, we do so no longer. [17] Therefore, if anyone is in Christ, the new creation has come: The old has gone, the new is here! [18] All this is from God, who reconciled us to himself through Christ and gave us the ministry of reconciliation: [19] that God was reconciling the world to himself in Christ, not counting people's sins against them. And he has committed to us the message of reconciliation."

THIS IS THE WORD OF THE LORD

2 Corinthians 10:3–6 (Chantel)

"³ For though we live in the world, we do not wage war as the world does. ⁴ The weapons we fight with are not the weapons of the world. On the contrary, they have divine power to demolish strongholds. ⁵ We demolish arguments and every pretension that sets itself up against the knowledge of God, and we take captive every thought to make it obedient to Christ. ⁶ And we will be ready to punish every act of disobedience, once your obedience is complete."

THIS IS THE WORD OF THE LORD.

Ephesians 3:14–19 (Pastor)

"¹⁴ For this reason I kneel before the Father, ¹⁵ from whom every family in heaven and on earth derives its name. ¹⁶ I pray that out of his glorious riches he may strengthen you with power through his Spirit in your inner being, ¹⁷ so that Christ may dwell in your hearts through faith. And I pray that you, being rooted and established in love, ¹⁸ may have power, together with all the Lord's holy people, to grasp how wide and long and high and deep is the love of Christ, ¹⁹ and to know this love that surpasses knowledge—that you may be filled to the measure of all the fullness of God."

THIS IS THE WORD OF THE LORD.

Ephesians 6:10–17 (Pastor)

"[10] Finally, be strong in the Lord and in his mighty power. [11] Put on the full armor of God, so that you can take your stand against the devil's schemes. [12] For our struggle is not against flesh and blood, but against the rulers, against the authorities, against the powers of this dark world and against the spiritual forces of evil in the heavenly realms. [13] Therefore put on the full armor of God, so that when the day of evil comes, you may be able to stand your ground, and after you have done everything, to stand. [14] Stand firm then, with the belt of truth buckled around your waist, with the breastplate of righteousness in place, [15] and with your feet fitted with the readiness that comes from the gospel of peace. [16] In addition to all this, take up the shield of faith, with which you can extinguish all the flaming arrows of the evil one. [17] Take the helmet of salvation and the sword of the Spirit, which is the word of God."

THIS IS THE WORD OF THE LORD.

Philippians 3:7–9 (Chantel)

"[7] But whatever were gains to me I now consider loss for the sake of Christ. [8] What is more, I consider everything a loss because of the surpassing worth of knowing Christ Jesus my Lord, for whose sake I have lost all things. I consider them garbage, that I may gain Christ [9] and be found in him, not having a righteousness of my own that comes from the law, but that which is through faith in Christ—the righteousness that comes from God on the basis of faith."

THIS IS THE WORD OF THE LORD.

Philippians 4:4–9 (Pastor)

"[4] Rejoice in the Lord always. I will say it again: Rejoice! [5] Let your gentleness be evident to all. The Lord is near. [6] Do not be anxious about anything, but in every situation, by prayer and petition, with thanksgiving, present your requests to God. [7] And the peace of God, which transcends all understanding, will guard your hearts and your minds in Christ Jesus. [8] Finally, brothers and sisters, whatever is true, whatever is noble, whatever is right, whatever is pure, whatever is lovely, whatever is admirable—if anything is excellent or praiseworthy—think about such things. [9] Whatever you have learned or received or heard from me, or seen in me—put it into practice. And the God of peace will be with you."

THIS IS THE WORD OF THE LORD.

2 Timothy 1:7 (Chantel)

"For the Spirit God gave us does not make us timid, but gives us power, love and self-discipline."

THIS IS THE WORD OF THE LORD.

THE HOLY GOSPEL READINGS

Matthew 16:24–27 (Pastor)

"²⁴ Then Jesus said to his disciples, "Whoever wants to be my disciple must deny themselves and take up their cross and follow me. ²⁵ For whoever wants to save their life will lose it, but whoever loses their life for me will find it. ²⁶ What good will it be for someone to gain the whole world, yet forfeit their soul? Or what can anyone give in exchange for their soul? ²⁷ For the Son of Man is going to come in his Father's glory with his angels, and then he will reward each person according to what they have done."

THIS IS THE GOSPEL OF OUR LORD.

John 16:33 (Chantel)

"I have told you these things, so that in me you may have peace. In this world you will have trouble. But take heart! I have overcome the world."

THIS IS THE GOSPEL OF OUR LORD.

Pastor: We now confess the words of The Apostle's Creed.[4]

All:

I believe in God, the Father Almighty,

maker of heaven and earth.

And in Jesus Christ, His only Son, our Lord,

who was conceived by the Holy Spirit,

born of the virgin Mary,

suffered under Pontius Pilate,

was crucified, died, and was buried.

He descended into hell.

The third day He rose again from the dead.

He ascended into heaven

and sits at the right hand of God the Father Almighty.

From thence He will come to judge the living and the dead.

I believe in the Holy Spirit,

the holy Christian Church,

the communion of saints,

the forgiveness of sins,

the resurrection of the body,

and the life † everlasting, Amen.

---

4 "Creeds," 2016, Concordia Lutheran Church, accessed Sept 25, 2020, http://concordia-lutheran.com/Creed.aspx.

THE SONG OF THANKSGIVING: "You Gave Me Hope" by Wess Morgan

Chantel: Naming and Acknowledging My Trusted and Faithful Care Circle Members

1. Triune GOD—Father, Son, Holy Spirit
2. One of my pastors
3. My therapist
4. A family member
5. A dear friend
6. ME—I showed up for myself!

Chantel: Affirmations from My Trusted Care Circle Members and Me (read aloud)

Affirmations from Trusted Care Circle member:

- I treat myself with kindness and patience.
- I am an important person.
- I am beginning to establish my limits.
- I am a friend to myself.
- I am a leader.
- I am a good example to others.
- I forgive others who have hurt me.
- I can enjoy leisure without guilt or anxiety.

- I am worthy.

- I deserve to be happy.

- I feel good about myself.

- I feel surrounded by love.

- I feel relaxed.

- I make wise choices.

- I am intelligent.

- I am witty.

- I am good-hearted.

- I can make good things happen.

- I am a resourceful person.

- I am non-judgmental.

- I am tactful in my dealings with others.

Affirmations from Trusted Care Circle Member:

- You have an absolute faith in God.

- You are one of the most caring, giving people I know; this was exemplified in how you took care of my husband.

- You have a special way about you with kids, in that even if they have never met you, they respond to your smile and cheerful demeanor.

- You are incredibly creative and can turn everyday items into things of beauty.

- You have a way with words that turns the ordinary into words of encouragement and inspiration.

Affirmations from Trusted Care Circle Member:

- You are loving.

- You are an excellent caregiver.

- You are kind-hearted and kind-spirited.

Affirmations from Me to myself:

- I am a child of the living God.

- I feel alive.

- I am present and living in the moment.

- I have healthy boundaries for others and myself.

- I choose to live with purpose.

- I choose healing in Christ every day.

- I am a survivor.

- I am an overcomer, in Christ Jesus.

- I take good care of others.

- I take good care of myself.

- I am a servant of the Lord.

- I have God's power in my inner being.

- I know and understand the deep love that Christ has for me.

- My life is full of the fullness of God that no one can take away.

- I can do more than I can ever imagine, with the help of God.

Pastor: Encouraging Letters and Prayers for Chantel from her Care Circle Members (while these were read aloud during the worship ceremony, they will remain private and not be shared in this book)

Chantel: Letter to Myself as a Child (written and read aloud by Chantel)

SAFE IN THE ARMS OF JESUS

Little Chantel,

You are so small and innocent. Your short brown hair shows off your beautiful almond-shaped eyes. Even at the tender age of eight years old, you are already acquainted with deep pain and grief. You have been hurt in ways that only God really knows and understands. He can see what you try so hard to hide from others—the pain that is deep down inside of us. Others could see this hurt and pain through your eyes, if only they would take the time to look closely enough to find it. They don't. And they won't, for many years to come.

We have also grown very accustomed to protecting ourselves, feeling the only way to do this is to pretend the pain does not exist. I can see that you are feeling alone, unloved, and abandoned in the midst of our grief and the difficulties that are going on inside of our life. But you are not forgotten or forsaken, at least not by everyone around you. God has placed a few, trusted people in your life; people who will love and guide us in the years to come. God sees what many others have missed—this is because He has been walking with us each step of the way, and He truly knows the pain and hurt we hold inside. You are His precious child, and He loves us beyond measure. Go to Him as you have done on so many occasions before now, allowing Him to comfort and envelop you in His loving embrace. It is safe there; no one can harm us while we are safe in the arms of Jesus.

Do not blame yourself for the things that are going on in our life, now (at such a young age) or in the future. The sexual assault and child sexual abuse was not your fault, and we are not to blame for this. The fact that no one asked you how you felt does not mean that it was your fault. The things we endured at the hands of the men who have sexually assaulted and abused us does not need to be the way we expect other men to treat us in the future. Above all, you need to know that God loves and treasures us—it is His view and treatment of us that should be foremost in our mind. Keep your eye on Him, and He will guide and comfort us along each step of our journey. Our first abuser is at fault for the evil that they chose to perpetrate against us during this already-difficult time in our young life. Our body sustained repeated sexual assault and child sexual abuse, but you did nothing, at all, to cause the abuse. You are not to blame for this either. You are not alone in your suffering. We are safe in the arms of Jesus.

As the years go by, the dysfunction and abuse continue. Your childhood, stolen from you and from me, seems to be like a crime that went unpunished. However, none of it was or is our fault. God is in control. And He has placed and will continue to place people into your path that can and will be there for us in ways others could not. Another abuser has now entered our life, but not because you did or said anything wrong. This additional act of evil against us was not of God, but He was there to comfort us in our pain and confusion. You let Him do that for us, and that was very brave. As the abuse continued and more abusers would enter into our life in the years to come, the pain, guilt, shame, and blame would pile up to the point of almost burying us alive. However, in and through it all, we remained resilient in Christ. As you cried out to Him to comfort you in our hurt and sorrow, He did. We were never alone. We were safe in the arms of Jesus.

As you entered into adulthood, you took with us all of the confusion and feelings related to our childhood. You knew no different, and I do not blame you. And, yet again, even more abusers perpetrated evil acts against us to fulfill their own selfish needs and desires. You did nothing to cause this, and the abuse was not our fault. Men would come into our life and bring with them betrayal and manipulation and lies. We did not deserve this. And it was not our fault.

We clung to our faith in God as we sought to fulfill His call on our life, even in the midst of our pain and suffering. And, eventually, He brought more people into our life who would help us understand how and, in some cases, why these things happened to us. God never intended for these sad occurrences and evil acts to be a part of our life. But God, who was and continues to be with us always, has brought healing into our life in ways you never imagined were possible, and He is using the evil for good. And I showed up for you, too—I showed up for you, I showed up for us, and I showed up for myself. As God tells us in His Word from the 30th Psalm, "⁵...weeping may stay for the night, but rejoicing (joy) comes in the morning...¹¹ You turned my wailing into dancing...¹² that my heart may sing your praises and not be silent." (v. 5, 11, 12)

It is now safe to come out and play, little Chantel. It is okay to laugh and smile, feel joy and peace, and to love without feeling guilty about it. You can now let go of the shame, blame, guilt, and self-doubt that we held on to for years because God's design has never been for us to hold on to these things to begin with. I want you to release us from the hurt and the pain that has been hanging on to us like a heavy curtain for years, dragging us down and holding us back. It is a very courageous thing to do. You are not to blame for the things that happened to us in our life. And we are not alone in our suffering. You are now free to love yourself, just as God loves you. There is hope and there is healing, little Chantel. And it all has been found, in and through Christ Jesus. His grace is enough. Believe in your heart that we are loved; we are treasured; we are whole; we are healed. We can receive God's best for us. I love you. I love us. And I love myself. No one can harm us. Praise be to God! No one can harm us ever again. We are truly safe in the arms of Jesus.

Chantel: "A Prayer of Thanksgiving and Praise and an Acknowledgment of Healing"—Embracing a Future in Christ Jesus

Most gracious Lord and heavenly Father, once again, we come before You and seek Your face. We are touched to the deepest points of our Spirit and soul by Your faithfulness and in and through Your abiding love and presence. We receive Your agape love and the hope that envelops us, each and every day we make the choice to seek after You. Thank You for this magnificent time with You, Lord. Thank You for Your true and spiritual healing. We are, indeed, surrounded by Your glory and renewed in body, soul, and spirit, strengthened for Your service.

Oh, Lord, I give thanks and praise to You for the following:

1. Thank you for giving me the strength to make the decision to find true healing in and through YOU and to get help for myself. When I told people over the past several years about the assault and abuse, I did not allow it to stop me as silence and unsupportive comments quickly followed my sharing. I know that it is imperative to speak the truth in love and for others

to receive it in that manner in order for true healing to take place. I kept going and moving forward in my healing process; I chose to put my name on the list and remain active in my healing process even when I hit emotional walls and felt as though I just could not go on in the healing process. I choose to heal and be whole in Christ each day. Thank You, Lord, for the continued strength to endure and rise above the circumstances of my past.

2. Thank You for helping me to develop healthy coping mechanisms, which includes doing for others what I can realistically do but also requiring them to do for themselves where I cannot or should not. Now, I no longer feel the need to be in control of things.

3. Thank You for helping me to replace the negative tapes in my mind with positive affirmations and the abundance of truth found in Your Word.

4. Thank You for allowing me to believe that the abuse happened. I established myself as a person (adult) in the present dealing with the abuse I suffered as a child and as a young adult.

5. Thank You for giving me the strength to show up for myself AND create a loving, nurturing, and safe environment for myself.

6. Thank You for giving me the strength to break the silence, speak my truth, and witness to others.

7. Thank You for helping me to know, understand, and believe that the abuse was not my fault and that I did nothing to cause it. Thank You for reaffirming in my soul, heart, and spirit that I did make the choice to forgive all of the abusers, for my sake and not theirs, thus releasing me from the associated fear and negativity of the past and the strongholds of the enemy.

8. Thank You for helping me to know, understand, and believe that I am not alone in my suffering—You believe and are with me, God, and You have placed others in my path who also empathize and/or can relate to my suffering from a firsthand perspective; I appreciate them and I appreciate and praise You.

9. Thank You for helping me to know, understand, and believe that I am a survivor AND that I can and will stand in my truth, to the glory of Your Holy Name.

10. Thank You for helping me to know, understand, and believe that I can trust myself and others by utilizing and calling on the godly discernment You have instilled in me.

11. Thank You for helping me to know, understand, and believe that I have placed the shame, blame, guilt, and self-doubt back onto my abusers where they belong! I know and trust that You will take it from here, God.

12. Thank You for helping me to know, understand, and believe that I have acknowledged my losses as well as my need and right to grieve them. I have expressed my related anger and rage in a healthy manner. I have control over my thoughts, feelings, and emotions—they DO NOT control me! I consciously and purposely choose Spirit over flesh, godly principle over preference.

13. Thank You for helping me to know, understand, and believe that I have found my voice and have taken back my power!

14. Thank You for helping me to know, understand, and believe that as a survivor of sexual assault and child

sexual abuse, my healing journey continues, and that I have made the conscious decision to be gentle with myself and look to You, LORD God, for my strength and guidance. If a future crisis arises, I can and will be able to handle it, with Your help.

15. Thank You for helping me to know, understand, and believe that I have created safe places for myself, which are my home, my "special" place, and my church sanctuary.

16. Thank You for helping me to know, understand, and believe that I have established and will maintain healthy boundaries for myself (and others), honoring my right to privacy. I am embracing and reveling in the fact that You, God, were with me during my entire grief process and healing journey, guiding, supporting, and comforting me, as only You can. You, my heavenly Father, were everything I needed You to be and more—You did not forsake me or abandon me, but You loved, comforted, and supported me right where I was and am. I praise You.

17. Thank You for allowing me to make the choice to open my heart to my future husband and a family

with him. I know that You will lead me to a beautiful Christian man, one who is upstanding in the Lord, who can be for me all that You need him to be. I know it will be someone who can care for me according to my needs and who will love, understand, and support me right where I am, being gentle with me and care for me unconditionally.

18. Thank You for allowing me to choose to minister to myself as a young child, letting the little girl within me know it is safe and okay to come out and play. I have shown up for her and she can now embrace our "new normal" and join me in living the life You purposed for us by standing in our truth and in Your truth and being the person that You created us to be.

19. Thank You for allowing me to make the choice to take better care of myself—mentally, emotionally, physically, spiritually, and socially—and embracing and striving to attain and fulfill Your best for me every day.

20. Thank You for allowing me to make the choice to no longer focus on what others think of me but to love and see myself as You love and see me.

21. Thank You for seeking me out and leading me to choose to keep my eye on You, allowing me to embrace and answer Your call on my life into mission work as You expand my existing ministry of service unto You, Lord. I will serve You wherever You lead me…and where You lead me, I will follow. I will serve You as a missionary, counseling with and ministering to women and children who are enslaved by sex trafficking and sexual assault and child sexual abuse, just as You have called me to do. I will write articles and letters of testimony and ministry books about surviving sexual assault and child sexual abuse. I will talk to women and children who have been sexually assaulted and abused and give them reassurance of a hope in Christ through my testimony of faith and healing. I will utilize my faith in Christ as a platform to promote hope and healing from sexual assault and child sexual abuse, and in a variety of other life struggles, in and through a saving relationship with Jesus. You will work through me to lead souls to Christ in this lost and lonely world, and allow me to let go

of the need to seek and have the support of those in my life who would choose, instead, to challenge me in the ministry to which You have called me, rather than support me in and through it.

I praise You for always being by my side, especially during the lonely nights as I lie awake and cry out to You. I thank You for instilling in me, at such a young age, an awareness of Your Presence. I acknowledge and give thanks for all the many times growing up when You provided ways for me to get to church and worship You, and for planting seeds of hope and godly love and Your Word in and on my heart. You knew I would need to call on You and Your Truth many times throughout my life, through all the tests and trials, to know and believe that You, my God, were with me, regardless of my circumstances. I clung to this Truth always, and I still do, each and every day. I have always felt Your presence, for You are Emmanuel, God with us. When I have been in crisis, wounded, broken wide open, or felt lost and all alone, it is You to whom I ran. You literally led me beside still waters throughout my life and restored my soul every time, and you still do that to this day. I just know that You are always with me. I have known and felt (and still do feel) Your presence with me, every day. And You were (and always are) right there waiting for me with open and loving arms outstretched. Your promises are true; You will never forsake me. You are always faithful to meet me right where I am.

In my adulthood, You have continued to bring people into my path who have ministered to me at the exact time I needed to receive it. I thank You for my trusted care circle members, all of whom have been named today and who have faithfully walked with me during these past few months of my healing journey as I have embraced and actively participated in my weekly therapy sessions and grief work. We are never alone in our suffering, and You showed this to me through my caregivers' loving actions each day. For this, I thank You.

Father, You have blessed me with an amazing ministry. You have provided to me many opportunities over the course of my lifetime, thus far, to minister to others and share Your hope, love, and truth. You have given me a wealth of knowledge, resources, and experience from which to minister. You have prepared me. In the midst of the past hurts and pain, You have taken my "mess" and turned it into a message of hope, in and through Christ Jesus. You have taken the trials and tests in my life and turned them into a testimony. You have repeatedly shown up in my life in such awe-inspiring ways, so much so that even an unbeliever would not be able to question the ways in which You have worked Your healing wonders in and through my life. You have worked and You continue to work, in and through me, to spread Your truth and hope to others in this lost and lonely world. Just as Your Word is God-breathed, You breathe new life into me each day. I am truly a new creation in Christ.

You have blessed me with four precious godchildren—Jocelyn, Jaeden, Lucas, and Riley—and I strive to serve and bring glory to You by continuing to minister to them, reminding them of who they are in Christ and that they belong to You, and by loving them fully and unconditionally, setting a godly example for their lives in Christ Jesus. May I continue to be Your witness to them, all the days of my life.

As I let go of the negativity of my past today and embrace and embark on a happy, healthy, abundant, and God-blessed future in You, Lord, I am humbled by Your mercy, clothed in Your righteousness and love, and graced by Your majesty. You have walked with me, led me to Your Word, which has served to speak to my hurt and pain, offered hope for my future in

You, released me from the fear related to my past, and obliterated my oppression. You have delivered me from anxiousness and worrisome behavior. You have lifted my feelings of depression. You have delivered me from a life of crisis and chaos. I am released. I am unburdened. I am loosed. You have created in me a clean heart; I have been renewed in body, soul, and spirit through Your grace and mercy.

You have forgiven my trespasses as I have forgiven those who have trespassed against me. I praise You, Father. I welcome the countless opportunities You will bring into my path from this point forward to spread Your love, speak Your truth, and share the hope of Christ with others. It is a blessing to serve You, God. My heart is truly open to hearing and receiving You. My spirit is one with You. I treasure our precious time together each morning, often in the early-morning hours before the day has awakened; and I appreciate being able to call out to You at various times throughout the day and to know that You are always there, seeking me as I am seeking You. I treasure the countless opportunities I have to serve others, especially those who are hurting. You have placed a burden on my heart to care for all, but mostly for women and children—those who are hurting, grieving, lost, abandoned, abused, forsaken, forgotten, and feeling unloved. True healing can only be found in You. So many are lost and hurting and need to know and hear this truth. I can (and will) do all things through Christ, who strengthens me. "The one who is in you is greater than the one who is in the world." (1 John 4:4) I receive and live in Your grace, receiving all of Your blessings. Your forgiveness of sins—past, present, and future; Your healing—of all diseases; Your protection—because I dwell in the secret place of the Most High God; Your compassion and loving kindness—a shield that is all around me; and Your renewing of youth—by keeping my eye on You and living in the righteousness of faith.

You are the Great I AM—You are not the great yesterday or the great tomorrow, but the Great I AM. There is a reason for this, which is the following: to be a reminder to myself and others to live in the present with You. Now. Today. And to seek You and Your will in our lives, always; to not get ahead of ourselves because You have it all under control. You are the same yesterday, today, and forever. May we always know and trust this in our hearts. I heard Your call on my life in my early 20s as You led me to serve You in so many ways over the past many years. I answered that call. And I hear You again, now, as You continue to confirm Your call on my life in so many new and blessed ways.

You have anointed me to serve You through prayer, service, and by leading souls to You in faith and through a hope in Christ Jesus. Here am I, Lord—use me, lead me, send me. Continue to speak Your truth through me. Your way is always best, and I seek Your best for me and in my life always. Father, we give You ultimate thanks and praise. We exalt You and glorify You; we bless Your name, God. You are the Lord of lords and the King of kings. You are the Name that is above every other name. We lift up this prayer of thanksgiving and praise to You, now, in Jesus's most precious name. Amen.

Pastor: *We now pray as our Father has taught us—The Lord's Prayer (Matthew 6:9–13, KJV).*

All:

"9 Our Father which art in heaven, Hallowed be thy name.

10 Thy kingdom come, Thy will be done in earth, as it is in heaven.

11 Give us this day our daily bread.

12 And forgive us our debts, as we forgive our debtors.

13 And lead us not into temptation, but deliver us from evil: For thine is the kingdom, and the power, and the glory, for ever. Amen."

THE RITE OF HOLY COMMUNION

THE BENEDICTION

Pastor:

"²⁴ The LORD bless you and keep you;

²⁵ the Lord make his face shine on you and be gracious to you;

²⁶ the LORD turn his face toward you and † give you peace."

(Numbers 6:24–26)

All: Amen.

THE SONG OF BLESSING, RECEIVING, AND ANOINTING: "More of You" by Wess Morgan

———•———

Creating this worship service outline and holding the blessing and releasing ceremony was very healing and freeing for me. It helped to release a lot of emotions. I felt a sense of relief, as if I now had a predetermined place in the Spirit to go back to where something essential had occurred in my healing process. At times, I felt intense sadness and loss, but also immense joy and peace rose up to meet me. I was able to overcome, with the help of the Lord (and the invaluable support of my pastor). This entire part of the healing process was very beneficial for me.

November 14, 2011

I held my blessing and releasing ceremony with my pastor yesterday. It was awesome, freeing, painful, emotional, releasing, and a new start. Today is the first day of my "new normal," and I feel so great! Now, I am focusing on moving forward in the light of healing and wholeness in Christ Jesus. I will be celebrating the completion of my formal therapy sessions following my last session with Catharine later this week. I am excited to focus on celebrating something instead of just coping or trying to get through a day. I have found my healing in Christ Jesus. I love myself. I am full of love, joy, and peace. All of this feels so awesome. Praise God.

November 17, 2011

I held my last session with my therapist, Catharine, today. I went into it with mixed feelings—I was excited to bring some formal closure to our time together yet conflicted about actually being done. It was a true emotional chasm: I acknowledged that not meeting with my therapist would be a loss—it had been a safe place for me to share openly, without judgment, for the past four months—but I was excited about what my future held in Christ, outside of these formal sessions. Our last session was bittersweet, but mostly sweet. I am so thankful for her. I have come a long way in my healing journey. Thanks and praise be to God.

November 20, 2011

One week out from my blessing and releasing ceremony and one week into my "new normal" way of life, and I feel great. I have continued to keep my eye on God and yield to Him in all things. The enemy is trying to steal my peace and joy, but I will not allow that to happen. I have had many opportunities during this past week to seek God or to allow the enemy to undo what I have worked so hard to accomplish. I will not allow the enemy to win.

I spent some time at my special place yesterday (in the woods). I love it there. I can feel things continue to come into focus in my life. I really am embracing the love I have for myself. I am excited for what my future holds. I spent some time this morning reading back over my entire journal. It is amazing to see the growth, journey, and healing that God has brought about in my life. It is so amazing. I love the Lord. I will focus my attention on God, my Father, and the fact that His timing is always perfect.

I feel that the best way to maintain healthy boundaries in my life is to pray for God's peace, grace, and joy to hover over a group, place, situation, or person, as this will allow Him to do His work in it/them/me. Mostly, I ask Him to fill me with that joy. The basic idea is not to live out of memory but to live in the present. I will continue to rise above, in and through Christ Jesus.

At some point following my blessing and releasing ceremony, I received the following feedback from a few of my trusted care circle members:

Feedback #1:

"The ceremony showed in CAPS your therapist's guidance and your hard work in bringing to the surface so many negative events, over such a long period of time. You did a great job organizing the ceremony. Hope for moving forward. Keep your head up."

Feedback #2:

"The ceremony was uplifting and encouraging. It was sad in parts to read what was said about some of your past, but it was very positive because I could see that you were giving everything up to God and allowing Him to take away your pain."

Feedback #3:

"It was a profound place that you invited me into, and I do not take it lightly that I was allowed into a very dark and unpleasant place so that God's Word of truth and grace might reign supreme. I understand that this is just a step in the healing, but I would hope a large step toward freedom as you live in the forgiveness received and given those who have harmed you. The thought that comes to mind is that Satan will be working hard to undo this work in your heart, calling it in to question and sending doubts about its effectiveness. May the Lord protect your heart and fan into flame the goodness that is replacing the darkness. As you already know, the people who have disappointed you and have not supported you most likely will not

change and will not be a source of healing. But the Lord is with you. He is your rock and strength. He will not disappoint."

———•———————•———————•———

At some point many years after completing this ceremony, I have gone back several times in my mind to this pivotal point in my life and healing journey, and the Lord has reminded me of the good work He did in my heart on that very day. He had created a demarcation line in the Spirit through the prophetic words and actions of this ceremony, and something had shifted in the Spirit and in me. You see, what one of my trusted care circle members said might occur, actually did occur; the enemy did try to undo what had been done during that ceremony, and someone very close to me has even tried to use this ceremony against me.

Let me be very clear on a few things: "Blessing and releasing" something in our life does not mean it did *not* occur; it means that what occurred no longer controls our life. It does not get swept under the rug, even though some people would desire for that to be the case and it would make life easier for them. It does not always need to die in silence, because every once in a while, we do need to speak the truth in love. God can work all things for good, and we can choose to live in the Light of Christ. God can and will use our life experiences in ways that we cannot possibly fathom, causing joy to arise within us, and purposing for others to receive healing from what we share, if we will only allow Him to do that. "Your sun will never set again, and your moon will wane no more; the LORD will be your everlasting light, and your days of sorrow will end." (Isaiah 60:20) Oh, yes, dear friends, lift your eyes up to the hills and see it: Your heart is opening up, more and more, to receiving the joy that comes in the morning.

Questions for Reflection

    1. Have I ever considered the need to "bless and release" things from my past? Who could help me to facilitate a worship ceremony like this? Has anyone ever tried to silence me and keep me from sharing my truth? (Note: You can find this entire "Blessing and Releasing Ceremony" as well as a clean (fill in the blank) version of the ceremony outline on our Hope

for the Soul Ministries website—when you are ready, you can then use it to create a worship service and ceremony that is personalized just for you and your spiritual and healing journey.)

2. What is(are) my purpose(s) for holding a blessing and releasing ceremony? What are my losses? Who are my abusers? What did my abuse consist of? What am I willing to let go of (and release it) to the Lord?

3. Which Scripture speaks to me the most, in terms of my own healing journey? Which praise and worship songs should I consider using in my blessing and releasing ceremony? Where could this ceremony take place?

4. Who are my trusted care circle members, and how have they supported me?

5. I will write a letter to myself as a child. How can (did) that provide healing to me?

Come into the Light

Gracious Lord and Heavenly Father, I acknowledge that there are numerous things from my past that I need to "bless and release" to You. I need You to show me how to create my own "blessing and releasing" ceremony, and lead me to whomever can best help me to facilitate it. If anyone has ever tried to silence me in my suffering, I am asking You to give me a voice and to walk with me through this part of my healing journey. I need You. Help me to connect with my purpose(s), define my losses, identify my abusers and the abuse I endured, and further identify the things I'm willing to let go of and release to You. Allow Your Word to rise up in my spirit and in my heart, and to be a lamp to my feet and a light unto my path. Remind me of those who have supported me, and help me to acknowledge them. Give me the strength to establish myself as an adult in the present dealing with the sexual assault and child sexual abuse of the past, and to write a letter to myself as a child. I need to be free from the pain. Help me to "bless and release" the things of the past, in whatever way that is best for me. I love You, and I praise You. I ask this all in Jesus's name. Amen.

Chapter 9

WHO WE ARE IN CHRIST:
OUR REAL IDENTITY

*"Yet to all who did receive him, to those who believed
in his name, he gave the right to become children of
God." (John 1:12)*

Have you ever asked God who you are, who you *really* are?
You should. He will tell you. And you might be surprised
by His response. In fact, I invite you to go to Him in prayer and
ask Him who you are. Write down His response in your journal.
Then, continue reading this chapter.

If I were to ask most people this question, their answers
might include some of the following: I am a mother, a father, a

son, a daughter; a teacher, a janitor, a lawyer; I am a babysitter, a caretaker, a provider; I am a good person, I am kind; I try to do the right thing. While these responses would definitely give me some idea as to the roles you fill in life, or the occupation you have chosen (or that has somehow chosen you), or some insight into the characteristics of your personality, these responses are not an indication of *who* you are. I believe in order to heal, truly and completely, we must know who we are in Christ, which is our real and complete identity. And this is not determined by how we feel—our identity, dear friends, is not based on feelings or emotions.

I know what God's Word tells me about our real identity. We are a new creation, His child, a saint, an heir of God, an instrument of His righteousness, forgiven, chosen, victorious, redeemed, reconciled, justified, secure, adopted, beloved, filled with joy and peace, granted true meaning in life, whole, complete, favored, blessed, healed. It is not what you say about yourself or what others say about you that causes something to be true; what God says about you is the real determining factor for truth. Throughout this chapter, we will read and study several words in a language different than standard English. We will use

Strong's Concordance for our ease of reference.[5] When we find our real identity in Christ and His resurrection (*dunamis*) power is in us, we cannot go back to being the victim. "No, in all these things we are more than conquerors through him who loved us." (Romans 8:37)

Let us explore God's Word and learn and study about who we truly are in Christ. We will review the various aspects of our real identity throughout this entire chapter. You should have your journal handy so you can continue to write down your thoughts as well as the answers to the Questions for Reflection at the end of each section. Let's get started!

9.1—WE ARE LOVED (by the Father)

In this first part of our Identity in Christ study, it seems natural that we would begin by focusing on the topic of love. Love is a fruit of the Spirit. God created us out of love. Love is who and what God **IS**. And in Chapter 6, we learned how to love again. At the core of our being, most everyone yearns to experience the

---

5 All words not in English in this chapter (such as Greek or Hebrew, etc.) can be found in *Strong's Concordance.*

feeling of being appreciated, needed, and *loved*. We are all a spirit being with a soul, which consists of our mind, our will, and our emotions and feelings, and all of this is contained in a human body. When we become a child of the Living God, our spirit becomes alive in Him and He in us. Our believing spirit allows us to be connected to the LORD God.

Quite often, a relationship with the Lord is based upon how someone feels instead of the truths and promises found in God's Word. "God is love." (1 John 4:16) The fact that we are loved should never be based off of how we feel about ourselves or by what someone says about us or how they treat us; feelings and emotions can be fleeting (and sometimes false), and others do not know us like God does. Perhaps you have or have had a difficult relationship with your earthly father and that has caused you to doubt God's love for you. Our Heavenly Father and our earthly father are not the same person. What God and His Word say about you is what really matters. God's love is unconditional and never-ending, and your behavior or performance does not determine whether you receive it. God is love, and He loves you. Period. End of discussion.

———•——————●——————•———

There are many ways to say or refer to "love" in the Hebrew language, the language of the Old Testament, but for the purpose of this particular study, we will focus only on the love between people or of people toward God (*ahab*) and the kindness of God toward people (*hesed*). Likewise, in the Greek language, the language of the New Testament, there are many ways to say or refer to "love." We will focus on God's expression of love for us (*agape* and *agapeo*) as extended to us through Holy Spirit. This agape love gives and sacrifices and expects nothing in return. It is eternal. We cannot love like this through our own power; Christ must dwell and work in and through us in order to bring it to fruition. You might be interested to know that the word love appears in the Bible nearly 700 times. Let us take a look at just a few of the examples of God as love and of His great love for us found throughout Scripture, both in the Old and New Testaments.

OLD TESTAMENT:

- "The LORD, the LORD, the compassionate and gracious God, slow to anger, abounding in **love** and faithfulness...." (Exodus 34:6; Numbers 14:18; Nehemiah 9:17; Psalm 103:8; Joel 2:13; Jonah 4:2)

- "...the Lord **loved** you...." (Deuteronomy 7:8)

- "Give thanks to the Lord, for he is good; his **love** endures forever." (1 Chronicles 16:34; Psalm 106:1; 118:1; 136:1)

- "But I trust in your unfailing **love**; my heart rejoices in your salvation." (Psalm 13:5)

- "Surely your goodness and **love** will follow me all the days of my life, and I will dwell in the house of the Lord forever." (Psalm 23:6)

- "I will be glad and rejoice in your **love**, for you saw my affliction and knew the anguish of my soul." (Psalm 31:7)

- "Your **love**, Lord, reaches to the heavens, your faithfulness to the skies." (Psalm 36:5; 57:10; 108:4)

- "Praise be to God, who has not rejected my prayer or withheld his **love** from me." (Psalm 66:20)

- "You, Lord, are forgiving and good, abounding in **love** to all who call to you." (Psalm 86:5)

- "For as high as the heavens are above the earth, so great is his **love** for those who fear him." (Psalm 103:11)

- "But you, Sovereign Lord, help me for your name's sake; out of the goodness of your **love**, deliver me." (Psalm 109:21)

- "May your unfailing **love** be my comfort, according to your promise to your servant." (Psalm 119:76)

- "...the Lord disciplines those he **loves**...." (Proverbs 3:12; Hebrews 12:6)

- "I **love** those who love me, and those who seek me find me." (Proverbs 8:17)

- "...yet my unfailing **love** for you will not be shaken." (Isaiah 54:10)

- "In his **love** and mercy he redeemed them...." (Isaiah 63:9)

- "I have **loved** you with an everlasting love." (Jeremiah 31:3)

- "Because of the Lord's great **love** we are not consumed, for his compassions never fail." (Lamentations 3:22)

NEW TESTAMENT:

- "For God so **loved** the world that he gave his one and only Son, that whoever believes in him shall not perish but have eternal life." (John 3:16)

- "Having **loved** his own who were in the world, he **loved** them to the end." (John 13:1)

- "Whoever has my commands and keeps them is the one who **loves** me. The one who **loves** me will be **loved** by my Father, and I too will **love** them and show myself to them." (John 14:21)

- "As the Father has **loved** me, so have I **loved** you. Now remain in my **love**." (John 15:9)

- "...the Father himself **loves** you because you have **loved** me and have believed that I came from God." (John 16:27)

- "And hope does not put us to shame, because God's **love** has been poured out into our hearts through the Holy Spirit, who has been given to us." (Romans 5:5)

- "But God demonstrates his own **love** for us in this: While we were still sinners, Christ died for us." (Romans 5:8)

- "And we know that in all things God works for the good of those who **love** him, who have been called according to his purpose." (Romans 8:28)

- "[35] Who shall separate us from the **love** of Christ? Shall trouble or hardship or persecution or famine or nakedness or danger or sword? [37] No, in all these things we are more than conquerors through him who loved us. [39]...neither height nor depth, nor anything else in all creation, will be able to separate us from the **love** of God that is in Christ Jesus our Lord." (Romans 8:35, 37, 39)

- "'...no eye has seen, no ear has heard, and no human mind has conceived'—the things God has prepared for those who **love** him." (1 Corinthians 2:9)

- "⁴ **Love** is patient, **love** is kind. It does not envy, it does not boast, it is not proud. ⁵ It does not dishonor others, it is not self-seeking, it is not easily angered, it keeps no record of wrongs. ⁶ **Love** does not delight in evil but rejoices with the truth. ⁷ It always protects, always trusts, always hopes, always perseveres." (1 Corinthians 13:4–7)

- "⁴ But because of his great **love** for us, God, who is rich in mercy, ⁵ made us alive with Christ even when we were dead in transgressions—it is by grace you have been saved." (Ephesians 2:4–5)

- "¹⁶ I pray that out of his glorious riches he may strengthen you with power through his Spirit in your inner being, ¹⁷ so that Christ may dwell in your hearts through faith. And I pray that you, being rooted and established in **love**, ¹⁸ may have power, together with all the Lord's holy people, to grasp how wide and long and high and deep is the **love** of Christ, ¹⁹ and to know this **love** that surpasses knowledge—that you may be filled to the measure of all the fullness of God." (Ephesians 3:16–19)

- "Therefore, as God's chosen people, holy and dearly **loved**, clothe yourselves with compassion, kindness, humility, gentleness and patience." (Colossians 3:12)

- "For we know, brothers and sisters **loved** by God, that he has chosen you...." (1 Thessalonians 1:4)

- "...brothers and sisters **loved** by the Lord...." (2 Thessalonians 2:13)

- "The grace of our Lord was poured out on me abundantly, along with the faith and **love** that are in Christ Jesus." (1 Timothy 1:14)

- "See what great **love** the Father has lavished on us, that we should be called children of God! And that is what we are. The reason the world does not know us is that it did not know him." (1 John 3:1)

- "⁹ This is how God showed his **love** among us: He sent his one and only Son into the world that we might live through him. ¹⁰ This is **love**: not that we loved God, but that he **loved** us and sent his Son as an atoning sacrifice for our sins. ¹⁶ God is **love**." (1 John 4:9–10, 16)

- "²⁰ But you, dear friends, by building yourselves up in your most holy faith and praying in the Holy Spirit, ²¹ keep yourselves in God's **love** as you wait for the mercy of our Lord Jesus Christ to bring you to eternal life." (Jude 1:20–21)

- "Those whom I **love** I rebuke and discipline. So be earnest and repent." (Revelation 3:19)

God's Word is so precious, and there is a wealth of truth found in it. ("Your Word is truth." (John 17:17) | "All Scripture is God-breathed…" (2 Timothy 3:16)). I encourage you to spend time in the Scriptures daily and meditate upon them. They will provide clarity and wisdom and speak God's Truth into every area of your life. By doing so, I assure you that you will receive a blessing and be a blessing to others, building up the body of Christ as you do so.

"And now these three remain: faith, hope and **love**. But the greatest of these is **love**" (1 Corinthians 13:13). Father loves you unconditionally. Take heart, dear friends. YOU. ARE. LOVED.

Questions for Reflection

1. Do you believe that God/Jesus loves you unconditionally?

2. Knowing that many of the relationships in your life are often performance based, what difference does it make to you to know that God/Jesus loves you no matter what?

3. Of the Scriptures shared above, which reveal(s) and speak(s) His Truth to you the most?

9.2—WE ARE CREATED TO LOVE (God and others)

It is not always easy to love others. I will be the first person to admit this. In our humanness, our feelings can get hurt, and it becomes harder and harder to love certain people in our lives. Perhaps they are unsupportive, selfish, or unloving. Perhaps they are incessantly thinking that they know what is best for you, above God's plan for your life. "In their hearts humans plan their course, but the Lord establishes their steps." (Proverbs 16:9)

However, God created us to love. That is where Christ comes in. Like us, Jesus was human, but He was also God incarnate, something we cannot claim. Unlike Jesus, you and I are not love. We can love, but we cannot do it perfectly. "A new command I give you: Love one another. As I have loved you, so you must love one another." (John 13:34) How do we do that? How do we love others?

In this second part of our study, let us look at additional types of love expressed in the Bible. Brotherly love (*phileo*) is a soulish type of love, connected through our emotions, experienced by both believers and non-believers alike. Family love (*storge*) is a Greek word that does not appear in the Bible, but there are several examples of this type of love (see Exodus 20:12; John 11:1–45). Spousal or sensual love between a husband and a wife (*eros*) is also a Greek word that does not appear in the Bible, but there are several examples of spousal love between a husband and wife (see 1 Corinthians 7:8–9; numerous passages in The Song of Solomon/Songs).

As Christians, we are to express both a soulish, familiar love and the spirit-led, unconditional love of Christ. Here are two of the Scriptures that incorporate both *(phileo)* and *(agape)* love:

- "Now that you have purified yourselves by obeying the truth so that you have sincere love (**phileo**) for each other, love (**agape**) one another deeply, from the heart." (1 Peter 1:22)

- "⁵ For this very reason, make every effort to add to your faith goodness; and to goodness, knowledge; ⁶ and to knowledge, self-control; and to self-control, perseverance; and to perseverance, godliness; ⁷ and to godliness, mutual affection (**phileo**); and to mutual affection, love (**agape**)." (2 Peter 1:5–7)

It is important to know and remember that loving God is also synonymous with obeying His Word; the two go hand in hand. So, once again, we turn to the Scriptures for examples of how we can love God, learn to love with the love of Christ, and love as we were created to love, all the while being mindful that "with God all things are possible," (Mark 10:27) and "apart from [God] you can do nothing." (John 15:5)

NEW TESTAMENT:

- "^{34} A new command I give you: **Love** one another. As I have **loved** you, so you must **love** one another. ^{35} By this everyone will know that you are my disciples, if you **love** one another." (John 13:34–35)

- "^{9} **Love** must be sincere. Hate what is evil; cling to what is good. ^{10} Be devoted to one another in **love**. Honor one another above yourselves." (Romans 12:9–10)

- "**Love** does no harm to a neighbor. Therefore, **love** is the fulfillment of the law." (Romans 13:10)

- "But whoever **loves** God is known by God." (1 Corinthians 8:3)

- "If I speak in the tongues of men or of angels, but do not have **love**, I am only a resounding gong or a clanging cymbal. ^{2} If I have the gift of prophecy and can fathom all mysteries and all knowledge, and if I have a faith that can move mountains, but do not have **love**, I am nothing. ³ If I give all I possess to the poor and give over my body to hardship that I may boast, but do not have **love**, I gain nothing. ⁴ **Love** is patient, **love** is kind. It does not envy, it does not boast, it is not proud. ⁵ It does not dishonor others, it is not self-seeking, it is not easily angered, it keeps no record of wrongs. ⁶ **Love** does not delight in evil but rejoices with the truth. ⁷ It always protects, always trusts, always hopes, always perseveres. ⁸ **Love** never fails. But where there are prophecies, they will cease; where there are tongues, they will be stilled; where there is knowledge, it will pass away. ⁹ For we know in part and we prophesy in part, ¹⁰ but when completeness comes, what is in part disappears. ¹¹ When I was a child, I talked like a child, I thought like a child, I reasoned like a child. When I became a man, I put the ways of childhood behind me. ¹² For now we see only a reflection as in a mirror; then we shall see face to face. Now I know in part; then I shall know fully, even as I am fully known. ¹³ And now these three remain: faith, hope and **love**. But the greatest of these is **love**." (1 Corinthians 13)

- "Do everything in **love**." (1 Corinthians 16:14)

- "For Christ's **love** compels us, because we are convinced that one died for all, and therefore all died." (2 Corinthians 5:14)

- "Finally, brothers and sisters, rejoice! Strive for full restoration, encourage one another, be of one mind, live in peace. And the God of **love** and peace will be with you." (2 Corinthians 13:11)

- "I have been crucified with Christ and I no longer live, but Christ lives in me. The life I now live in the body, I live by faith in the Son of God, who **loved** me and gave himself for me." (Galatians 2:20)

- "You, my brothers and sisters, were called to be free. But do not use your freedom to indulge the flesh; rather, serve one another humbly In **love**." (Galatians 5:13)

- "22 But the fruit of the Spirit is **love**, joy, peace, forbearance, kindness, goodness, faithfulness, 23 gentleness and self-control." (Galatians 5:22–23)

- "Be completely humble and gentle; be patient, bearing with one another in **love**." (Ephesians 4:2)

- "[15] Instead, speaking the truth in **love**, we will grow to become in every respect the mature body of him who is the head, that is, Christ. [16] From him the whole body, joined and held together by every supporting ligament, grows and builds itself up in **love**, as each part does its work." (Ephesians 4:15–16)

- "[1] Follow God's example, therefore, as dearly **loved** children [2] and walk in the way of **love**, just as Christ **loved** us and gave himself up for us as a fragrant offering and sacrifice to God." (Ephesians 5:1–2)

- "[25] Husbands, **love** your wives, just as Christ **loved** the church and gave himself up for her [26] to make her holy, cleansing her by the washing with water through the word, [27] and to present her to himself as a radiant church, without stain or wrinkle or any other blemish, but holy and blameless. [28] In this same way, husbands ought to **love** their wives as their own bodies. He who **loves** his wife loves himself. [29] After all, no one ever hated their own body, but they feed and care for their body, just as Christ does the church— [30] for we are members of his body. [31] 'For this reason a man will leave his father and mother and be united to his wife, and the two will become one flesh.' [32] This is a profound mystery—but I am talking about Christ and the church. [33] However, each one of you also must **love** his wife as he loves himself, and the wife must respect her husband." (Ephesians 5:25–33)

- "[9] And this is my prayer: that your **love** may abound more and more in knowledge and depth of insight, [10] so that you may be able to discern what is best and may be pure and blameless for the day of Christ, [11] filled with the fruit of righteousness that comes through Jesus Christ—to the glory and praise of God." (Philippians 1:9–11)

- "Therefore, if you have any encouragement from being united with Christ, if any comfort from his **love**, if any common sharing in the Spirit, if any tenderness and compassion, [2] then make my joy complete by being like-minded, having the same **love**, being one in spirit and of one mind." (Philippians 2:1–2)

- "Finally, brothers and sisters, whatever is true, whatever is noble, whatever is right, whatever is pure, whatever is **lovely**, whatever is admirable—if anything is excellent or praiseworthy—think about such things." (Philippians 4:8)

- "[12] Therefore, as God's chosen people, holy and dearly **loved**, clothe yourselves with compassion, kindness, humility, gentleness and patience. [13] Bear with each other and forgive one another if any of you has a grievance against someone. Forgive as the Lord forgave you. [14] And over all these virtues put on **love**, which binds them all together in perfect unity." (Colossians 3:12–14)

- "May the Lord make your **love** increase and overflow for each other and for everyone else...." (1 Thessalonians 3:12)

- "...for you yourselves have been taught by God to **love** each other." (1 Thessalonians 4:9)

- "...and the **love** all of you have for one another is increasing." (2 Thessalonians 1:3)

- "...pursue righteousness, godliness, faith, **love**, endurance and gentleness." (1 Timothy 6:11)

- "For the Spirit God gave us does not make us timid, but gives us power, **love** and self-discipline." (2 Timothy 1:7)

- "…be hospitable, one who **loves** what is good, who is self-controlled, upright, holy and disciplined." (Titus 1:8)

- "23 Let us hold unswervingly to the hope we profess, for he who promised is faithful. 24 And let us consider how we may spur one another on toward **love** and good deeds, 25 not giving up meeting together, as some are in the habit of doing, but encouraging one another—and all the more as you see the Day approaching." (Hebrews 10:23–25)

- "Anyone who **loves** their brother and sister lives in the light, and there is nothing in them to make them stumble." (1 John 2:10)

- "Do not **love** the world or anything in the world. If anyone **loves** the world, **love** for the Father is not in them." (1 John 2:15)

- "For this is the message you heard from the beginning: We should **love** one another." (1 John 3:11)

- "¹⁴ We know that we have passed from death to life, because we **love** each other. Anyone who does not **love** remains in death. ¹⁵ Anyone who hates a brother or sister is a murderer, and you know that no murderer has eternal life residing in him. ¹⁶ This is how we know what **love** is: Jesus Christ laid down his life for us. And we ought to lay down our lives for our brothers and sisters. ¹⁷ If anyone has material possessions and sees a brother or sister in need but has no pity on them, how can the **love** of God be in that person? ¹⁸ Dear children, let us not **love** with words or speech but with actions and in truth." (1 John 3:14–18)

- "⁷ Dear friends, let us **love** one another, for **love** comes from God. Everyone who **loves** has been born of God and knows God. ⁸ Whoever does not **love** does not know God, because God is **love**. ⁹ This is how God showed his **love** among us: He sent his one and only Son into the world that we might live through him. ¹⁰ This is **love**: not that we **loved** God, but that he **loved** us and sent his Son as an atoning sacrifice for our sins. [11] Dear friends, since God so **loved** us, we also ought to **love** one another. [12] No one has ever seen God; but if we **love** one another, God lives in us and his **love** is made complete in us. [13] This is how we know that we live in him and he in us: He has given us of his Spirit. [14] And we have seen and testify that the Father has sent his Son to be the Savior of the world. [15] If anyone acknowledges that Jesus is the Son of God, God lives in them and they in God. [16] And so we know and rely on the **love** God has for us. God is **love**. Whoever lives in **love** lives in God, and God in them. [17] This is how **love** is made complete among us so that we will have confidence on the day of judgment: In this world we are like Jesus. [18] There is no fear in **love**. But perfect **love** drives out fear, because fear has to do with punishment. The one who fears is not made perfect in **love**. [19] We **love** because he first **loved** us. [20] Whoever claims to **love** God yet hates a brother or sister is a liar. For whoever does not **love** their brother and sister, whom they have seen, cannot **love** God, whom they have not seen. [21] And he has given us this command: Anyone who **loves** God must also **love** their brother and sister." (1 John 4:7–21)

- "² This is how we know that we **love** the children of God: by **loving** God and carrying out his commands. ³ In fact, this is **love** for God: to keep his commands. And his commands are not burdensome, ⁴ for everyone born of God overcomes the world. This is the victory that has overcome the world, even our faith. ⁵ Who is it that overcomes the world? Only the one who believes that Jesus is the Son of God." (1 John 5:2–5)

- "And this is **love**: that we walk in obedience to his commands. As you have heard from the beginning, his command is that you walk in **love**." (2 John 1:6)

- "²⁰ But you, dear friends, by building yourselves up in your most holy faith and praying in the Holy Spirit, ²¹ keep yourselves in God's **love** as you wait for the mercy of our Lord Jesus Christ to bring you to eternal life." (Jude 1:20–21)

When Jesus was asked what the greatest commandment was, "[37] Jesus replied: '**Love** the Lord your God with all your heart and with all your soul and with all your mind.' [38] This is the first and greatest commandment. [39] And the second is like it: '**Love** your neighbor as yourself.'" (Matthew 22:37–39; Mark 12:30–31; Luke 10:27) Jesus said that the entire law was dependent upon these two commandments. It is also important to know and understand that, as believers, we live under grace and not the law, because of Jesus's sacrifice on the cross and His subsequent fulfillment of the law. There must be a balance of law and grace. And it is this very grace that allows us to love God and others with a godly love.

Caring is Christ's love in action. I encourage you now to spend time in prayer and in His Word daily. Go forth and serve the Lord our God and others, in and through this very love. After all, dear friends, we are created to love.

Questions for Reflection

1. Do you love God? How do you know this? How do others know this? How do you express this love to God?

2. How often do you say "God/Jesus loves you" to others? What kind of difference would/does it make in their lives...and in yours...if you did/do this?

3. How do you show God's love to others? What are some ways (both tangible and intangible) in which you can express Christ's love to others in this coming week?

4. Whom is the Lord leading you to love in a godlier way? Spend some time with God in prayer and make a list of those people—then express Christ's love to them in thought, word, and deed. (Note: Meditating upon the above Scriptures will help in this exercise.)

5. Of the Scriptures shared above, which reveal(s) and speak(s) His Truth to you the most?

9.3—WE ARE ACCEPTED CHILDREN OF THE LIVING GOD

In and through the first two parts of our Identity in Christ study, we have established a solid foundation and understanding of being loved by God and having been created to love. God created us in such a way that we need a relationship with Him, our Creator, and we need human relationships. He did not create us to be alone.

We were created in relationship, for relationship, and through relationship.

In relationship:

"God saw that [His Creation] was good." (Genesis 1:4, 10, 12, 18, 21, 25)

For relationship:

"God saw all that He had made, and behold, it was very good." (Genesis 1:31)

And through relationship:

"Then the LORD God said, 'it is not good for the man to be alone.'" (Genesis 2:18)

It is important to know and understand that Jesus was willing to risk the fear of failure and rejection. Jesus was secure in who He was and in His relationship with the Father. Because of this, He found a release from the fear of failure and the fear of rejection to do the Father's will.

Jesus had a sense of **provision**.

Jesus had a sense of **purpose**.

Jesus had a sense of **peace**.

Jesus also had a **power of identity**.

- "³ Jesus knew that the Father had put all things under his power, and that he had **come from God** and was returning to God; ⁴ so he got up from the meal, took off his outer clothing, and wrapped a towel around his waist. ⁵ After that, he poured water into a basin and began to wash his disciples' feet, drying them with the towel that was wrapped around him." (John 13:3–5)

- Jesus understood "For even the Son of Man did not come to be served, but to serve, and to give his life as a ransom for many." (Matthew 20:28; Mark 10:45)

———•——————•——————•———

Jesus knew who He was (and IS) because of His relationship, in and through and with the Father. By extension, we can also know who we are, because of the personal relationship we have with God through Jesus and because of the identity we have established and are establishing in Christ. So, Jesus knew who He was and who He is. Who are you?

You are loved, you were created to love, and you are an accepted child of the living God. But how do we know this is true?

WE MUST UNDERSTAND THAT WE ARE ALL SINNERS.

- "²¹ But now apart from the law the righteousness of God has been made known, to which the Law and the Prophets testify. ²² This righteousness is given through faith in Jesus Christ to all who believe. There is no difference between Jew and Gentile, ²³ **for all have sinned and fall short of the glory of God,** ²⁴ and all are justified freely by his grace through the redemption that came by Christ Jesus. ²⁵ God presented Christ as a sacrifice of atonement, through the shedding of his blood—to be received by faith. He did this to demonstrate his righteousness, because in his forbearance he had left the sins committed beforehand unpunished— ²⁶ he did it to demonstrate his righteousness at the present time, so as to be just and the one who justifies those who have faith in Jesus." (Romans 3:21–26)

WE MUST PAY A WAGE FOR OUR SIN, UNDERSTANDING THAT JESUS TOOK OUR SIN ON HIMSELF BY DYING ON A CROSS.

- **"For the wages of sin is death, but the free gift of God is eternal life in Christ Jesus our Lord."** (Romans 6:23)

WE MUST BELIEVE THAT JESUS CHRIST IS GOD WHO CAME IN THE FLESH TO DIE FOR OUR SINS, AND WE MUST RECEIVE HIM AS OUR SAVIOR, LORD, RULER, AND KING.

- "⁹ The true light that gives light to everyone was coming into the world. ¹⁰ He was in the world, and though the world was made through him, the world did not recognize him. ¹¹ He came to that which was his own, **but his own did not receive him. ¹² Yet to all who did receive him, to those who believed in his name, he gave the right to become children of God—** ¹³ children born not of natural descent, nor of human decision or a husband's will, but born of God." (John 1:9–13)

———•———

WE MUST ASK JESUS CHRIST TO COME INTO OUR HEART—AS HE STANDS AT THE DOOR, KNOCKING—AND BE LORD OF OUR LIFE; BELIEVE HE LOVES US AND DIED FOR US; ASK FOR HIS FORGIVENESS; BELIEVE HE ROSE AGAIN FROM THE DEAD TO GIVE US ETERNAL LIFE; AND THANK HIM FOR LOVING US AND GIVING US SUCH A PRECIOUS GIFT—OUR ETERNAL SALVATION THROUGH HIS FINISHED WORK ON THE CROSS.

- "[19] Those whom I love I rebuke and discipline. So be earnest and repent. [20] Here I am! I stand at the door and knock. If anyone hears my voice and opens the door, I will come in and eat with that person, and they with me. [21] To the one who is victorious, I will give the right to sit with me on my throne, just as I was victorious and sat down with my Father on his throne." (Revelation 3:19–21)

WE MUST BELIEVE, REPENT, AND RECEIVE. THIS GIVES US THE RIGHT TO BECOME ACCEPTED CHILDREN OF THE LIVING GOD, RECEIVING THE GIFT OF THE HOLY SPIRIT—THE NEW BIRTH, THE NEVER-ENDING LIFE OF GOD.

- "And Peter said to them, 'Repent and be baptized every one of you in the name of Jesus Christ for the forgiveness of your sins, and you will receive the gift of the Holy Spirit.'" (Acts 2:38)

If you have chosen to do the above—to reconcile yourself to God through Christ Jesus our Lord—you have become an accepted child of the living God. (Note: You were given an opportunity, at the end of Chapter 1, to pray a prayer of salvation. If you chose not to do that then but you desire to do that now, kindly go back to Chapter 1 and then rejoin the Identity study when you are done.)

As with anything we encounter in this life (situations, questions, the need for understanding, etc.), we turn, once again, to God's Word for the answers, for the proof that this aspect of our identity in Christ is, indeed, true. "[His] word is truth." (John 17:17) | "All Scripture is God-breathed..." (2 Timothy 3:16) | "[His] word is a lamp to [our] feet and a light to [our] path." (Psalm 119:105)

OLD & NEW TESTAMENTS:

- "You are the **children of the LORD your God....**" (Deuteronomy 14:1)

- "[12] Yet to all who did receive him, to those who believed in his name, he gave the right to become **children of God**— [13] children born not of natural descent, nor of human decision or a husband's will, but born of God." (John 1:12–13)

- "Jesus answered, 'Very truly I tell you, no one can enter the kingdom of God unless they are born of water and the Spirit. Flesh gives birth to flesh, but the Spirit gives birth to spirit.'" (John 3:5–6)

- "...¹⁵ that everyone who believes may have eternal life in him...¹⁸ Whoever believes in him is not condemned, but whoever does not believe stands condemned already because they have not believed in the name of God's one and only Son." (John 3:15, 18)

- "When the Gentiles heard this, they were glad and honored the word of the Lord; and all who were appointed for eternal life believed." (Acts 13:48)

- "¹⁴ For those who are led by the Spirit of God are the **children of God**. ¹⁵ The Spirit you received does not make you slaves, so that you live in fear again; rather, the Spirit you received brought about your **adoption to sonship**. And by him we cry, *"Abba*, Father." ¹⁶ The Spirit himself testifies with our spirit that **we are God's children**. ¹⁷ Now if we are **children**, then we are heirs—heirs of God and co-heirs with Christ, if indeed we share in his sufferings in order that we may also share in his glory....²⁸ And we know that in all things God works for the good of those who love him, who have been called according to his purpose.

²⁹ For those God foreknew he also predestined to be conformed to the image of his Son, that he might be the firstborn among many brothers and sisters. ³⁰ And those he predestined, he also called; those he called, he also justified; those he justified, he also glorified." (Romans 8:14–17, 28–30)

(NOTE: **Adoption to sonship** is neutral and pertaining to both men and women, so it applies to all of us. Jesus is the only begotten Son of God (John 3:16) and we are **adopted** into God's family through Christ Jesus.)

- "Accept one another, then, just as **Christ accepted you**, in order to bring praise to God." (Romans 15:7)

- "Now you are the body of Christ, and each one of you is a part of it." (1 Corinthians 12:27)

- "²⁶ So in Christ Jesus you are all **children of God** through faith, ²⁷ for all of you who were baptized into Christ have clothed yourselves with Christ." (Galatians 3:26–27)

- "⁴ But when the set time had fully come, God sent his Son, born of a woman, born under the law, ⁵ to redeem those under the law, that we might receive

adoption to sonship. [6] Because you are his sons, God sent the Spirit of his Son into our hearts, the Spirit who calls out, *"Abba,* Father." [7] So you are no longer a slave, but **God's child**; and since **you are his child**, God has made you also an heir." (Galatians 4:4–7)

- "[3] Praise be to the God and Father of our Lord Jesus Christ, who has blessed us in the heavenly realms with every spiritual blessing in Christ. [4] For **he chose us** in him before the creation of the world to be holy and blameless in his sight. In love [5] he predestined us for **adoption to sonship** through Jesus Christ, in accordance with his pleasure and will— [6] to the praise of his glorious grace, which he has freely given us in the One he loves." (Ephesians 1:3–6)

- "Therefore, as **God's chosen people**, holy and dearly loved, clothe yourselves with compassion, kindness, humility, gentleness and patience." (Colossians 3:12)

- "[4] But when the kindness and love of God our Savior appeared, [5] he saved us, not because of righteous things we had done, but because of his mercy. He saved us through the washing of rebirth and renewal by the Holy Spirit, ⁶ whom he poured out on us generously through Jesus Christ our Savior, ⁷ so that, having been justified by his grace, we might become heirs having the hope of eternal life." (Titus 3:4–7)

- "¹⁷ Every good and perfect gift is from above, coming down from the Father of the heavenly lights, who does not change like shifting shadows. ¹⁸ He chose to give us birth through the word of truth, that we might be a kind of firstfruits of all he created." (James 1:17–18)

- "For you have been born again, not of perishable seed, but of imperishable, through the living and enduring word of God." (1 Peter 1:23)

- "²⁸ And now, **dear children**, continue in him, so that when he appears we may be confident and unashamed before him at his coming. ²⁹ If you know that he is righteous, you know that everyone who does what is right has been born of him." (1 John 2:28–29)

- "See what great love the Father has lavished on us, that we should be called **children of God**! And that is what we are! The reason the world does not know us is that it did not know him. ² Dear friends, now **we are children of God**, and what we will be has not yet been made known. But we know that when Christ appears, we shall be like him, for we shall see him as he is." (1 John 3:1–2)

- "¹⁸ We know that anyone born of God does not continue to sin; the One who was born of God keeps them safe, and the evil one cannot harm them. ¹⁹ We know that **we are children of God**, and that the whole world is under the control of the evil one. ²⁰ We know also that the Son of God has come and has given us understanding, so that we may know him who is true. And we are in him who is true by being in his Son Jesus Christ. He is the true God and eternal life." (1 John 5:18–20)

If you have ever felt rejected, please know that it is a ploy of the enemy to steal your peace and joy. God has not rejected you. If you have ever felt alone and unwanted, please know that the enemy—the devil—is the father of all lies. God wants you. God's love surrounds you; you can choose to live in His Presence always. If you have ever felt as though you do not belong, please know that you do. You are one in whom Christ dwells, one redeemed by Jesus Christ and adopted into sonship with the Father.

Today, may you find peace in His Presence and comfort in knowing that you are an accepted child of the Living God.

Questions for Reflection

1. Have you ever felt rejected, unwanted, or as though you do not belong? What does it mean to you to know that these are all lies and that you are an accepted child of the Living God, adopted into His sonship?

2. How did Jesus's provision, purpose, and peace prepare Him for what He was called to do? What is **your** provision, purpose, and peace? How does knowing all of this change your life and how you serve God and relate to others?

3. Of the Scriptures shared above, which reveal(s) and speak(s) His Truth to you the most?

———•——————•——————•——

9.4— We Are Equipped with the Full Armor of God (to come up against the attacks of our enemy the devil)

THE SPIDER AND THE WASP

One day, I came upon a spider living in a windowsill. (For the purpose of this fourth part of our study, we will refer to the spider as our enemy the devil.) He was brown and furry with extremely long legs, and he was about the size of a half dollar. His web was somewhat of a masterpiece, shaped like a hammock with well-rounded bottom and sides, which were equivalent to a thin layer of cotton candy (and probably just as sticky). His preys' lifeless bodies strewn all across this web, there was nothing alive besides him. Suffice it to say, the enemy-spider appeared to have been taking up residence in this place for quite some time.

As I passed by a second time, which was only a few minutes later, I noticed that a wasp had become stuck in the web. (For the purpose of this part of our study, we will refer to the wasp as a believer; that's us, if we have accepted Jesus Christ as our Lord and Savior.) Immediately, I became mindful that the believing-wasp had become ensnared, was completely vulnerable, and did not see the trap that the enemy-spider had set. It appeared utterly defenseless, as though there was no hope to escape.

The enemy-spider was in a dark hole on the left edge of the windowsill, where he had been waiting to spring on his prey without warning. His craftiness was extremely obvious. He had been lying in wait for his next victim, sneaky, ruthless, and ready to attack.

- **"Your enemy the devil prowls around like a roaring lion looking for someone to devour." (1 Peter 5:8b)**

What happened over the course of the next hour or so was like a dance. The believing-wasp had flown into the enemy-spider's web, and it had become visibly stuck. The enemy-spider came out of his dark hole, pounced on the believing-wasp, and danced all around it, trying to encircle the wasp until it was totally and seemingly defenseless. The believing-wasp fought back, fluttering its wings and jabbing at the enemy-spider, trying to wound him and somehow get free. The enemy-spider would occasionally retreat to his dark hole, only to return and repeat this attacking dance again later. Repeatedly, he tried to tire out the believing-wasp. As this battle went on, the believing-wasp, through its veritable struggle to get free, was indeed wearing down.

- **"The thief comes only to steal and kill and destroy; I have come that they may have life, and have it to the full." (John 10:10)**

Our enemy the devil, comes to **STEAL** our peace, joy, and confidence; **KILL** through accident or illness; and, **DESTROY** through fear, doubt, and unbelief. Our peace, joy, and confidence are in Christ—not in worldly or fleshy things— though the enemy would certainly try to convince us otherwise. God's Word tells us how to come up against enemy attacks made through fear, doubt, and unbelief.

FEAR:

- God's Word says, "For [I have] not given [you] a spirit of timidity or fear, but of power and of love and of a sound mind." (2 Timothy 1:7)

DOUBT:

- "⁵ If any of you lacks wisdom, you should ask God, who gives generously to all without finding fault, and it will be given to you. ⁶ But when you ask, you must believe and not doubt, because the one who doubts is like a wave of the sea, blown and tossed by the wind. ⁷ That person should not expect to receive anything from the Lord." (James 1:5–7)

UNBELIEF (we will look at two examples):

- "¹⁹ Without weakening in his faith, he [Abraham] faced the fact that his body was as good as dead—since he was about a hundred years old—and that Sarah's womb was also dead. ²⁰ Yet he did not waver through unbelief regarding the promise of God, but was strengthened in his faith and gave glory to God, ²¹ being fully persuaded that God had power to do what he had promised." (Romans 4:19–21)

- In relation to the Israelites Moses was leading out of Egypt to the Promised Land, it is written, "¹⁸ And to whom did God swear that they would never enter his rest if not to those who disobeyed? ¹⁹ So we see that they were not able to enter, because of their unbelief." (Hebrews 3:18–19)

———•———————•———————•———

Against the attacks of the enemy, God's Word instructs us to prepare as follows:

- "10 Finally, be strong in the Lord and in his mighty power. 11 Put on the full armor of God, so that you can take your stand against the devil's schemes. 12 For our struggle is not against flesh and blood, but against the rulers, against the authorities, against the powers of this dark world and against the spiritual forces of evil in the heavenly realms. 13 Therefore put on the full armor of God, so that when the day of evil comes, you may be able to stand your ground, and after you have done everything, to stand. 14 Stand firm then, with the belt of truth buckled around your waist, with the breastplate of righteousness in place, 15 and with your feet fitted with the readiness that comes from the gospel of peace. 16 In addition to all this, take up the shield of faith, with which you can extinguish all the flaming arrows of the evil one. ¹⁷ Take the helmet of salvation and the sword of the Spirit, which is the word of God." (Ephesians 6:10–17)

- "³ For though we live in the world, we do not wage war as the world does. ⁴ The weapons we fight with are not the weapons of the world. On the contrary, they have divine power to demolish strongholds. ⁵ We demolish arguments and every pretension that sets itself up against the knowledge of God, and we take captive every thought to make it obedient to Christ. ⁶ And we will be ready to punish every act of disobedience, once your obedience is complete." (2 Corinthians 10:3–6)

———•———•———

Those who insist on living outside of God's Perfect Will also open themselves up to the attacks of the enemy.

- "⁹ When you enter the land the LORD your God is giving you, do not learn to imitate the detestable ways of the nations there. ¹⁰ Let no one be found among you who sacrifices their son or daughter in the fire, who practices divination or sorcery, interprets omens, engages in witchcraft, [11] or casts spells, or who is a medium or spiritist or who consults the dead." (Deuteronomy 18:9–11)

- "You belong to your father, the devil, and you want to carry out your father's desires. He was a murderer from the beginning, not holding to the truth, for there is no truth in him. When he lies, he speaks his native language, for he is a liar and the father of lies." (John 8:44)

Eternal salvation and spiritual freedom are not rooted in mediums, psychics, horoscopes, false religions, or ungodly living. Just one view of the latest television guide from the newspaper or one scroll through your social media newsfeed reveals to us how the enemy is working through various shows and forms of media. We see shows about cheating, lying, and selfish living, with a focus on worldly things and fleshy desires. This is certainly not godly, kingdom living. It is also true that electronic devices and all forms of media are subject to evil use by the enemy, too. We can and should be alert, making wise decisions as to what we put into our bodies, minds, and spirits and what we spend our time doing.

- "¹⁹ Do you not know that your bodies are temples of the Holy Spirit, who is in you, whom you have received from God? You are not your own; ²⁰ you were bought at a price. Therefore, honor God with your bodies." (1 Corinthians 6:19–20)

Sometimes we can sustain enemy attacks through others, especially from those who are closest to us. And Jesus certainly was not immune to this when He walked the earth.

- "¹⁴ Therefore, since we have a great high priest who has ascended into heaven, Jesus the Son of God, let us hold firmly to the faith we profess. [15] For we do not have a high priest who is unable to empathize with our weaknesses, but we have one who has been tempted in every way, just as we are—yet he did not sin. [16] Let us then approach God's throne of grace with confidence, so that we may receive mercy and find grace to help us in our time of need." (Hebrews 4:14–16)

———————•———————

I encourage you to draw close to the Lord Jesus Christ in your time of great need, for He truly knows what it is like to be:

—in pain

—suffering

—abandoned

—physically abused

—tired

—humiliated

Call upon the Lord. There is power in the name of Jesus, in the blood of Jesus, and in God's Word:

- "⁷ Cast all your anxiety on him because he cares for you. ⁸ Be alert and of sober mind. Your enemy the devil prowls around like a roaring lion looking for someone to devour. ⁹ Resist him, standing firm in the faith, because you know that the family of believers throughout the world is undergoing the same kind of sufferings." (1 Peter 5:7–9)
- "Therefore, keep watch, because you do not know on what day your Lord will come." (Matthew 24:42)
- "Watch and pray so that you will not fall into temptation. The spirit is willing, but the flesh is weak." (Matthew 26:41)
- "Therefore, there is now no condemnation for those who are in Christ Jesus." (Romans 8:1)

- "[37] No, in all these things we are more than conquerors through him who loved us. [38] For I am convinced that neither death nor life, neither angels nor demons, neither the present nor the future, nor any powers, [39] neither height nor depth, nor anything else in all creation, will be able to separate us from the love of God that is in Christ Jesus our Lord." (Romans 8:37–39)

- "So then, let us not be like others, who are asleep, but let us be awake and sober." (1 Thessalonians 5:6)

- "But the Lord stood at my side and gave me strength, so that through me the message might be fully proclaimed and all the Gentiles might hear it. And I was delivered from the lion's mouth." (2 Timothy 4:17)

- "Submit yourselves, then, to God. Resist the devil, and he will flee from you." (James 4:7)

- "Therefore, with minds that are alert and fully sober, set your hope on the grace to be brought to you when Jesus Christ is revealed at his coming." (1 Peter 1:13)

It is imperative to remember that the enemy attempted to place himself above the LORD our God:

- "¹³ You [Satan] said in your heart, "I will ascend to the heavens; I will raise my throne above the stars of God; I will sit enthroned on the mount of assembly, on the utmost heights of Mount Zaphon. ¹⁴ I will ascend above the tops of the clouds; I will make myself like the Most High." ¹⁵ But you are brought down to the realm of the dead, to the depths of the pit." (Isaiah 14:13–15)

- "The one who does what is sinful is of the devil, because the devil has been sinning from the beginning. The reason the Son of God appeared was to destroy the devil's work." (1 John 3:8)

Jesus defeated sin, death, and our enemy the devil, in and through His finished work on the cross. Hallelujah!

- And that's why St. Paul wrote: "¹⁷ Therefore, if anyone is in Christ, the new creation has come: The old has gone, the new is here! ¹⁸ All this is from God, who reconciled us to himself...." (2 Corinthians 5:17–18a)

Now, some of you may be wondering what had happened to that believing-wasp from our story above. Well, when I came back later in the day, the wasp was nowhere to be found. It had escaped from the web and the clutches of the enemy-spider! Yay!

- "²⁵ About midnight Paul and Silas were praying and singing hymns to God, and the other prisoners were listening to them. ²⁶ Suddenly there was such a violent earthquake that the foundations of the prison were shaken. At once all the prison doors flew open, and everyone's chains came loose. ²⁷ The jailer woke up, and when he saw the prison doors open, he drew his sword and was about to kill himself because he thought the prisoners had escaped." (Acts 16:25–27)

———————●———————

Death certainly does not discriminate and is ready to ensnare any who fall into its trap. Later that same day, I noticed another insect's lifeless body caught up in the enemy-spider's web. This is why we must stay alert and be prepared, putting on the full armor of God so we can stand firm against the enemy's attacks!

———————●———————

- "The sting of death is sin, and the power of sin is the law." (1 Corinthians 15:56) However, as (v. 57) goes on to state: "Thanks be to God! He gives us the victory through our Lord Jesus Christ."
- "I have told you these things, so that in me you may have peace. In this world you will have trouble. But take heart! I have overcome the world." (John 16:33)

Yes, Jesus defeated sin, death, and our enemy the devil. Because of that, we have the assurance of victory in Christ Jesus, regardless of what the enemy may attempt to bring against us in this life. Jesus is always greater!

Hallelujah, dear friends! Hallelujah, indeed!

Questions for Reflection

1. How is the enemy trying to steal, kill, or destroy you and your life?

2. What are you doing to contribute to this? What will you commit to now changing in your life?

3. What does it mean to you to know that Jesus truly understands your pain and suffering?

4. How does knowing that Jesus already defeated sin, death, and our enemy the devil, in and through His finished work on the cross, help you in/on your spiritual journey?

5. Of the Scripture shared above, which reveal(s) and speak(s) His Truth to you the most?

9.5—WE ARE COMPLETE IN CHRIST JESUS

In a very popular movie from the mid-90s, one of the main characters tells her boyfriend, "You complete me." Millions of fans, including me, found it to be a very romantic saying. Now, looking back, I find it to be quite sad and confusing. Certainly, people can add to our lives in many positive ways, but the only person who can truly complete us is Jesus Christ.

- "[9] For in Christ all the fullness of the Deity lives in bodily form, [10] and in Christ you have been **brought to fullness**. He is the head over every power and authority." (Colossians 2:9–10)

Who completes you?

———·————●————·———

Before we move forward in this fifth part of our Identity in Christ study, we need to review what we have learned previously. Over the course of the first four parts of our study, we have been learning about what God's Word says in relation to who we are in Christ. Thus far, we have established the following biblical truths about our identity:

—we are loved

—we have been created to love

—we are accepted children of the living God

—we are equipped with the full armor of God (to come up against the attacks of our enemy the devil)

———·————●————·———

We are also complete in Christ Jesus. But how do we know this latter aspect of our identity in Christ is really true? In the Greek language, there are five different words for "complete" that we will take a look at in this particular study: complete *(pleroo)*, completion *(pleroma)*, full assurance *(plerophoria)*, complete *(holokleros)*, and complete *(teleioo)*. As we have done in each study in our series thus far, we will turn, once again, to God's Word to teach us, this time, about our **complete** nature in Christ:

———•———•———•———

- "¹⁰ If you keep my commands, you will remain in my love, just as I have kept my Father's commands and remain in his love. ¹¹ I have told you this so that my joy may be in you and **that your joy may be complete (pleroo)**. ¹² My command is this: Love each other as I have loved you." (John 15:10–12)

- "²³ In that day you will no longer ask me anything. Very truly I tell you, my Father will give you whatever you ask in my name. ²⁴ Until now you have not asked for anything in my name. Ask and you will receive, and **your joy will be complete (pleroo)**. ²⁵ 'Though I have been speaking figuratively, a time is coming when I will no longer use this kind of language but will tell you plainly about my Father.'" (John 16:23–25)

- "²² I have given them the glory that you gave me, that they may be one as we are one— ²³ I in them and you in me—**so that they may be brought to complete (teleioo) unity**. Then the world will know that you sent me and have loved them even as you have loved me. ²⁴ 'Father, I want those you have given me to be with me where I am, and to see my glory, the glory you have given me because you loved me before the creation of the world.'" (John 17:22–24)

- "¹⁴ For this reason I kneel before the Father, ¹⁵ from whom every family in heaven and on earth derives its name. ¹⁶ I pray that out of his glorious riches he may strengthen you with power through his Spirit in your inner being, ¹⁷ so that Christ may dwell in your hearts through faith. And I pray that you, being rooted and established in love, ¹⁸ may have power, together with all the Lord's holy people, to grasp how wide and long and high and deep is the love of Christ, ¹⁹ **and to know this love that surpasses knowledge—that you may be filled to the measure of all the fullness (pleroma) of God.**" (Ephesians 3:14–19)

- "Therefore if you have any encouragement from being united with Christ, if any comfort from his love, if any common sharing in the Spirit, if any tenderness and compassion, ² then **make my joy complete (pleroo)** by being like-minded, having the same love, being one in spirit and of one mind. ³ Do nothing out of selfish ambition or vain conceit. Rather, in humility value others above yourselves...." (Philippians 2:1–3)

- "² My goal is that they may be encouraged in heart and united in love, so **that they may have the full riches of complete (plerophoria) understanding**, in order that they may know the mystery of God, namely, Christ, ³ in whom are hidden all the treasures of wisdom and knowledge." (Colossians 2:2–3)

- "² Consider it pure joy, my brothers and sisters, whenever you face trials of many kinds, ³ because you know that the testing of your faith produces perseverance. ⁴ Let perseverance finish its work so **that you may be mature (teleios) and complete (hololeros)**, not lacking anything. ⁵ If any of you lacks wisdom, you should ask God, who gives generously to all without finding fault, and it will be given to you." (James 1:2–5)

- "²²You see that [Abraham's] faith and his actions were working together, and **his faith was made complete (teleioo)** by what he did. ²³And the scripture was **fulfilled (pleroo)** that says, 'Abraham believed God, and it was credited to him as righteousness,' and he was called God's friend." (James 2:22–23)

- "⁴Whoever says, 'I know him,' but does not do what he commands is a liar, and the truth is not in that person. ⁵But if anyone obeys his word, love for God is **truly made complete (teleioo)** in them. This is how we know we are in him: ⁶Whoever claims to live in him must live as Jesus did." (1 John 2:4–6)

- "¹¹Dear friends, since God so loved us, we also ought to love one another. ¹²No one has ever seen God; but if we love one another, God lives in us and **his love is made complete (teleioo)** in us. ¹³This is how we know that we live in him and he in us: He has given us of his Spirit." (1 John 4:11–13)

- "[16] And so we know and rely on the love God has for us. God is love. Whoever lives in love lives in God, and God in them. [17] **This is how love is made complete (teleioo) among us** so that we will have confidence on the day of judgment: In this world we are like Jesus. [18] There is no fear in love. But perfect love drives out fear, because fear has to do with punishment. The one who fears is not made perfect in love." (1 John 4:16–18)

It is because of our **complete** nature in Christ that "in him and through faith in him we may approach God with freedom and confidence." (Ephesians 3:12) You need not look to anyone or anything else to complete you, dear friends. You are, indeed, complete in Christ Jesus. Glory be to God for this great blessing!

Questions for Reflection:

1. To this point in your life, what have you been looking to in hope of it completing you?

2. What needs to change in you or your life, and how will you go about making those changes?

3. What does it mean to you—and to your spiritual journey—to be complete in Christ Jesus?

4. With whom can you share this great blessing and good news of a complete nature in Christ?

5. Of the Scriptures shared above, which reveal(s) and speak(s) His Truth to you the most?

9.6—WE ARE SECURE IN CHRIST JESUS

Oftentimes, as we discussed at the beginning of this chapter, identity is who we are in the world: our name, occupation, role, or character. How do you define yourself? How are you beginning to define yourself? What constitutes your identity? From where do you derive your security? As we have been working through this Identity in Christ study, it is my fervent hope that, more and more, your real identity is rooted in Him.

———·————————·————————·———

We have already established the following truths about who we are in Christ:

—we are loved

—we have been created to love

—we are accepted children of the living God

—we are equipped with the full armor of God (to come up against the attacks of our enemy the devil)

—we are complete in Christ Jesus

———·————————·————————·———

We also have a security in Christ, and God's Word reveals this Truth to us all:

YOU ARE BORN AGAIN.

- "³ Jesus replied, 'Very truly I tell you, no one can see the kingdom of God unless they are **born again**.'

⁴ 'How can someone be born when they are old?' Nicodemus asked. 'Surely they cannot enter a second time into their mother's womb to be born!' ⁵ Jesus answered, 'Very truly I tell you, no one can enter the kingdom of God unless they are **born of water and the Spirit**. ⁶ Flesh gives birth to flesh, but the Spirit gives birth to spirit.'" (John 3:3–6)

- "We know that anyone **born of God** does not continue to sin; the One who was born of God keeps them safe, and the evil one cannot harm them." (1 John 5:18)

YOU ARE A NEW CREATION.

- "¹⁷ Therefore, if anyone is in Christ, the **new creation** has come: The old has gone, the new is here! ¹⁸ All this is from God, who reconciled us to himself through Christ and gave us the ministry of reconciliation: ¹⁹ that God was reconciling the world to himself in Christ, not counting people's sins against them. And he has committed to us the message of reconciliation." (2 Corinthians 5:17–19)

YOU ARE A CHILD OF GOD, AN HEIR OF GOD/CO-HEIR WITH CHRIST.

- "²⁶ So in Christ Jesus you are all **children of God** through faith, ²⁷ for all of you who were baptized into Christ have clothed yourselves with Christ. ²⁸ There is neither Jew nor Gentile, neither slave nor free, nor is there male and female, for you are all one in Christ Jesus. ²⁹ If you belong to Christ, then you are Abraham's seed, and **heirs** according to the promise." (Galatians 3:26–29)

- "¹² Yet to all who did receive him, to those who believed in his name, he gave the right to become **children of God**— ¹³ children born not of natural descent, nor of human decision or a husband's will, but born of God." (John 1:12–13)

- "⁶ Because you are his sons, God sent the Spirit of his Son into our hearts, the Spirit who calls out, *"Abba,* Father." ⁷ So you are no longer a slave, but **God's child**; and since you are **his child**, God has made you also an **heir**." (Galatians 4:6–7)

- "Now if we are **children**, then we are **heirs**—heirs of God and co-heirs with Christ, if indeed we share in his sufferings in order that we may also share in his glory." (Romans 8:17)

YOU ARE CHOSEN...

- "For we know, brothers and sisters loved by God, that he has **chosen** you...." (1 Thessalonians 1:4)

...AND YOU BELONG TO GOD.

- "²¹ Now it is God who makes both us and you stand firm in Christ. He anointed us, ²² **set his seal of ownership on us**, and put his Spirit in our hearts as a deposit, guaranteeing what is to come." (2 Corinthians 1:21–22)

YOU ARE JESUS'S FRIEND.

- "[14] You are my **friends** if you do what I command. [15] I no longer call you servants, because a servant does not know his master's business. Instead, I have called you **friends**, for everything that I learned from my Father I have made known to you. [16] You did not choose me, but I chose you and appointed you so that you might go and bear fruit—fruit that will last—and so that whatever you ask in my name the Father will give you." (John 15:14–16)

YOU ARE FREE FROM CONDEMNATION.

- "Therefore, there is now **no condemnation** for those who are in Christ Jesus, [2] because through Christ Jesus the law of the Spirit who gives life has set you free from the law of sin and death. [3] For what the law was powerless to do because it was weakened by the flesh, God did by sending his own Son in the likeness of sinful flesh to be a sin offering. And so he condemned sin in the flesh, [4] in order that the righteous requirement of the law might be fully met in us, who do not live according to the flesh but according to the Spirit." (Romans 8:1–4)

- "In him and through faith in him we may approach God with freedom and confidence." (Ephesians 3:12)

YOU HAVE A GOD WHO WORKS ON YOUR BEHALF.

- "And we know that in all things **God works for the good** of those who love him, who have been called according to his purpose." (Romans 8:28)

- "…being confident of this, that he who began a good work in you will carry it on to completion until the day of Christ Jesus." (Philippians 1:6)

YOU HAVE A GOD WHO IS FOR YOU; YOU ARE MORE THAN A CONQUEROR; NOTHING CAN SEPARATE YOU FROM HIM.

- "[31] What, then, shall we say in response to these things? If **God is for us**, who can be against us? [32] He who did not spare his own Son, but gave him up for us all—how will he not also, along with him, graciously give us all things? [33] Who will bring any charge against those whom God has chosen? It is God who justifies. [34] Who then is the one who condemns? No one. Christ Jesus who died—more than that, who was raised to life—is at the right hand of God and is also interceding for us. [35] Who shall separate us from the love of Christ? Shall trouble or hardship or persecution or famine or nakedness or danger or sword? [36] As it is written: 'For your sake we face death all day long; we are considered as sheep to be slaughtered.' [37] No, in all these things we are **more than conquerors** through him who loved us. [38] For I am convinced that neither death nor life, neither angels nor demons, neither the present nor the future, nor any powers, [39] neither height nor depth, nor anything else in all creation, will be able to **separate** us from the love of God that is in Christ Jesus our Lord." (Romans 8:31–39)

- "But thanks be to God, who always leads us as captives in Christ's triumphal procession and uses us to spread the aroma of the knowledge of him everywhere." (2 Corinthians 2:14)

YOUR CITIZENSHIP IS IN HEAVEN.

- "[18] For, as I have often told you before and now tell you again even with tears, many live as enemies of the cross of Christ. [19] Their destiny is destruction, their god is their stomach, and their glory is in their shame. Their mind is set on earthly things. [20] But **our citizenship is in heaven**. And we eagerly await a Savior from there, the Lord Jesus Christ, [21] who, by the power that enables him to bring everything under his control, will transform our lowly bodies so that they will be like his glorious body." (Philippians 3:18–21)

- "Since, then, you have been raised with Christ, set your hearts on **things above**, where Christ is, seated at the right hand of God. [2] Set your minds on **things**

above, not on earthly things. ³ For you died, and your life is now hidden with Christ in God. ⁴ When Christ, who is your life, appears, then you also will appear with him in glory.... ¹² Therefore, as God's chosen people, holy and dearly loved, clothe yourselves with compassion, kindness, humility, gentleness and patience." (Colossians 3:1–4, 12)

YOU ARE ONE SPIRIT WITH THE LORD.

- "¹⁸ For through him we both have access to the Father by one Spirit. ¹⁹ Consequently, you are no longer foreigners and strangers, but fellow citizens with God's people and also members of his household...." (Ephesians 2:18–19)

- "But whoever is united with the Lord is **one with him in spirit**...Now you are the body of Christ, and each one of you is a part of it." (1 Corinthians 6:17; 12:27)

YOU HAVE A SPIRIT OF POWER AND LOVE.

- "For the Spirit God gave us does not make us timid, but gives us **power**, **love** and self-discipline." (2 Timothy 1:7)

YOU HAVE HOPE IN CHRIST.

- "We have this **hope** as an anchor for the soul, firm and **secure**." (Hebrews 6:19a)

In this day and age, with uncertainty, doubt, and chaos abounding in this world, we must not lose sight of who we are in Christ, and that to which the Lord has called us. We belong to Him; He has secured our future and us; our names are written on the palms of His hands. God loves you. You are His. You are secure in Christ Jesus, dear friends. May this Truth—knowing and believing who you are in Christ—uplift and sustain you in the days ahead.

Questions for Reflection

1. What constitutes your identity?

2. From where does your security come?

3. How have these two aspects of who and what you are changed over the course of this study, thus far?

4. Who needs to hear this Truth? What is preventing you from sharing it?

5. Of the Scriptures shared above, which reveal(s) and speak(s) His Truth to you the most?

9.7—WE ARE SIGNIFICANT IN CHRIST JESUS

Significance. That word certainly brings up a plethora of thoughts such as: What is the meaning of significance? How does that apply to me? Do I even measure up? In life, many people just want to know if they matter at all to anyone. What is the meaning of your life? How do you apply to this world? To whom do you *really* matter and hold some type of significance?

Thus far in our study, we have learned the following truths about who we are in Christ:

>   —we are loved
>
>   —we have been created to love
>
>   —we are accepted children of the living God
>
>   —we are equipped with the full armor of God (to come up against the attacks of our enemy the devil)
>
>   —we are complete in Christ Jesus
>
>   —we are secure in Christ Jesus

We are also significant in Christ Jesus. What does God's Word tell us about this significance in Him and in Jesus? Let's take a look.

YOU ARE SALT AND LIGHT; CHILDREN OF THE LIGHT.

- "^{13} You are the **salt** of the earth. But if the salt loses its saltiness, how can it be made salty again? It is no longer good for anything, except to be thrown out and trampled underfoot. [14] "'You are the **light** of the world. A town built on a hill cannot be hidden.'" (Matthew 5:13–14)

- "[5] You are all **children of the light** and children of the day. We do not belong to the night or to the darkness. [6] So then, let us not be like others, who are asleep, but let us be awake and sober." (1 Thessalonians 5:5–6)

YOU ARE CREATED TO BEAR FRUIT.

- "I am the true vine, and my Father is the gardener. [2] He cuts off every branch in me that bears no fruit, while every branch that does bear fruit, he prunes so that it will be even more fruitful. [3] You are already clean because of the word I have spoken to you. [4] Remain in me, as I also remain in you. No branch can bear fruit by itself; it must remain in the vine. Neither can you bear fruit unless you remain in me. [5] 'I am the vine; you are the branches. If you remain in me and I in you, you will bear much fruit; apart from me you can do nothing.'" (John 15:1–5)

———•————————•———————•———

YOU ARE NOT SLAVES TO SIN, BUT SLAVES TO RIGHTEOUSNESS.

- "¹⁸ You have been set free from sin and have become **slaves to righteousness**.... ²² But now that you have been set free from sin and have become slaves of God, the benefit you reap leads to holiness, and the result is eternal life." (Romans 6:18, 22)

- "¹⁷ Therefore, if anyone is in Christ, the new creation has come: The old has gone, the new is here! ¹⁸ All this is from God, who reconciled us to himself through Christ and gave us the ministry of reconciliation: ¹⁹ that God was reconciling the world to himself in Christ, not counting people's sins against them. And he has committed to us the message of reconciliation. ²⁰ We are therefore Christ's ambassadors, as though God were making his appeal through us. We implore you on Christ's behalf: Be reconciled to God. ²¹ God made him who had no sin to be sin for us, so that in him we might become the **righteousness** of God.... As God's co-workers we urge you not to receive God's grace in vain." (2 Corinthians 5:17–21; 6:1)

———————•————————•————————•———————

YOU ARE CALLED TO LIVE A LIFE WORTHY OF YOUR CALLING, WHICH WAS CREATED FOR A PURPOSE.

• "² Surely you have heard about the administration of God's grace that was given to me for you, ³ that is, the mystery made known to me by revelation, as I have already written briefly. ⁴ In reading this, then, you will be able to understand my insight into the mystery of Christ, ⁵ which was not made known to people in other generations as it has now been revealed by the Spirit to God's holy apostles and prophets. ⁶ This mystery is that through the gospel the Gentiles are heirs together with Israel, members together of one body, and sharers together in the promise in Christ Jesus....As a prisoner for the Lord, then, I urge you to

live a life worthy of the calling you have received."
(Ephesians 3:2–6; 4:1)

- "...for it is God who works in you to will and to act in order to fulfill his good **purpose**....I can do all this through him who gives me strength." (Philippians 2:13; 4:13)

———————•———————

YOU ARE CALLED TO LIVE PURE AND GODLY LIVES.

- "Don't you know that you yourselves are God's temple and that God's Spirit dwells in your midst? Do you not know that **your bodies are temples of the Holy Spirit**, who is in you, whom you have received from God? You are not your own...." (1 Corinthians 3:16; 6:19)

- "Therefore, holy brothers and sisters, who share in the heavenly calling, fix your thoughts on Jesus, whom we acknowledge as our apostle and high priest....We have come to share in Christ, if indeed we hold our original conviction firmly to the very end....[4] Marriage [between a husband and wife] should be honored by all, and the marriage bed kept **pure**, for God will judge the adulterer and all the sexually immoral. [5] Keep your lives free from the love of money and be content with what you have, because God has said, 'Never will I leave you; never will I forsake you.' [6] So we say with confidence, 'The Lord is my helper; I will not be afraid. What can mere mortals do to me?'" (Hebrews 3:1, 14; 13:4–6)

- "[4] As you come to him, the living Stone—rejected by humans but chosen by God and precious to him— [5] you also, like living stones, are being built into a spiritual house to be a holy priesthood, offering spiritual sacrifices acceptable to God through Jesus Christ. [6] For in Scripture it says: 'See, I lay a stone in Zion, a chosen and precious cornerstone, and the one who trusts in him will never be put to shame.' [7] Now to you who believe, this stone is precious. But to those who do not believe, 'The stone the builders rejected has become the cornerstone,' [8] and, 'A stone that causes people to stumble and a rock that makes them fall.' They stumble because they disobey the

message—which is also what they were destined for.
⁹ But you are a chosen people, a royal priesthood, a holy nation, God's special possession, that you may declare the praises of him who called you out of darkness into his wonderful light. ¹⁰ Once you were not a people, but now you are the people of God; once you had not received mercy, but now you have received mercy. ¹¹ Dear friends, I urge you, as foreigners and exiles, to **abstain from sinful desires**, which wage war against your soul." (1 Peter 2:4–11)

- "³ His divine power has given us everything we need for a **godly life** through our knowledge of him who called us by his own glory and goodness. ⁴ Through these he has given us his very great and precious promises, so that through them you may participate in the divine nature, having escaped the corruption in the world caused by evil desires. ⁵ For this very reason, make every effort to add to your faith goodness; and to goodness, knowledge; ⁶ and to knowledge, self-control; and to self-control, perseverance; and to perseverance, godliness; ⁷ and to godliness, mutual affection; and to mutual affection, love. [8] For if you possess these qualities in increasing measure, they will keep you from being ineffective and unproductive in your knowledge of our Lord Jesus Christ. [9] But whoever does not have them is nearsighted and blind, forgetting that they have been cleansed from their past sins. [10] Therefore, my brothers and sisters, make every effort to confirm your calling and election. For if you do these things, you will never stumble, [11] and you will receive a rich welcome into the eternal kingdom of our Lord and Savior Jesus Christ." (2 Peter 1:3–11)

YOU ARE CHOSEN TO BE IN FELLOWSHIP AND PARTNERSHIP WITH JESUS CHRIST.

- "[11] In him we were also **chosen**, having been predestined according to the plan of him who works out everything in conformity with the purpose of his will, [12] in order that we, who were the first to put our hope in Christ, might be for the praise of his glory." (Ephesians 1:11–12)

- "⁴ I always thank my God for you because of his grace given you in Christ Jesus. ⁵ For in him you have been enriched in every way—with all kinds of speech and with all knowledge— ⁶ God thus confirming our testimony about Christ among you. ⁷ Therefore you do not lack any spiritual gift as you eagerly wait for our Lord Jesus Christ to be revealed. ⁸ He will also keep you firm to the end, so that you will be blameless on the day of our Lord Jesus Christ. ⁹ God is faithful, who has called you into **fellowship** with his Son, Jesus Christ our Lord." (1 Corinthians 1:4–9)

- "³ I thank my God every time I remember you. ⁴ In all my prayers for all of you, I always pray with joy ⁵ because of your partnership in the gospel from the first day until now, ⁶ being confident of this, that he who began a good work in you will carry it on to completion until the day of Christ Jesus." (Philippians 1:3–6)

YOU ARE CREATED TO DO GOOD WORKS.

- "[6] And God raised us up with Christ and seated us with him in the heavenly realms in Christ Jesus…[8] For it is by grace you have been saved, through faith—and this is not from yourselves, it is the gift of God—[9] not by works, so that no one can boast. [10] For we are God's handiwork, created in Christ Jesus to do **good works**, which God prepared in advance for us to do." (Ephesians 2:6, 8–10)

- "[19] Nevertheless, God's solid foundation stands firm, sealed with this inscription: 'The Lord knows those who are his,' and, 'Everyone who confesses the name of the Lord must turn away from wickedness.' [20] In a large house there are articles not only of gold and silver, but also of wood and clay; some are for special purposes and some for common use. [21] Those who cleanse themselves from the latter will be instruments for special purposes, made holy, useful to the Master and prepared to do any **good work**." (2 Timothy 2:19–21)

God's Word also tells us that when we doubt anything, we can surely call upon Him for clarity:

- "If any of you lacks **wisdom**, you should ask God, who gives generously to all without finding fault, and it will be given to you." (James 1:5)

As believers, we are those in whom Christ dwells. We live in this world, though we are not of or from it. And while we are here, we are to serve God in this kingdom and keep an eternal mindset in relation to our home in heaven, the place where our citizenship is located. Satan desires to undermine us—and he will—if we don't know who we are! God calls us all to do His will in this lost and lonely world. And you may recall that "[Jesus] did not come to be served, but to serve others." (Matthew 20:28; Mark 10:45)

You need to know these truths about your real identity:

You are a saint; born again of imperishable and incorruptible seed; a new creation; complete in Christ; a child of God.

You are one with the Lord; a temple of the Holy Spirit; forgiven and eternally redeemed; seated with Christ in heavenly places; you are hidden with Christ in God; a citizen of heaven.

You are dead to sin and alive to God in Christ Jesus; free from guilt and condemnation; righteous, holy, blameless; strong in the Lord and in the power of His might.

You are loved with an everlasting love.

You are the head and not the tail; blessed with all spiritual blessings; joint heir with Jesus Christ; chosen by God; anointed; God's royal ambassador.

You are a king and a priest of the Most High God; bold as a lion; more than a conqueror; a testimony of God's grace.

You are a city set on a hill that cannot be hidden; a tree planted by rivers of living water, with branches whose leaves will not wither.

You are called to be salt and light in this world; to bear fruit; to be slaves to righteousness; to live a life worthy of your calling (godly and pure); to be in fellowship and partnership with Jesus Christ; to do good works.

How are you serving the LORD and others? Think about that as you come to realize, more and more, that you are truly significant in Christ Jesus. God created you for a purpose. However, if you carry the wrong identity, you will abort your purpose. Shine on, dear friends! Connect to and fulfill your God-given purpose! Now, go forth in this very light to serve the Lord our God.

Questions for Reflection:

1. To this point, how have you been defining your significance?

2. What is the meaning of your life? Did you realize that you were created for a purpose?

3. You are significant in Christ Jesus. What does this truth mean to you? Who else in your life needs to

hear this truth?

4. How can you serve the Lord on a much deeper level knowing what you now know about your true significance (and your real identity in Christ)?

5. Of the Scriptures shared above, which reveal(s) and speak(s) His Truth to you the most?

9.8—WE ARE CREATED TO PRAY

Many people think of praying only when they are in need or when they want something. Why is that? Why is it that most people only go to the Lord to ask for things, thinking that is all there is to prayer? God does not want us to only come to him in prayer when we are in need. He wants a relationship with us, too, an intimate relationship that includes prayer in both good times and in not-so-good times. God wants all of us. He wants to have a beautiful conversation with us in and through prayer.

Why do you pray?

This is the last study in our Identity in Christ series. To review what we have established so far, we have learned the following truths about who we are in Christ:

—we are loved

—we have been created to love

—we are accepted children of the living God

—we are equipped with the full armor of God (to come up against the attacks of our enemy the devil)

—we are complete in Christ Jesus

—we are secure in Christ Jesus

—we are significant in Christ Jesus

We are also created to pray.

In the Greek language, the word for pray is *proseuchomai.* Praying, from a biblical perspective, means that we are **moving toward a goal or destination** (God) to **make our request** (prayer, petition, supplication, etc.) **known to** Him. We can pray by prayer and **supplication** (prayer for ourselves) or by prayer and **petition** (prayer for others), doing so with thanksgiving, exchanging our human wishes for His divine will and persuasion through faith. At the same time, we are **in local proximity with the Father** (He is in our midst; we are in His Presence). We pray to spend time with our Creator. Peace resides in His Presence; it is a beautiful place to be.

———•———

- "⁶ Do not be anxious about anything, but in every situation, by prayer and petition, with thanksgiving, present your requests to God. ⁷ And the peace of God, which transcends all understanding, will guard your hearts and your minds in Christ Jesus." (Philippians 4:6–7)

———•———

Perhaps you have often wondered if God even hears you when you pray. "This is the confidence we have in approaching

God: that if we ask anything according to his will, he hears us."
(1 John 5:14)

———·————————●————————·———

How does God answer prayer?

    1. Yes.

    2. Not now (remember that a delay is not a denial).

    3. No, or in a way that you did not expect.

*There is always a proper, godly timing for answered prayer.

———·————————●————————·———

Why does God answer prayer?

    1. To show that He is real.

    2. To build your faith.

    3. To build your faith in His Word.

    4. To show that He loves you and cares for you.

    5. So that your joy may be full.

———·————————●————————·———

So, why should we pray?

Some of the main reasons that I choose to pray each day are as follows:

- It is beautiful, intimate communication with God.

- It is an opportunity to listen, have a discussion with God, give thanks, praise and worship Him…not just ask for things.

- It is for God's benefit, for our benefit, for the benefit of others.

- It is for a personal relationship with Him; it will not grow without communication, and God wants our fellowship and our time.

- Because prayer is a privilege.

- It can bring about a renewal of our mind and a true heart change.

- It helps us to be more Christ-like.

- Because prayer was necessary for Jesus (and the disciples) and, therefore, it must be even more imperative for us.

- It allows us to show dependence on the Lord.

- We can bask in His Presence.

- We can humble ourselves in His Presence.

- We can build ourselves up.

- It builds up the body of Christ.

- We can change for the better; prayer doesn't always change things for us, but it can change us for things.

- In the powerful words of one of my favorite pastors: "If we are not praying, we are spiritually asleep!"

Many people in the Bible also prayed:

- "God is spirit, and his worshipers must **worship** in the Spirit and in truth." (John 4:24)

- "⁴ So Moses chiseled out two stone tablets like the first ones and went up Mount Sinai early in the morning, as the LORD had commanded him; and he carried the two stone tablets in his hands. ⁵ Then the LORD came down in the cloud and stood there with him and proclaimed his name, the LORD. ⁶ And he passed in front of Moses, proclaiming, 'The LORD, the LORD, the compassionate and gracious God, slow to anger, abounding in love and faithfulness, [7] maintaining love to thousands, and forgiving wickedness, rebellion and sin. Yet he does not leave the guilty unpunished; he punishes the children and their children for the sin of the parents to the third and fourth generation.' [8] Moses bowed to the ground at once and **worshiped**." (Exodus 34:4–8)

- Just as the angel reassured Daniel, we, too, can be sure from the first moment of our prayers that they are heard in heaven: "Then he continued, 'Do not be afraid, Daniel. Since the first day that you set your mind to gain understanding and to humble yourself before your God, **your words were heard**, and I have come in response to them.'" (Daniel 10:12).

———————•————————•————————— • ——

Jesus prayed…

- "After he had dismissed them, he went up on a mountainside by himself to **pray**." (Matthew 14:23a)

- "Very early in the morning, while it was still dark, Jesus got up, left the house and went off to a solitary place, where he **prayed**." (Mark 1:35)

- "But Jesus often withdrew to lonely places and **prayed**." (Luke 5:16)

- "[42] 'Father, if you are willing, take this cup from me; yet not my will, but yours be done.' [43] An angel from heaven appeared to him and strengthened him. [44] And being in anguish, he **prayed** more earnestly, and his sweat was like drops of blood falling to the ground. [45] When he rose from prayer and went back to the disciples, he found them asleep, exhausted from sorrow." (Luke 22:42–45)

- "Jesus said, 'Father, forgive them, for they do not know what they are doing....'" (Luke 23:34)

———·———————●———————·———

And as Paul had prayed in Ephesians 3:14–21, let this also be our prayer:

- "¹⁴ For this reason I kneel before the Father, ¹⁵ from whom every family in heaven and on earth derives its name. ¹⁶ I **pray** that out of his glorious riches he may strengthen you with power through his Spirit in your inner being, ¹⁷ so that Christ may dwell in your hearts through faith. And I pray that you, being rooted and established in love, ¹⁸ may have power, together with all the Lord's holy people, to grasp how wide and long and high and deep is the love of Christ, ¹⁹ and to know this love that surpasses knowledge—that you may be filled to the measure of all the fullness of God. ²⁰ Now to him who is able to do immeasurably more than all we ask or imagine, according to his power that is at work within us, ²¹ to him be glory in the church and in Christ Jesus throughout all generations, for ever and ever! Amen."

Why do you pray? How do you pray?

REMEMBER HOW OUR FATHER HAS TAUGHT US TO PRAY:

- "⁵ And when thou prayest, thou shalt not be as the hypocrites are: for they love to pray standing in the synagogues and in the corners of the streets, that they may be seen of men. Verily I say unto you, they have their reward. ⁶ But thou, when thou prayest, enter into thy closet, and when thou hast shut thy door, pray to thy Father which is in secret; and thy Father which seeth in secret shall reward thee openly. ⁷ But when ye pray, use not vain repetitions, as the heathen do: for they think that they shall be heard for their much speaking. ⁸ Be not ye therefore like unto them: for your Father knoweth what things ye have need of, before ye ask him. ⁹ After this manner therefore pray ye: Our Father which art in heaven, Hallowed be thy name. ¹⁰ Thy kingdom come, Thy will be done in earth, as it is in heaven. ¹¹ Give us this day our daily bread. ¹² And forgive us our debts, as we forgive our debtors. ¹³ And lead us not into temptation, but deliver us from evil: For thine is the kingdom, and the power, and the glory, for ever. Amen. [14] For if ye forgive men their trespasses, your heavenly Father will also forgive you." (Matthew 6:5–14, King James Version)

———•———————•———————•———

Prayer guards our spirit, while watching guards our heart.

———•———————•———————•———

DON'T TRIP UP IN THE LAST DAYS; STAY IN THE LIGHT:

- "[35] Be dressed ready for service and keep your lamps burning, [36] like servants waiting for their master to return from a wedding banquet, so that when he comes and knocks, they can immediately open the door for him." (Luke 12:35–36)

———•———————•———————•———

WE CAN LEARN FROM THE PARABLE OF THE TEN VIRGINS:

- "At that time the kingdom of heaven will be like ten virgins who took their lamps and went out to meet the bridegroom. [2] Five of them were foolish and five were wise. [3] The foolish ones took their lamps but did not take any oil with them. [4] The wise ones, however, took oil in jars along with their lamps. [5] The bridegroom was a long time in coming, and they all became drowsy and fell asleep. [6] At midnight the cry rang out: 'Here's the bridegroom! Come out to meet him!' [7] Then all the virgins woke up and trimmed their lamps. [8] The foolish ones said to the wise, 'Give us some of your oil; our lamps are going out.' [9] 'No,' they replied, 'there may not be enough for both us and you. Instead, go to those who sell oil and buy some for yourselves.' [10] But while they were on their way to buy the oil, the bridegroom arrived. The virgins who were ready went in with him to the wedding banquet. And the door was shut. [11] Later the others also came. 'Lord, Lord,' they said, 'open the door for us!' ¹²But he replied, 'Truly I tell you, I don't know you.' ¹³Therefore keep watch, because you do not know the day or the hour." (Matthew 25:1–13)

PRAY THAT WE ARE WORTHY TO ESCAPE ALL THESE THINGS:

- "Be always on the watch, and pray that you may be able to escape all that is about to happen, and that you may be able to stand before the Son of Man." (Luke 21:36)

- "So, when you, a mere human being, pass judgment on them and yet do the same things, do you think you will escape God's judgment?" (Romans 2:3)

- "While people are saying, 'Peace and safety,' destruction will come on them suddenly, as labor pains on a pregnant woman, and they will not escape." (1 Thessalonians 5:3)

- "...how shall we escape if we ignore so great a salvation? This salvation, which was first announced by the Lord, was confirmed to us by those who heard him." (Hebrews 2:3)

We can remember what God's Word says in the fourth chapter of Philippians: "Do not be anxious about anything, but in every situation, by prayer and petition, with thanksgiving, present your requests to God." (v. 6) We can take to heart God's Words from 1 Thessalonians 5: "Rejoice always, pray continually, give thanks in all circumstances; for this is God's will for you in Christ Jesus." (v. 16–18) And we can choose to believe "…that in all things God works for the good of those who love him, who have been called according to his purpose." (Romans 8:28)

Father hears our prayers: "Praise be to God, who has not rejected my prayer or withheld his love from me." (Psalm 66:20) However, He does not have a chance to answer them, according to His will, if we never ask. He wants to have an intimate relationship with us through prayer and time spent in His Word. He also wants us to pray to Him in good times and in bad. God is waiting to love you and for you to love Him. Go to Him in prayer, dear friends. Do it today.

Questions for Reflection

1. How do you pray?

2. Why do you pray?

3. How does knowing that God hears and answers your prayers, according to His will, help you on your spiritual journey?

4. How is your identity changing? How does praying help you to become more Christ-like?

5. Of the Scriptures shared above, which reveal(s) and speak(s) His Truth to you the most?

Our identity is a reflection of who we are and in what we have in our being. Now that you have completed this Identity in Christ study series and we are ending this chapter, how do you define yourself? Who are you? Who does God say that you are? As survivors of sexual assault and child sexual abuse, we must know what our real identity is: It is who we are in Christ Jesus. If we define ourselves by any other measure, we will come up short.

We are a created being, led by Father to do many things, living out of and by God's will in purity and humility. As you continue moving forward on your healing journey, remember that as your real identity comes into sharper focus you move closer and closer to God. Cloaked in humility, when we draw close to the Lord, He will draw close to us (see James 4:8a). Ultimately, your identity will be tied to whatever you give your heart to. Let that be God! What you think in your heart, so you are (see Proverbs 23:7). Divine healing takes on an entirely new and different meaning when you live out of your real identity in Christ, dear friends. Embrace it!

Come into the Light

Gracious Lord and Heavenly Father, I'm learning about who I really am—about my real identity in Christ. No one has ever told me these things before...not like You have revealed them to me today. I'm overwhelmed. It has wrecked me to know that, for so long, I was living contrary to Your will for me...not seeing myself the way that You see me. That changes, starting today. Help me to start living out of my real identity in Christ—this is who I *really* am. I want to know more of You, more of Your Word. Fill me with Your Truth. I desire to see myself the way that You see me, through Your eyes. Lead me in the way I am to go, Lord. I want to know You more. In Jesus's name, I pray. Amen.

Chapter 10

OUR HEALING IN CHRIST: FORGIVENESS, RECONCILIATION, AND DELIVERANCE

"LORD my God, I called to you for help, and you healed me." (Psalm 30:2)

I feel that I was blessed with a strong faith walk from a very young age, and I had felt the Lord calling me to Him and into ministry since my early 20s. In the dark hours, amid the painful experiences and repeated instances of sexual assault and child sexual abuse, my God was with me. Each night. Each day. Always. He was the One on whom I could always count to comfort me in my deep sorrow. Our healing comes from God through His Son Jesus Christ and in the power and presence of His Holy Spirit.

The enemy lied to me about the sexual assault and child sexual abuse, not only convincing me that it was my fault or that I had done something to cause it but also convincing me that the assault and abuse was "mine" whenever someone would ask me about it or encourage me to let it go. This was pure deception. I remember talking to one of my pastors before formal therapy had begun with my therapist and telling him that I could never let the pain go because it was *mine*. What I meant, at the time, was that it had happened to *me*. It was a deeply profound and personal experience. What I realized in time was that, although the sexual assault and child sexual abuse had happened to me, it was not something that I needed to hold on to. Nothing about sexual assault or child sexual abuse is ours! Yes, we had the experience and nothing will ever change that truth, but God never intended for us to keep it all hidden. The enemy used this tactic to control me, to keep me living in the past, and to prevent me from living the life that God had planned for me. Not talking about the sexual assault or child sexual abuse is akin to being in a self-prison.

God's Word tells us that we only need to ask and believe, and the doors of the past will open so healing can take place within us.

- "⁷ Ask and it will be given to you; seek and you will find; knock and the door will be opened to you. ⁸ For everyone who asks receives; the one who seeks finds; and to the one who knocks, the door will be opened. ⁹ 'Which of you, if your son asks for bread, will give him a stone? ¹⁰ Or if he asks for a fish, will give him a snake? ¹¹ If you, then, though you are evil, know how to give good gifts to your children, how much more will your Father in heaven give good gifts to those who ask him!'" (Matthew 7:7–11)

- "²³ Truly I tell you, if anyone says to this mountain, 'Go, throw yourself into the sea,' and does not doubt in their heart but believes that what they say will happen, it will be done for them. [24] Therefore I tell you, whatever you ask for in prayer, believe that you have received it, and it will be yours. [25] And when you stand praying, if you hold anything against anyone, forgive them, so that your Father in heaven may forgive you your sins." (Mark 11:23–25)

- "If you remain in me and my words remain in you, ask whatever you wish, and it will be done for you." (John 15:7)

FORGIVENESS AND RECONCILIATION

God gave me the strength to forgive all of the abusers who had perpetrated evil acts against me; I did that for my sake, unbeknownst to them. I had actually done a majority of the forgiveness process prior to entering into formal therapy. Most people, including survivors even, do not agree that we should forgive those who have sexually assaulted or abused us; they say it is unnecessary or impossible to do that. However, in order to truly be set free, we must forgive. "Forgive one another if any of you has a grievance against someone. Forgive as the Lord forgave you." (Colossians 3:13) This is a commandment from the Lord.

Many people believe that forgiveness only involves a person asking for forgiveness from someone else, and the person who had been wronged granting that forgiveness. This is only a part of the forgiveness process. True forgiveness is much more than that. In fact, true forgiveness is not just saying, "I'm sorry," and the other person saying, "I forgive you." True forgiveness does not even require the person to whom you are granting forgiveness to be alive, in the same room with you, or even aware of what you are doing. True forgiveness is a unilateral process between God and us. True forgiveness is not keeping lists of wrongdoings (see 1 Corinthians 13). When we have experienced true forgiveness, we no longer walk in the past. We do not recite those former lists of wrongdoings. We do not continue to use those lists as a weapon against the person who had wronged us to begin with. If we are to walk in true forgiveness, we need to forgive, let go and let God, honestly from our heart, and do as God always does with us: remember the sins no more. We are not excusing the behavior or saying that it didn't occur. We are freeing ourselves from holding on to the pain any longer or being controlled by it. True forgiveness can only be achieved with the help of God.

You may not want to hear this, but there is something that we have in common with the people who abused or betrayed us: We are all sinners. Yes, we are all sinners. This is the great equalizer. Wow. You mean to say that in the area of sin we are the same? Yes. And, generally speaking, if you can find something in common with someone else (even a perpetrator), it really does put things in the correct spiritual perspective. It's a tough pill to swallow; I get that. But it doesn't make what I'm saying any less true. Think about it.

True forgiveness is God's best for all of us. However, if you do not think God has forgiven you, you will not forgive others. "…Freely you have received; freely give." (Matthew 10:8) Forgiveness allows us to begin to come out of the darkness as the Light of Christ shines upon the situation with which we are dealing. "⁵ This is the message we have heard from him and declare to you: God is light; in him there is no darkness at all. [6] If we claim to have fellowship with him and yet walk in the darkness, we lie and do not live out the truth. [7] But if we walk in the light, as he is in the light, we have fellowship with one another, and the blood of Jesus, his Son, purifies us from all sin. [8] If we claim to be without sin, we deceive ourselves and the truth is not in us. [9] If we confess our sins, he is faithful and just and will forgive us our sins and purify us from all unrighteousness." (1 John 1:5–9)

I know that in my own life when I chose to forgive with the help of God, it freed me from the chains of the enemy that had been holding me captive. I asked the Lord to do this good work in and through me, in my heart, and He did. In some cases, I had to walk this out purposefully and repeatedly, choosing to forgive anew each day. Some of the forgiveness was easier to walk out than others. This forgiveness encompassed many people in my life, not just the sexual violence perpetrators. In some instances, it was and continues to be a daily process of forgiveness, giving and receiving, and understanding that Jesus died to give me freedom from the past. I wanted that. Deeply. I want that for you, too. Completely. Truly, forgiveness is a heart matter, and we must allow the Lord to get to the root of our heart in order for the deep forgiveness to take place. We should all desire to be ministers of reconciliation on whatever levels it is needed. Do you want to be free, or don't you? Do you want to be healed, or don't you? Do you want to be whole, or don't you? The choice is yours, dear friends.

———•————————•————————•———

Through Christ, we also have the ministry of reconciliation. "[11] Since, then, we know what it is to fear the Lord, we try to persuade others. What we are is plain to God, and I hope it is also plain to your conscience. [12] We are not trying to commend ourselves to you again, but are giving you an opportunity to take pride in us, so that you can answer those who take pride in what is seen rather than in what is in the heart. [13] If we are 'out of our mind,' as some say, it is for God; if we are in our right mind, it is for you. [14] For Christ's love compels us, because we are convinced that one died for all, and therefore all died. [15] And he died for all, that those who live should no longer live for themselves but for him who died for them and was raised again. [16] So from now on we regard no one from a worldly point of view. Though we once regarded Christ in this way, we do so no longer. [17] Therefore, if anyone is in Christ, the new creation has come: The old has gone, the new is here! [18] All this is from God, who reconciled us to himself through Christ and gave us the ministry of reconciliation: [19] that God was reconciling the world to himself in Christ, not counting people's sins against them. And he has committed to us the message of reconciliation. [20] We are therefore Christ's ambassadors, as though God were making his appeal through us. We implore you on Christ's behalf: Be reconciled to God. [21] God made him who had no sin to be sin for us, so that in him we might become the righteousness of God." (2 Corinthians 5:11–21) Through Christ Jesus, we are reconciled, redeemed, justified and sanctified—truly, we are reconciled to Him in all things, whether on earth or in heaven (see Colossians 1:19–22; Romans 5).

God was instrumental in putting the people in my life that would ultimately walk with me on the path toward healing. I have shared quite a bit about those people already. I chose (and I still do choose) to trust that the LORD God holds my true healing, as well as me, in the palms of His hands, and it is my fervent prayer for you to be able to believe this for yourself. "And when you stand praying, if you hold anything against anyone, forgive them, so that your Father in heaven may forgive you your sins." (Mark 11:25). It's not always advisable, or ideal, to seek reconciliation with a perpetrator or abuser. That is a personal decision, and it should be made with the utmost care and consideration on a case-by-case basis. Just like the pursuit of justice, reconciliation is your choice; you pursue something for what it looks like for you. That is between you and the Lord. But I'm encouraging you to at least consider it as an option in your healing process. Even if the other person is not involved, you can be reconciled to Christ.

God's touch can be a gentle caress if we will lay down our wills and agendas and let Him work. True forgiveness is freeing, loving, and healing. By withholding forgiveness from those who perpetrated sexual violence against you, the only person you are hurting is yourself. I encourage you to seek the Lord and allow Him to do a profound, deep, forgiving work in you today. He will bring about a complete restoration in your life. When we seek Him in truth, when He can see the content and intentions of our heart and they are honest and sincere, He can and will do a good work, in and through us. Forgive. Bless and release. Let it all go to the Lord. Do it today. It truly is God's best for us, dear friends.

———•———

DELIVERANCE

———•———

As a direct result of the sexual assault and child sexual abuse through which we have suffered, many spiritual strongholds and negative tapes can enter into the heart and soul of a survivor. These strongholds keep us from experiencing God's best in our lives. The negative tapes play repeatedly until we believe what they say. Spiritual strongholds and negative tapes leave a wake of fear, oppression, and self-doubt in their path. Nevertheless, God can obliterate and deliver us from it all! Our self-esteem, self-respect, self-image, and self-worth take a heavy blow following sexual assault or child sexual abuse. However, no one else can define our worth unless we give him or her the power to do that.

Throughout the mission field, I've ministered to and counseled with numerous women and children, a majority of whom have sustained some form of sexual violence in their lives.

Typically, this includes some form of human sex trafficking, sexual assault, or child sexual abuse. A number of counselees have also been victimized by demonic and satanic ritual sexual abuse, which involves human ritual sacrifice, bestiality, and many other forms of physical and sexual torment. A portion of these survivors are also suffering from some form of dissociation, spiritual heart fragmentation, and various physical, emotional, and mental incapacities and challenges. The wounds go deep. But, in Christ, there is healing for everyone.

November 27, 2011

I have been recovering some lost memories from my childhood years over the past week or so. As a direct result of some of these recovered memories, I now can see why certain people in my life could not fully support me as I wanted or needed them to.

I am continuing to replace the negative tapes with positive affirmations and truth from God's Word.

I realize that sexual assault and child sexual abuse sometimes exist in bloodlines and travel through generations, and it must be dealt with on that level. I have been under severe spiritual attack for the past several days. However, I continue to keep my eye on God and yield to Him for my strength to endure. I know the enemy is attacking me because of the call on my life, my destiny in Christ, and what the Lord is going to continue to do in and through me. My God is greater! I rebuke Satan, in Jesus's name.

———————————●———————————

An abundance of damage occurs in the life of a sexual assault and child sexual abuse survivor. We are survivors, but some days it seems like we exist rather than survive. On most days, it can actually feel like we are drowning. God wants us to survive, thrive, and overcome through Christ Jesus. How do we do that when so much damage has occurred? As painful as it may be, we need to assess the damage. This damage can include: obsessive-compulsive disorder (OCD); posttraumatic stress disorder (PTSD); complex traumatic stress disorder (CTSD); a need for control; symptoms of depression and anxiety; fear; isolation; cutting; eating disorders (anorexia, bulimia, binge eating); paranoia; flashbacks; triggers; nightmares; regressive behavior (thumb-sucking, rocking, bed-wetting). This list only touches the surface, as the full list is too lengthy to include in this book. However, it should be understood that the damage caused by sexual violence is and can be quite extensive.

Many coping mechanisms can come out of pain and suffering. As we discussed previously, some are positive, some are negative, and some have both positive and negative elements. One of the coping mechanisms that numerous survivors suffer from is weight gain, generally stemming from an addiction to food. In other instances, not wearing makeup or wearing unflattering clothes or clothes of the opposite sex is a way for many survivors to remove an association with their God-given gender. In most of these cases, the enemy has brought a spiritual stronghold of confusion into their mind, as wearing flattering clothes and garnering the attention and positive comments of others can be uncomfortable to receive. "For God is not the author of confusion, but of peace, as in all the churches of the saints." (1 Corinthians 14:33, NKJV) Other survivors can often dress provocatively because they desire the wrong kind of attention. In most of these cases, the enemy has brought a spiritual stronghold of sensuality into their heart and soul. Not taking care of our body leaves a door open to the enemy; as believers, our body is a temple of Holy Spirit (see 1 Corinthians 6:19–20). Many survivors also experience exposure to pornography during sexual assault or child sexual abuse, and this can result in a future sexual addiction. It is easy to see, just through these few examples, that what is on the inside manifests outwardly.

Premarital sex is a huge problem in the world today. "And when Shechem the son of Hamor the Hivite, the prince of the land, saw her, he seized her and lay with her and humiliated her." (Genesis 34:2) Many survivors enter into erratic or unstable relationships as a direct result of the sexual assault and child sexual abuse perpetrated against them. More spiritual strongholds related to damaged emotions result in multiple, failed relationships, some of which involve both marriage and divorce and some of which involve living together outside of marriage. If someone is not willing to commit to you in marriage, they are not worthy of a long-term relationship. However, no one should ever enter into marriage inadvisably or lightly. Not every person is marriage material, especially when he or she comes into a relationship carrying so many broken pieces from their past. God is capable of restoring them, and there is always hope in Christ. However, marriage is a holy covenant between one man and one woman, and it deserves reverence and respect, not to be twisted and perverted by the enemy.

Grief work and healing are difficult, but we have already established that with God all things are possible. That said, most people, survivors included, continue to live in spiritual captivity and brokenness. Without spiritual healing and deliverance, dysfunctional cycles, generational patterns, and ancestral curses will continue to plague people. Think about the woman at the well (see John 4). We do not even know her name. And isn't that the point? By not knowing her name, anyone reading this passage of scripture can insert herself into the story. In this particular passage of Scripture, we read that a Samaritan woman went to the well to gather water. There she encountered Jesus. He spoke to her first, asking her to give Him a drink. She is caught off guard because Jews (Jesus) did not associate with or speak to Samaritans (the woman at the well). Jesus, however, was not concerned with anything other than her spiritual well-being. Jesus offers her the Living Water, and she accepts. He tells her who He is and offers her encouragement. Jesus knows that this woman has been married five times and is presently living with a man outside of marriage. It's the first time anyone has bothered to see her. Jesus sees her for who she really is: a child of God. He sees her potential and brings restoration. He was letting her know that she mattered. Her pain mattered. He showed her that He cared, that He loved her. Subsequently, she is changed. She leaves the well to go and tell others about the Lord and about what He can do for them.

———·———————●———————·———

God is in the restoration business, but many are content with their ungodly lifestyles, regardless of how they came to live that way. "Are they ashamed of their detestable conduct? No, they have no shame at all; they do not even know how to blush." (Jeremiah 6:15) God is able to deliver us from the clutches of the enemy, including spiritual strongholds and afflictions of any kind. Why would we continue in sin, defeat, and spiritual bondage when we can experience freedom and healing in Christ Jesus? Sometimes, this has more to do with our relationship, or our location, to God than we may realize.

Think about what God inquired of Adam in the third chapter of Genesis: "Where are you?" (v. 9) Adam and Eve had been in the garden, and both had sinned against God by eating from the Tree of the Knowledge of Good and Evil, which had been forbidden by God. Immediately, Adam and Eve knew that they had done something wrong, that something was different. However, when God asked Adam where he was, God was not trying to determine "where" Adam was, exactly, because God knows all things. God was trying to get Adam to determine where he was in relation to God. By sinning, Adam and Eve had changed their location to God. They had been in good standing, living a perfect life, which God had created for them (and for all of us). But when they knowingly sinned against God, they were no longer in this perfect standing with God. They had changed their location. Where are you?

We need to examine our relationship with and to God. It is about our location in proximity to God. It is not about His grasp on us, which is a constant; it is about our grasp on Him, especially when we change our location. God's Word tells us, "but I am afraid that just as Eve was deceived by the serpent's cunning, your minds may somehow be led astray from your sincere and pure devotion to Christ." (2 Corinthians 11:3) Do not allow that to happen to you, dear friends. And, if it has, you can choose to return to your First Love: God. Envision the blood of Jesus, a healing and anointing oil of Holy Spirit, and the resurrection (*dunamis*) power of Jesus washing over your entire being—body, soul, spirit. Through Jesus's redemptive work on the cross, we return to a "right" position with God. Restoration comes to our location in relation to Father, and we are then able to live out of His best for us. Restoration and reconciliation are, indeed, a beautiful thing!

When sexual assault or child sexual abuse occurs, the effects on the victim's body can be confusing. I spoke in Chapter 1 about feeling conflicted regarding one of my perpetrators; I felt as though I needed to protect them, which prevented me from talking to anyone about the abuse. This shows how twisted sexual violence can become. Sexual violation perpetrated against your will causes your body to function in a certain manner. In essence, it can feel very much like your body is betraying you. We need to understand that a plethora of chemicals are surging through our bodies during sexual assault and child sexual abuse. This is the way our bodies were designed to react to the stimulus, good or bad. Regarding the neurobiology of trauma and sexual assault on the survivor, many physical and physiological changes are occurring in the body, as various chemicals are released through the act of sexual relations. This is when the "fear circuitry" kicks in, causing the prefrontal cortex—known as the decision-making part of the brain—to be bypassed entirely.

Let's take a closer look at the chemicals involved in this process. First, there are *adrenaline* and *cortisol,* two key hormones involved with the stress response during sexual violence. When we are in danger, these hormones drive a host of physiological changes that kick our fight-or-flight nervous system into gear and pump the brakes on our rest-and-digest nervous system. This results in a burst of energy, redirecting blood to vital organs and functions and shutting down everything else. Next, there is *dopamine,* a neurochemical associated with pleasure that is released outside of the victim's control. Then, there is *oxytocin,* a powerful chemical that bonds us to others. This is released through touch and is used by the body to increase positive feelings, especially in times of sexual violation when parts of our mind and body are pulling away from the trauma and experience of the assault or abuse. Next, there is *vasopressin,* a long-term bonding chemical, which plays an important role in sexual assault and child sexual abuse that occurs over longer periods of time, such as months or years. Finally, there are *opiates,* natural morphine that is released into the body in order to compensate for the victim's physical and emotional pain, effectively numbing all emotions.[6]

What is imperative for all of us to understand is that, while these chemicals are surging through the physical body and bonding the survivor to the perpetrator on a physical level, there is also a spiritual bonding taking place simultaneously. The bonding, on both the physical and spiritual levels, creates great difficulty for the survivor. There is now a serious bond between the victim and the perpetrator that must be dealt with. In order to break that spiritual bond, it must be severed appropriately and completely.

Sexual assault and child sexual abuse survivors can develop something referred to as heart strings, or unhealthy and ungodly soul ties. These unhealthy, ungodly soul ties develop between ourselves and each one of the perpetrators that sexually violate us. Ungodly soul ties actually form between anyone with whom we engage in sexual relations, consensual or non-consensual. They can form through emotions, too. Since these ungodly soul ties are spiritual and emotional, that means that

6 Smith, Deborah, 2017, "What Judges Need to Know about the Neurobiology of Sexual Assault," National Center for State Courts, https://www.ncsc.org/trends/monthly-trends-articles/2017/what-judges-need-to-know-about-the-neurobiology-of-sexual-assault.

we can also create healthy soul ties (i.e., husband and wife, parent and child, siblings, etc.). From a deliverance standpoint, it is imperative to understand how ungodly soul ties work on a spiritual level. It's also important to know and understand that, when a trauma or emotional wounding occurs, it damages our spiritual heart. This wounding creates what is called a heart part, a part of your spiritual heart actually breaks off and is in need of healing. Broken hearts are a real thing. But, dear friends, there is spiritual healing available for you.

Here are several Scripture from God's Word on the subjects of heart parts and soul ties:

- "[14] By his power God raised the Lord from the dead, and he will raise us also. [15] Do you not know that your bodies are members of Christ himself? Shall I then take the members of Christ and unite them with a prostitute? Never! [16] Do you not know that he who unites himself with a prostitute is one with her in body? For it is said, 'The two will become one flesh.' [17] But whoever is united with the Lord is one with him in spirit. [18] Flee from sexual immorality. All other sins a person commits are outside the body, but whoever sins sexually, sins against their own body." (1 Corinthians 6:14–18)

- "After David had finished talking with Saul, Jonathan became one in spirit with David, and he loved him as himself." (1 Samuel 18:1)

- "For the word of God is alive and active. Sharper than any double-edged sword, it penetrates even to dividing soul and spirit, joints and marrow; it judges the thoughts and attitudes of the heart." (Hebrews 4:12)

- "[1] Now Dinah, the daughter Leah had borne to Jacob, went out to visit the women of the land. [2] When Shechem son of Hamor the Hivite, the ruler of that area, saw her, he took her and raped her. [3] His heart was drawn to Dinah daughter of Jacob; he loved the young woman and spoke tenderly to her." (Genesis 34:1–3)

- "³ Do not intermarry with them. Do not give your daughters to their sons or take their daughters for your sons, ⁴ for they will turn your children away from following me to serve other gods, and the LORD's anger will burn against you and will quickly destroy you." (Deuteronomy 7:3–4)

- "He heals the brokenhearted and binds up their wounds." (Psalm 147:3)

In your journal, consider writing down the names of anyone with whom you have created an unhealthy or ungodly soul tie through consensual or non-consensual sexual relations or other emotional wounding. I did this. I also made a list based on emotional wounding to my spiritual heart, resulting in a broken heart part. I'm encouraging you to do that, too. When I did this (made these lists) I needed to remember that God knows the contents of my heart, so complete honesty was the wisest approach. Also, I was aware that it's natural for some emotions to come to the surface. At times, there were a lot of emotions. That is okay. I just let them come to the extent that I was comfortable and able to process them. If you need help processing, just ask a trusted spiritual advisor for additional help. This spiritual exercise really helped me to identify and let go of the unhealthy connections to those from my past (and present) that had been somehow holding me back from experiencing God's best for my life. Emotional and spiritual wounding creates heavy burdens. Receiving healing from the Lord provides peace and allows joy to arise.

Find a place where you are safe and can be alone with the Lord. Enter into prayer. Then, follow the steps below to break any negative, unhealthy, ungodly soul ties and receive spiritual healing for your spiritual heart. (Note: You will do this soul tie–breaking and spiritual heart healing exercise—steps 1 through 5—for *each* person on your list. Again, if and as you need help processing, do consider asking a trusted spiritual advisor to assist you in walking out your healing. For many readers, prayer may be a new concept. It may be something you don't do often. You may feel intimidated. Don't. Just ask for the help that you need. There's healing waiting for you.)

BREAKING ALL UNHEALTHY, UNGODLY SOUL TIES AND RECEIVING SPIRITUAL HEART HEALING

1. In the power of the Holy Spirit, call forth all of the heart parts in you that have a connection through sexual or emotional bonds or wounding.

2. In the power of the Holy Spirit, send all of your damaged heart parts to Jesus for healing, covering them in the blood of Jesus, applying a healing and anointing oil and a resurrection (*dunamis*) power of Jesus to this area of your soul and heart (you will say all of this, aloud or to yourself, in prayer).

3. In the power of the Holy Spirit, ask the Lord Jesus (as it is His will) to heal and return all healed heart parts back to you. Heart parts can be healed and whole and stay with Jesus. This doesn't make you less-than, if He decides to keep a heart part; it just means, while this part of your heart is now healed, you no longer need it here on earth. Don't be alarmed if this should occur. If you are meant to have the now-healed heart

part returned to you, it will happen. God knows.

4. In the power of the Holy Spirit, sever all ungodly soul ties on both ends—theirs and yours—and also cover each person in the blood of Jesus. (You will say all of this aloud or to yourself in prayer.)

5. In the power of the Holy Spirit, thank God for the healing that He now has purposed to take place in your heart and soul, closing your prayer as you normally would in Jesus's name. (Note reminder: Take your time. You will want to be as thorough as possible and allow the Lord to do a good and complete work in your heart and soul. It also may be necessary to do just a few. Then, take a break. Then, do more, as you are able. Don't feel the need to rush through this.) (Additional note reminder: You will do this soul tie-breaking and spiritual heart healing exercise—steps 1 through 5—for *each* person on your list.)

Sometimes it's necessary to go deeper in your spiritual deliverance. For you, it may look something like this: (you will pray to cut off the following, saying) "I cut off all ungodly soul ties, demonic cords, demonic strongholds, devils, demons, evil spirits and their entire kingdoms, demonic chains, and all things demonic from my eye gates, ear gates, mouth/tongue/throat gates, physical/spiritual heart gates, mind/will/emotions (soul), conscience, spirit, entire physical body and all of my organs, entire spiritual being and all of my flesh, from my vaginal/penile, nipple, belly, nasal and anal gates, from all of my spiritual gates, and all of my spiritual doors, in Jesus's name."

You may also desire to remove the trauma in your physical body that has manifested because of the original sexual or emotional wounding. Sometimes you know the trauma is there because you feel it in a certain part of your physical body— muscles, organs, etc. For you, it may look something like this: (you will pray, saying) "I bind any and all trauma in my physical body that has come in through physical or emotional wounding, and I loose it (release it, command it to go) from my body, in Jesus's name."

I always recommend that, once a person comes to terms with the fact that we are all sinners in need of a Savior, a part of your daily faith walk should include a regular confession and repenting of personal sins, transgressions, and iniquities. This confession is done through prayer to the LORD God. Then, knowing what God's Word says about forgiveness (when we confess our sins, He is faithful to hear our confessions, forgive our sins, and remember them no more) we can receive full absolution in Christ and walk in spiritual freedom. This is a beautiful thing, dear friends.

Still, some people desire an even deeper deliverance. In these special cases, it is recommended that you seek out a reputable deliverance minister, someone who is walking closely with the Lord and who is trained in spiritual and biblical deliverance to help you on your journey to spiritual freedom in the Lord. Regardless, everyone needs some level of spiritual deliverance, and I encourage you to avail yourself to the process.

———•—————————•—————————•———

As a direct result of the sexual assault and child sexual abuse I endured, I was afflicted with numerous spiritual strongholds. Some of the strongholds I experienced included sadness, suicidal thoughts, defeat; fear; failure; addictions (to pornography and food); bitterness, anger; torment, pain, suffering; obsessions, compulsions, perfectionism; control; guilt. Additionally, some of the disorders I developed were quite debilitating. I wet my bed until I was about 12 years old. I turned to food to comfort myself and ease damaged emotions. I experienced nightmares and flashbacks quite frequently. At some point, I received a medical diagnosis of a mild-to-moderate form of (OCD). The obsession (thought) and the compulsion (action) drive this behavior. Thoughts about perfectionism consumed my mind. I desperately needed to control the outcome of things. I was particularly obsessive about the arrangement of items in my house or on a table in a restaurant. Overall, I did these things because I felt the need to control things or people because my life, otherwise, was so out of control. All of this stemmed from the sexual assault and child sexual abuse I had endured throughout my life. There also were numerous times during my life when many close to me would tease me, ostracize me, or talk about me behind my back because of this behavior. They did not understand, and many times they did not *want* to understand. This was very hurtful to me. Perhaps you can relate to this in some way.

Strongholds are incorrect, false, or negative thinking or thought patterns: those that come from the enemy, and those that are about God, which are not based in reality. The sexual violence we suffer through is trauma. Trauma is actually a coffin located inside of our thinking process. Satan puts us in a prison in our soul (mind, will, emotions, and feelings). But Jesus comes with a key in the shape of a cross. He is the One who can free us from the spiritual bonds and chains that bind us. The shame, blame, guilt, self-doubt, etc.—all gone! Medical conditions—all gone! Physical ailments—all gone! Often, the physical ailments we experience are really trauma-based, somatic reactions. This can include headaches, stomach problems, ulcers, etc. When the trauma is removed, the ailment is also removed. Dear friends, we are living below our spiritual inheritance—below our God-given potential—when we allow the enemy to put us in a prison. However, God will do something, in and through us, on the other side. If you ask Him to remove the spiritual strongholds in your life that are holding you captive, He is faithful to do it! He is a healer. And His love for you is never-ending.

Below, please find a list of demonic strongholds, which is derived from, expounded upon, and excerpted from a spiritual stronghold list I came across some years ago.[7] Kindly understand

7 "Seven Prayers That Heal the Heart," 2020, Communion with God Ministries, accessed Sept 25, 2020, https://www.cwgministries.org/seven-prayers-heal-heart-adopted-interceeding-others.

that this is not an exhaustive list but is a helpful place to begin. Perhaps, as you pray about it, the Lord will reveal more insight to you (I have added a few strongholds to this list, within each category, over the years). In your journal, as you go through each list, write down each spiritual stronghold in each separate category that you feel applies to you and your spiritual journey. We will be using this list for a spiritual exercise shortly.

———•————•————•———

DEMONIC STRONGHOLDS

- **Abandonment:**
  - desertion, orphan spirit, divorce, rejection, neglect, victimization, blocked intimacy, not valuing people/relationships/ending relationships, burning bridges, isolation, loneliness, self-pity

- **Addictions:**
  - alcohol, tobacco, drugs, food, sugar, coffee, chocolate/sweets, pornography, sex, flirtation, junky magazines/websites/TV shows/movies, overeating, drinking too much alcohol, anything you cannot do in moderation

- **Anger:**

  - hatred, malice, rage, murder, temper, cursing, vengeance, retaliation, violence, abuse, cruelty, sadism, unforgiveness, bitterness, resentment, being judgmental or critical, taking offense easily, irritability, anger towards men or women, anger towards mother or father, anger towards authority, anger/resentment towards God, orphan spirit

- **Depression:**

  - rejection, despair, defeat, helplessness, hopelessness, sadness, self-pity, withdrawal, suicidal thoughts/actions

- **Fear:**

  - fear of man, fear of authority, doubt/unbelief, dread, worry, anxiety, fear the worst will happen, fear of various illnesses like cancer, fear people will get angry with you or won't like you, orphan spirit, spirit of false responsibility, spirit of rush

- **Financial lack:**

  - belief in poverty, robbing God by not tithing, not believing in covenant blessings, greed, covetousness, debt, dishonesty, idolatry of possessions, failure

- **Grief:**
  - sorrow, despair, heartbreak, loss, pain, suffering, torment, weeping, anguish, agony, destruction

- **Lying:**
  - cheating, theft, deception, trickery, untrustworthiness, adultery, emotional adultery, denial, self-deception, secretiveness, hiding purchases/activities/relationships, orphan spirit, harlotry

- **Mental instability:**
  - mental illness, obsessions, compulsions, perfectionism, confusion, anxiety, panic, hysteria, paranoia, schizophrenia, insanity

- **Pride:**
  - arrogance, disdain, selfishness, control/pushiness, independence, callousness/lack of concern for others, gossip, harlotry

- **Procrastination:**
    - sloth, laziness, distraction/confusion/lack of focus, not thinking things through before acting or speaking or writing emails, lack of organization/preparation, lateness/tardiness, missing appointments/phone calls

- **Sensuality:**
    - lust, fantasizing/coveting another's mate, flirtation, premarital sex, sexual abuse, fornication/adultery/emotional adultery, demonic sex, pornography, strings on the heart (unhealthy soul ties), perversion, bondage/control, rape, incest, harlotry

- **Shame:**
    - anger, condemnation, disgrace, embarrassment, guilt, hatred, self-hate, self-pity, withdrawal, hiding/antisocial, timidity/fear, inferiority

---

Again, I want to encourage you to take the necessary time to write down in your journal which spiritual strongholds are affecting you, not only the main category (**in bold type**) but also those subcategories within each main category. This is *very* important. You want to move forward on your healing journey without all of the unnecessary spiritual baggage. The enemy does not want you to do this. However, if you are afflicted with any of the spiritual strongholds on the list above, ask God to help you remove them from your life. He is more than capable to do it, and He is faithful to restore your soul. Let Him do that for you today, dear friends.

———•————————•———•———

Exercise: (this is set up as a prayer) Using the spiritual stronghold list that you created in your journal, address each "main category" (**in bold type**) separately (one "group" at a time); with the help of the Lord, we are now going to remove everything within each main category that pertains to you, as it relates to the spiritual strongholds that are present in your heart and soul:

1. In the power of the Holy Spirit, I grab hold of the demonic stronghold root cluster of (fill in the blank—**anger, abandonment, etc....but choose**

to work on only <u>one</u> main category at a time) and I pull it out, roots and all, from my soul. (Note: You will use a prophetic act of actually "pulling" the stronghold root out of the stomach/ belly area of your physical body. You may (will likely) feel some (physical and spiritual) resistance. That is to be expected. Continue pulling until you feel no more resistance in your stomach/belly area. It's also quite common to experience some or a lot of emotions as you do this prophetic act. Take your time. There is no hurry.)

2. In the power of the Holy Spirit, I cut off ungodly soul ties, demonic cords, demonic strongholds, devils, demons, evil spirits and their entire kingdoms, demonic chains, and all things demonic between me and the demonic stronghold root cluster of (fill in the blank—**anger, abandonment, etc....again, only choosing to work on only <u>one</u> main category at a time)**.

3. In the power of the Holy Spirit, I repent, break and renounce, cut off any and all rights, any and all ties,

yokes of bondage, and the power and presence of the evil spirits.

4. In the power of the Holy Spirit, I release the fire of God into all of these areas of my soul, and I ask the Lord to fill me with Holy Ghost fire, Holy Ghost oil, and the power and presence of Holy Spirit—into the spiritual root systems, the hidden and empty places, the entirety of my physical body and spiritual being, etc.

5. I give thanks, and I ask this all in Jesus's name. (Note: You will complete this list (1–5) for each "main category" in the list above, as it pertains to you and the spiritual healing that you need or desire to receive from the Lord. Take your time, and be thorough.)

———•——————————•—————— •———

God's Word tells us that, as children of God, we can live by the Spirit and not by the flesh:

- "¹² Therefore, brothers and sisters, we have an obligation—but it is not to the flesh, to live according to it. ¹³ For if you live according to the flesh, you will die; but if by the Spirit you put to death the misdeeds of the body, you will live. ¹⁴ For those who are led by the Spirit of God are the children of God. ¹⁵ The Spirit you received does not make you slaves, so that you live in fear again; rather, the Spirit you received brought about your adoption to sonship. And by him we cry, '*Abba,* Father.' ¹⁶ The Spirit himself testifies with our spirit that we are God's children. ¹⁷ Now if we are children, then we are heirs—heirs of God and co-heirs with Christ, if indeed we share in his sufferings in order that we may also share in his glory." (Romans 8:12–17)

God is in control, and many of you may be asking yourselves, "How is a God who loves me able to allow something bad, such as sexual assault and child sexual abuse, to happen to me?" Please understand that there is evil and sin in the world. An act of sexual assault or child sexual abuse is NOT from God. "No temptation has overtaken you except what is common to mankind. And God is faithful; he will not let you be tempted beyond what you can bear. But when you are tempted, he will also provide a way out so that you can endure it." (1 Corinthians 10:13) Everyone has free will. Sometimes people use that free will to harm others. But God allows us to go through something so we can be a testimony to others. He asks, "I am the LORD, the God of all mankind. Is anything too hard for me?" (Jeremiah 32:27) We can choose to trust Him to bring us out of anything, including sexual and spiritual bondage.

The enemy attacks your desire for God to the point that there is just no giving God anything. Press through. Trust the Lord. God has great plans for you. Ask yourself the following question: What am I willing to do in order to get in God's Presence? Fall in love with Jesus again or for the first time. Fall in love with and have faith in the Jesus of today, who He *really* is and not the historical Jesus that you have only heard about. Jesus wants to have a personal relationship with you and love you. Let Him. He will renew the faith within you.

───•──────●─────•───

- "²⁸ Do you not know? Have you not heard? The LORD is the everlasting God, the Creator of the ends of the earth. He will not grow tired or weary, and his understanding no one can fathom. ²⁹ He gives strength to the weary and increases the power of the weak. ³⁰ Even youths grow tired and weary, and young men stumble and fall; ³¹ but those who hope in the LORD will renew their strength. They will soar on wings like eagles; they will run and not grow weary; they will walk and not be faint." (Isaiah 40:28–31)

───•──────●─────•───

Ask God if you have any ungodly beliefs. "It is for freedom that Christ has set us free. Stand firm, then, and do not let yourselves be burdened again by a yoke of slavery." (Galatians 5:1) In your journal, write down God's responses to your question, making a list of any ungodly beliefs that God reveals to you. This should also include any ungodly oaths, vows, covenants, and agreements you have made. Then, give them all up to God. Ask Him to renew your mind and bring about a true heart change in you. Ask Him to show you what truth in His Word can replace the lies you have been believing. He is faithful to do it.

———•———————•———————•———

- "What causes fights and quarrels among you? Don't they come from your desires that battle within you? [2] You desire but do not have, so you kill. You covet but you cannot get what you want, so you quarrel and fight. You do not have because you do not ask God. [3] When you ask, you do not receive, because you ask with wrong motives, that you may spend what you get on your pleasures. [4] You adulterous people, don't you know that friendship with the world means enmity against God? Therefore, anyone who chooses to be a friend of the world becomes an enemy of God. [5] Or do you think Scripture says without reason that he jealously longs for the spirit he has caused to dwell in us? [6] But he gives us more grace. That is why Scripture says: 'God opposes the proud but shows favor to the humble.' [7] Submit yourselves, then, to God. Resist the devil, and he will flee from you. [8] Come near to God and he will come near to you." (James 4:1–8)

————•————————•————————•————

Enemy attacks can often occur because of your destiny and the call on your life. However, God's Word tells us "[The devil] intended to harm me, but God intended it for good...." (Genesis 50:20) Your past is not the whole story of your life. Do not act like what the devil did to you is greater than what Jesus did in you when He saved you; the yoke the enemy had on you is not more powerful than the ability of God to free you from it. Remember: "The one who is in you is greater than the one who is in the world." (1 John 4:4) God changes your nature when He moves on the inside of you. Once God moves on the inside of you so powerfully, you cannot go back, even if you wanted to. Keep. Moving. Forward.

- "⁶ Humble yourselves, therefore, under God's mighty hand, that he may lift you up in due time. ⁷ Cast all your anxiety on him because he cares for you. ⁸ Be alert and of sober mind. Your enemy the devil prowls around like a roaring lion looking for someone to devour. ⁹ Resist him, standing firm in the faith, because you know that the family of believers throughout the world is undergoing the same kind of sufferings. ¹⁰ And the God of all grace, who called you to his eternal glory in Christ, after you have suffered a little while, will himself restore you and make you strong, firm and steadfast." (1 Peter 5:6–10)

It is time to storm the gates of hell. It is time to recover what the enemy has taken from you. It is time to war, spiritually, and ask the Lord to war on your behalf. It's time to be free.

- "[10] Finally, be strong in the Lord and in his mighty power. [11] Put on the full armor of God, so that you can take your stand against the devil's schemes. [12] For our struggle is not against flesh and blood, but against the rulers, against the authorities, against the powers of this dark world and against the spiritual forces of evil in the heavenly realms." (Ephesians 6:10–12)

There is a hierarchy of the devil, which is operating under him and his authority: rulers (principalities); authorities (powers); powers of this dark world (darkness); spiritual forces of evil (spiritual wickedness in high places). We must war in the Spirit.

- "[3] For though we live in the world, we do not wage war as the world does. [4] The weapons we fight with are not the weapons of the world. On the contrary, they have divine power to demolish strongholds. ⁵ We demolish arguments and every pretension that sets itself up against the knowledge of God, and we take captive every thought to make it obedient to Christ. ⁶ And we will be ready to punish every act of disobedience, once your obedience is complete." (2 Corinthians 10:3–6)

———————•———————

Dear friends, we are not ignorant of the enemy's devices, and we can move forward in faith. The devil is very real, but so is God. And God is greater (see again, 1 John 4:4)! It is possible to grasp this the most when we know who we are in Christ, which is our real identity, and we can stand in God's truth to war against the enemy.

Think of it like an eagle doing battle with a snake. If the eagle and the snake did battle on the ground, the snake would win, without question. However, what if the eagle grabbed the snake and lifted him into the air? Now the eagle has the upper hand. Our battle with our enemy the devil is no different. Remember, we do not wage war as the world does; our battles are spiritual (see Ephesians 6:12, above). Remember, also, that God does war on our behalf. When we live out of who we are in Christ, the victory is most certainly ours because the battle belongs to the Lord (see 1 Chronicles 20:15). Rejoice, dear friends! Rejoice!

The devil walks back and forth (see 1 Peter 5:8), but God's eyes go back and forth "for the eyes of the LORD range throughout the earth to strengthen those whose hearts are fully committed to him." (2 Chronicles 16:9) Who is greater? Who is more powerful? The LORD our God is. Seek Him. Do it today. Your healing and deliverance are coming.

———•————————•————•———

- "I have told you these things, so that in me you may have peace. In this world you will have trouble. But take heart! I have overcome the world!" (John 16:33)

———•————————•————•———

We must get rid of unnecessary things and stand firm in times of testing, just as Job proclaimed following a testing from God: "...when he has tested me, I will come forth as gold!" (Job

23:10) For most of us, the clarity we are seeking comes about most readily when we renew our minds (*metanoia*), bringing about a true heart change. "²² You were taught, with regard to your former way of life, to put off your old self, which is being corrupted by its deceitful desires; ²³ to be made new in the attitude of your minds; ²⁴ and to put on the new self, created to be like God in true righteousness and holiness." (Ephesians 4:22–24) "…put on the new self, which is being renewed in knowledge in the image of its Creator." (Colossians 3:10) "Do not conform to the pattern of this world, but be transformed by the renewing of your mind. Then you will be able to test and approve what God's will is—his good, pleasing and perfect will." (Romans 12:2)

Teach us, oh Lord, what we are to do. Give us power to grow up into You! "¹⁶ I pray that out of his glorious riches he may strengthen you with power through his Spirit in your inner being, ¹⁷ so that Christ may dwell in your hearts through faith. And I pray that you, being rooted and established in love, ¹⁸ may have power, together with all the Lord's holy people, to grasp how wide and long and high and deep is the love of Christ, ¹⁹ and to know this love that surpasses knowledge—that you may be filled to the measure of all the fullness of God!" (Ephesians 3:16–19)

Help us to remember that You are greater than anything that the enemy tries to bring against us. "⁹ Therefore God exalted him to the highest place and gave him the name that is above every name, ¹⁰ that at the name of Jesus every knee should bow, in heaven and on earth and under the earth, ¹¹ and every tongue acknowledge that Jesus Christ is Lord, to the glory of God the Father." (Philippians 2:9–11) We have victory in Christ. "…No weapon forged against you will prevail!" (Isaiah 54:17)

When Jesus died on the cross for the forgiveness of our sins, along with His bruised, bloodied, and battered body, He nailed all of our fears, pain, illness, and physical and emotional affliction—anything negative we have suffered, are suffering, or will ever suffer—to the cross. Therefore, when we seek deliverance, we must not forget about addressing the sin of offense. A sin of offense is any offense that you have not let go of yet. We are to forgive everyone for the things they do to us; this, we have already established. However, when we hold on to that "thing," it becomes a sin of offense. In other words, perhaps you have been able to forgive someone with the help of God, but you have been holding on to offense against that person. This is still sinning. If so, I encourage you to deal with that today.

In your journal, make a list of anyone against whom you have been holding a sin of offense. Then, enter into prayer, confess the sin of offense including the person's name and the situation, asking the Lord to forgive you for holding on to this sin. Next, apply the resurrection (*dunamis*) power of Jesus to your soul, as well as the oil of Holy Spirit for healing and anointing. Then, let the offense go to the Lord; remember it no more. Ask the Lord to cover you, the other person, and the entire situation in the blood of Jesus. As you close in prayer, thank the Lord for the good work He has done in you.

———•——————•——————•———

God desires to come up against your enemies:

- "⁵ Your love, LORD, reaches to the heavens, your faithfulness to the skies. ⁶ Your righteousness is like the highest mountains, your justice like the great deep. You, LORD, preserve both people and animals. ⁷ How priceless is your unfailing love, O God! People take refuge in the shadow of your wings. ⁸ They feast on the abundance of your house; you give them drink from your river of delights. [9] For with you is the fountain of life; in your light we see light. [10] Continue your love to those who know you, your righteousness to the upright in heart. [11] May the foot of the proud not come against me, nor the hand of the wicked drive me away. [12] See how the evildoers lie fallen— thrown down, not able to rise!" (Psalm 36:5–12)

DEMONS AND THE OCCULT

Many believers and unbelievers alike are involved in the occult and afflicted by demon spirits. Please understand that there is a drastic difference between being possessed (something that is only possible for an *unbeliever*) and being negatively influenced by demons; it's the latter of the two that I'm referencing here. Most people do not know demonization is even going on. Moreover, some people do not even care. Others like the power that their demons give them. However, we must become aware. Many people in this world are in need of deliverance. Everyone, at some point in their life and for a variety of reasons, is in need of spiritual deliverance.

———•————————•————————•———

- "⁹ When you enter the land the LORD your God is giving you, do not learn to imitate the detestable ways of the nations there. ¹⁰ Let no one be found among you who sacrifices their son or daughter in the fire, who practices divination or sorcery, interprets omens, engages in witchcraft, ¹¹ or casts spells, or who is a medium or spiritist or who consults the dead. ¹² Anyone who does these things is detestable to the LORD; because of these same detestable practices the LORD your God will drive out those nations before you. ¹³ You must be blameless before the LORD your God." (Deuteronomy 18:9–13)

OCCULT ACTIVITY

Occult activity includes, but is not limited to, the following:

- astrology
- birth signs
- blood covenants (tattoos, pacts, etc.)
- crystals
- dowsing (water, oil, etc.)
- Eastern meditation (yoga, mantras, etc.)
- enchanting
- fortune-telling
- drugs (cocaine, heroin, marijuana, etc.)
- most non-Christian, heavy metal, and hard rock music
- horoscopes
- hypnosis
- incantations
- karma
- levitation
- lucky charms

- mediums

- mind control

- numerology

- ouija boards

- pagan rights

- palmistry (palm reading)

- psychic healing

- reincarnation

- seances

- sorcery

- spells

- star signs

- superstitions

- tarot cards

- tea-leaf reading

- UFO fixation

- witchcraft

- zodiac signs

————•———————————•————————————•————

This is certainly not an exhaustive list of occult activities, but it does give us a good grasp on the activities that are associated with the occult. If you are or have been involved in any of these occult activities, you are in need of spiritual deliverance. "I will destroy your witchcraft and you will no longer cast spells." (Micah 5:12)

————•———————————•————————————•————

DEMON SPIRITS

These are some examples of demon spirits (in no particular order):

- perversion
- lust
- strings on the heart (soul ties)
- rage
- witchcraft
- infirmity
- defeat
- sadness
- gossip

- anger

- panic

- confusion

- isolation

- anxiety

- perfectionism

- pride

- resentment

- bitterness

- poverty

- theft

- pain

- suffering

- destruction

- rejection

- deception

- control

- depression

- suicidal thoughts

- bodily pain

- fear

- hopelessness

- betrayal

Again, this is certainly not an exhaustive list of demon spirits, but it gives you a good idea. If you are experiencing any of these afflictions, you are in need of spiritual deliverance.

DELIVERANCE PRAYER—REPENT, RENOUNCE, BREAK, BLESSING

It is God's desire to set you free from all demonic strongholds, occult activity, and demonic spirits. If this is your desire, too, please pray the following prayer of deliverance. In preparation, go back to each of the lists in this chapter in order to determine what you should include in your prayer of deliverance.

Gracious Lord and Heavenly Father, You are the Creator of Life. It is my desire to walk in the Light of Christ. I come before You, now, to repent for my own personal sin in allowing the spirit of death, demonic strongholds (read your list above), occult activity (read your list above), and demonic spirits (read your list above) to have any place in my life or in me. I repent of any involvement my family had in any of these areas, too. I repent for any actions or choices I made that gave anyone other than You power over me. You are my God. I want nothing to do with any of these spirits, strongholds, or activity. I renounce all of their deceptive works. I, now, repent of and break all words, curses, oaths, vows, and agreements with these spirits, known or unknown, that I spoke or that were spoken over me, giving anyone other than You access or power in my life, Lord. I break all actions, agreements, covenants and blood covenants, sacrifices and blood sacrifices with these spirits, and I break every connection, influence, or tie in my family with these spirits. Lord Jesus, come to me now and fill me with Life—Your life-giving and abundant power and Presence. Be all things to me. I ask You to bring new life to my body, my soul (mind, will, emotions), and all of the relationships in my life. In the mighty name of Jesus Christ, I pray. Amen!

———•———————•———————•———

Rejoice, dear friends! If you have prayed this prayer, with a sincere heart, God has just delivered you from death and brought you into new Life. All glory to God. I am grateful to God for helping us to fight the enemy. Please allow Him to do a good work, in and through you. You will not regret it. "Thanks be to God, who delivers me through Jesus Christ our Lord!" (Romans 7:25)

———•———————•———————•———

January 6, 2012

The Lord is opening my eyes to many things going on around me. Everything continues to make complete sense to me. Wow! God is so amazing. I am so thankful as He continues to reveal more and more things to me about my healing journey.

February 5, 2012

I began a three-day spiritual retreat on Friday. I am seeking the Lord, spending time in His Word, praying, etc. It is a blessing to have these special times with God. Today, I have an acute awareness in my spirit, in that I am continually coming out of spiritual bondage! Praise God from whom all blessings flow.

Throughout my journey, the Lord granted deliverance to me on a few different occasions. Although that day of coming out of spiritual bondage did not arrive until I was 40 years old, I continued to seek the Lord and believe in Him. I was delivered from all obsessive thoughts and compulsive behaviors, depressive symptoms, and even a severe phobia of spiders (this was rooted in fear). Literally, every sickness, disease, infection, affliction, infirmity, illness, pain, virus, bad bacteria, germ, fever, and abnormality was removed from me by the Lord. I was healed on every level: physical, mental, emotional, spiritual, and social. When there is spiritual healing that takes place, God can (and will) bring spiritual deliverance, too.

———•———————⬤———————•———

Dear friends, healing is hard work, but I have done the hard work already. I completed an abundance of written and oral exercises as directed by my therapist, in private and on my own time. I actively participated in twelve therapy sessions in Catharine's office over the course of four months, sharing about my experiences and purging the negative memories, thoughts, emotions, and feelings. I advocated for myself and for my own healing when many others would not. I eventually found my voice and used it to find my own healing. The Lord has healed me completely. Yes, it was hard work, but I kept going; you can do it, too. Now, I can focus on my future and the plans God has for the remainder of my life on this earth.

It's important to remember that whole people are not carrying around bitterness, resentment, and anger. God releases us from all of that (see Luke 6:37). He goes to the root and releases the fruit. God does not cause bad things to happen to you, but He can and will use those things and turn them around for your good. "Instead of your shame you will receive a double portion, and instead of disgrace you will rejoice in your inheritance. And so you will inherit a double portion in your land, and everlasting joy will be yours." (Isaiah 61:7)

I still have some days or moments within a day that are difficult, when something may trigger an unpleasant memory, but those instances do not occur as much as they did before I sought help for myself, granted complete forgiveness, sought reconciliation in and through the Lord, and received a profound level of spiritual deliverance and healing. I now have the tools to overcome. I have a deep and unfailing faith that tells me of my healing in Christ Jesus. My chains are gone; I am free! I have received this deep level of healing because I make the choice to heal anew in Christ Jesus each day. Dear friends, you can make the same choice to forgive. Be reconciled to Jesus and walk in divine healing, and watch as your joy arises, too.

———— • —————————— • —————————— • ————

Questions for Reflection

1. What is my definition of forgiveness? What could my life look like if I was able to forgive completely (with the help of God)?

2. Who do I need to forgive (with the help of God)? What is holding me back (if anything) from walking

in forgiveness? Have I been holding onto offense against anyone? Was I aware that this is sin (which separates me from God)?

3. What are the negative tapes that play repeatedly in my mind? How can I find ways to remove and tape over those messages with positive, life-affirming messages?

4. Have I ever assessed the damage that sexual assault and child sexual abuse have done to me and brought into my life? Am I open to doing that now? What are the coping mechanisms that I have developed— negative and positive (remembering that some are both negative and positive)? What spiritual strongholds are present in my life?

5. Did I actively participate in the exercises in this chapter? Is there anything holding me back from seeking and receiving complete spiritual deliverance? If I engaged in and received spiritual deliverance, what did that look like for me? What is different in me and in my life now? If I feel that more (and a deeper level of) deliverance is needed, what is my plan to achieve that?

Come into the Light

Gracious Lord and Heavenly Father, I acknowledge that there are people I need(ed) to forgive. Thank You for showing me what that truly looks like and helping me to walk in that, each day. I need Your help—I can't do it alone. You are faithful to also forgive me, and I thank You for Your grace and mercy. As You have revealed to me all of the negative tapes that have been playing in my mind, I am thankful to You for removing them from me and replacing them with positive and life-affirming messages (and Your Word). Sexual assault and child sexual abuse caused a lot of damage in my life, but I am thankful to You for bringing healing into my life—the removal of spiritual strongholds and the receiving of spiritual deliverance. Continue to do a good work in me, Lord. I am so thankful. This, I pray, in Jesus's name. Amen.

Chapter 11

CELEBRATING AND NAVIGATING OUR "NEW NORMAL"

*"Whether you turn to the right or to the left, your ears
will hear a voice behind you, saying,
'This is the way; walk in it.'" (Isaiah 30:21)*

When my formal therapy had ended, I took the time to celebrate with one of my trusted care circle members. The overall thought was to allow the child in both of us to come out and play—I loved this idea. She and I went to McDonald's and ordered Happy Meals for lunch. We spent time at a local children's science museum, playing and having fun—the child in us truly did come out to play that day. We also went to see a movie. It was a wonderful way to celebrate such a significant milestone in my life and in my healing journey, something that needed to be acknowledged and truly embraced. She had taken this journey with me, as had a few others who were also part of my trusted care circle, and it was a blessing to share in the day with her. God had truly done a good work, in and through me, and it was imperative to my ongoing healing process to mark the occasion in a special and meaningful way. What will you do to celebrate the significant milestones in your healing journey? I encourage you to write down some ideas in your journal and begin making plans, when the time is right. As always, the Lord will guide you and direct your steps if you ask Him for His help. Just remember to make it memorable.

———·————————●————————·———

Just a few years ago, I was faced with the "unknowns" of sexual violence. A significant amount of healing had taken place, but something occurred that had threatened to unravel some of what had been accomplished. I'm going to go out on a limb here and say that I'm not alone in this. Now, it might look a bit different for each person, but for me, it looked like this: I suddenly had an overwhelming feeling that a doctor who had treated me back in the late 90s had possibly violated me sexually. I had come to this realization when many survivors were disclosing about sexual abuse occurring in the gymnastics world. I could not remember any details; it was just a feeling I had. I came to refer to these feelings and anything else like it as the "unknowns" of my healing journey. Vague memories that were incomplete. Feelings that won't go away. The feeling in the pit of your stomach that something just isn't right. How would I possibly handle and make sense out of all of this? I had received a significant amount of healing to that point; would or could this potentially be a setback from which I could not recover?

I did the only thing I knew how to do. I had to surrender to the Lord the things I knew and the things that I didn't know. You see, dear friends, there's something I know for sure: We can trust an uncertain past or future to a very certain God. He knows all things, and He's already gone ahead of us to prepare the way forward. Even when we can't see around the corner, God is already there. He knows the beginning from the end. He is our soft place to fall. When things don't make sense, we can find peace in knowing that He does. He makes a way where there seems to be no way. "He gives power to the weak and strength to the powerless. Even youths will become weak and tired, and young men will fall in exhaustion. But those who trust in the LORD will find new strength. They will soar high on wings like eagles. They will run and not grow weary. They will walk and not faint." (Isaiah 40:29–31 NLT) I *could* do this, and the Lord would help me. He will do the same for you.

As I continue to move forward on my healing journey, I glean a great deal of strength from a solid support system: the LORD God, my pastors and church family, the members of my trusted care circle, my Stephen Minister, some of my family members, and various trusted friends. I am so very encouraged by the counselees and mentees that we help through the ministry. I continue to focus on maintaining healthy boundaries for myself. And I practice an assortment of spiritual disciplines on a regular basis (remembering my daily "Self-care with God"). I am gentle with myself. I declare and decree spiritual proclamations from God's Word over my life, the ministry to which the Lord has called me, and over myself. "I lift up my eyes to the hills—where does my help come from? ² My help comes from the LORD, the Maker of heaven and earth." (Psalm 121:1–2)

We need to remember to surrender our life to God continually. Our daily prayers should include dying to self; a daily emptying of self; a new infilling of Holy Spirit, the fruit of the Spirit and the gifts of the Spirit; a deep desire for God's will to be done. In the Bible, Paul tells us that he "dies to self, daily" (see 1 Corinthians 15:31). We can also read in God's Word about dying to self, which means to put to death the "old man" and allow the "new man" (the new, renewed spirit within you) to rise up in us as a result of being born again in Christ Jesus (see Ephesians 4:22–24).

———————•———————•———————

- "³ Jesus replied, 'Very truly I tell you, no one can see the kingdom of God unless they are born again.' ⁴ 'How can someone be born when they are old?' Nicodemus asked. 'Surely, they cannot enter a second time into their mother's womb to be born!' ⁵ Jesus answered, 'Very truly I tell you, no one can enter the kingdom of God unless they are born of water and the Spirit.

⁶ Flesh gives birth to flesh, but the Spirit gives birth to spirit. ⁷ You should not be surprised at my saying, 'You must be born again.' ⁸ The wind blows wherever it pleases. You hear its sound, but you cannot tell where it comes from or where it is going. So it is with everyone born of the Spirit.'" (John 3:3–8)

———————•————————•————————•———————

Do not allow your faith to become lukewarm. God's Word tells us that He finds many of us are neither hot nor cold about our faith in Him, and He goes on to say that He will spit us out of His mouth (see Revelation 3:15–16). Do not allow this to happen, dear friends. Instead, proclaim that your sinful nature has been crucified in Christ (see Galatians 5:24). Then, exclaim the following for all to hear: "I have been crucified with Christ and I no longer live, but Christ lives in me. The life I now live in the body, I live by faith in the Son of God, who loved me and gave himself for me!" (Galatians 2:20)

God will get you to where He wants you to go. Surrender and submit to Him. When you do that—when you are hidden in Christ, and He guards your heart and mind in Christ Jesus—it will be more difficult for the enemy to reach you. I have found that it is more difficult to catch something that is in motion. Keep. Moving. Forward.

———•———————•————————•———

Create safe places for yourself. I created safe places for myself early on in life. As a child, those spaces were near the crick and at my grandmother's home. During the formal part of my healing journey as an adult, those spaces were my home, my church sanctuary, and my special place in a wooded area next to a creek in a public park. He leads me beside still water and restores my soul. Eventually, I was able to realign with my one, true safe place in the Secret Place of the Most High, with the Lord, finding my rest in Him and under His wing. *This was His deepest desire for me all along, dear friends.* He desires this for you, too.

———•———————•————————•———

- "Whoever dwells in the shelter of the Most High will rest in the shadow of the Almighty. [2] I will say of the LORD, 'He is my refuge and my fortress, my God, in whom I trust.'" (Psalm 91:1–2)

In my own healing process, in addition to reading my Bible and listening to praise and worship music, I have found the following activities to be some of the most valuable forms of treatment.

- Practicing various forms of art: jewelry making, drawing, and painting. All of these give me a creative outlet.

- Taking long walks in the park, in the woods, or in the country. I find that this is very calming to my soul.

- Journaling. This allowed me to put a voice to the pain and suffering related to the sexual assault and child sexual abuse in writing, which I then shared aloud with someone I could trust (my therapist, Catharine). Now, I have also stepped out in faith and shared them with the whole world in this book, in the hope that it will help others on their healing journey. I still journal on a daily basis.

Perspective is so important. And, as I have looked back over the past several years, I realize many key things. The memories and feelings related to each instance of sexual assault and child sexual abuse had haunted me. I could not manage to escape them. I was confused and filled with *false* shame, blame, guilt, and self-doubt. For many years, I lived in constant fear, suffering from complex and posttraumatic stress disorder as well as numerous other afflictions from which God completely healed me. Many different things triggered and exacerbated the deep-seated emotions and feelings I was experiencing. Over time, I became numb and completely gutted. I understand now that this was a time of condition and victimization. However, I eventually moved into a time of transition, going from victim to survivor. I learned that sexual violence had affected virtually every area of my life: relationships, educational endeavors, and business pursuits. Eventually, with the help of God, I was able to find the courage to seek help, further my education, and start a new career.

In September 2002, I completed Stephen Ministry and Stephen Ministry Leadership training and began serving in volunteer ministry, in a variety of ministries, in my (then) home church, and in the surrounding community in Kansas. Nine years later, I received therapy and counseling through a local sexual assault center. With the invaluable help of my therapist, Catharine, I purged and reconciled related memories and feelings, created and maintained healthy boundaries, and climbed out of the deep, dark hole I had been in for a majority of my life to that point. I established myself as an adult in the present dealing with the sexual assault and child sexual abuse of the past. In June 2012, I began serving in full-time ministry and missions. The following year, I completed Christian (Biblical) counselor training. Eventually, I found that I had entered into a time of position as an overcomer in Christ. In April 2017, the Lord led me to start a ministry, Hope for the Soul Ministries (H4tS). When we move from a place of "why me?" to a place of "who needs my story?" we can be used mightily by the Lord to help others.

For the past several years, it has been and continues to be my great blessing to be able to counsel with, minister to, and share the gospel and the hope of the Lord Jesus Christ with women and children who are lost, suffering, and affected by sexual assault, child sexual abuse, and human sex trafficking throughout a mission field in the United States and on the continent of Asia. I hope to share more about my ministry and missional journey in future books.

Through the work of the H4tS ministry, we disciple the disciple, meaning that we lead someone to Christ (if this is their choice) and, then, we teach them how to lead others to the Lord. Just as we have received Christ Jesus as Lord, we must continue to encourage others to live in Him (see Colossians 2:6). We help survivors seek justice in terms of what justice looks like for them, but we trust God to bring the justice ultimately. We speak for those who can't speak for themselves. We help others find their voice and encourage them to use it to find their own healing. We focus on trauma-informed and trauma-capable care, which are imperative to the overall success of enabling the survivor to move forward in their own healing process. We find that this predominantly encompasses the areas of sexual violence, domestic violence, and homelessness—one or more of these situations predisposes a person to the other, oftentimes.

Through our advocacy work, we seek to educate everyone on the atrocity of sexual violence. I believe we all need to have an active role in creating awareness. We can petition lawmakers to pass laws and form public policy that punishes the perpetrators, not the victims, and delivers swift and significant consequences. As a society, we all need to advocate for victims and survivors, giving them a voice until they can find and use their own and reminding them that they are not alone in their suffering. We need to send the message that we will not tolerate violence against women or children, sexual or otherwise, anywhere or anytime. One time is one time too many, and victims deserve to seek justice.

We need to focus on prevention. We need to teach our sons and daughters how to treat others with love and respect and not as a commodity or a means through which one achieves selfish gratification. We need to ensure that we are teaching children to use the correct names for private body parts (i.e., vagina and penis) so they are not confused by other made-up terminology. Doing so will likely make grooming children more difficult for perpetrators—knowledge is power. We need to advise children and adults that we do not keep secrets—this is where the devil hides out, in secrets. We also need to encourage families to actively engage with various service organizations in their community while children are at a young age so that there is less chance of a breach in their hedge of protection. Connecting with and participating in community events will help to foster the types of safe, caring relationships that aid in prevention. We need to love one another. We need to challenge the cultural norms, because when we find and address the source of false beliefs and ritualistic mindsets, we can achieve culture change and stop the insidious cycle of assault and abuse. Together, we can make a difference!

—————•—————•—————•—————

As a missionary of hope, I need you to know that you are not alone in your suffering, and you are not required to suffer in silence. Share. Learn. Forgive. Release. Heal. It takes time to heal, but I encourage you to stay focused on bringing healing and wholeness to the broken and captive places inside of you. The sexual assault and child sexual abuse you endured is not your fault. You did not do anything to cause it. You *were* a victim, but you *are* a survivor. Keep. Moving. Forward. Healing from sexual assault and child sexual abuse is difficult, but it is entirely possible. I am living proof. With the help of the Lord

Jesus Christ, I have learned to love, trust, and hope again; and I have reached a point of healing and wholeness, forgiveness and reconciliation, peace and contentment.

To put things into their proper perspective, I will point out that this book encompasses only a part of my healing journey—approximately seven months of journal entries, events, and personal milestones. However, the Lord accomplished a significant amount of healing during this time (and beyond). He helped me to become whole again, and He allowed joy to rise up in my heart. Some of the ways that He did this were to show me how to experience joy again—real joy, in Him. From the addition of incorporating more colors into my wardrobe, to engaging in fun, playful activity, such as stopping to play at a splash park or joining in on youth group activities throughout the mission field, to resuming various activities that had once been enjoyable and brought so much joy into my life, the Lord was showing me how to find joy in the morning. How refreshing! Yes, my heart had learned how to allow joy to arise, even in the midst of great suffering. I was and am truly living and loving life again.

———·———————●———————·———

What does YOUR "new normal" look like?

———·———————●———————·———

God can take us from *condition* (sexual assault and child sexual abuse) to *transition* (divine and spiritual, mental, physical, and emotional healing, in all forms) to *position* (living the life He has for us, helping others to find their way, and proclaiming the good works of Jesus through the preaching of The Good News— the Gospel of the Lord Jesus Christ). It is all good news. Dear friends, there is hope and there is healing, and His name is Jesus, "Let all that I am wait quietly before God, for my hope is in Him." (Psalm 62:5)

Moving forward, we need to see God as our One and only Source of all things. He is our Supplier and our Provision, our Healer and our Redeemer. As we are obedient to Him, He will bless us and give us what we need. Jesus Christ is our Firm Foundation, "for no one can lay a foundation other than the one already laid—Jesus!" (1 Corinthians 3:11) Remember: Your self-worth and your identity are not tied up in being a survivor.

Your real identity is who you are in Christ (see again, Chapter 9). When things become difficult—and they will—it's easy to gravitate towards what we know and what we have always done. But God's Word tells us that a fool repeating his folly is like a dog who goes back to his own vomit (see Proverbs 26:11; Peter 2:22). God is doing a new thing. Let's keep moving forward, with the Lord and in His strength. I welcome you to continue to walk into the new.

God knows the end from the beginning (see Isaiah 46:10), and He makes it known. He knows the plans He has for us—and they are amazing (see Jeremiah 29:11). "⁵Trust in the LORD with all your heart and lean not on your own understanding; ⁶in all your ways submit to him, and he will make your paths straight." (Proverbs 3:5–6). At the edge of the Red Sea, the Israelites did not know what to do. At various times in our journey toward healing from sexual assault and child sexual abuse, we may not know what to do either. Then God says, "Be still, and know that I am God; I will be exalted among the nations, I will be exalted in the earth." (Psalm 46:10) God made a way for the Israelites, a way where there seemed to be no way. God did what only He could do. He can and will do that for us, too.

At some point in my healing journey many years ago, I wrote a poem. It speaks to how I felt about a lot of aspects of my healing journey, and about my faith walk with the Lord. I'd like to share that with you now.

FINALLY, I HAVE ARRIVED

The radiant sun shines through the billowy clouds, Like the first light that wakes a darkened room. And as the soft rays gently permeate the vibrant sky, They speak to me, as if to say, "finally, I have arrived."

Breaking through the clouds is a genuine and renewing life experience That brings with it a just reward—one that offers strength and self-love. It brings about a manifestation that, in and of itself, makes the world a better place. A life begins anew—a godly and worldly woman is reborn.

The imperious shrouds of life as she knew it fall in scattered mounds all around her, And it only takes a second that, in all honesty, seems like an eternity To make her way through them to the illuminated pathway for which she has been prepared. For it is on this journey that she will take no superfluous belongings.

Growing ever stronger in her faith, she makes her way through life on a journey That can only reflect her purposeful steps and those of her gracious Lord. Looking toward the sky, she feels the warmth of the sun's rays on her face, Gently shining down on her soft, radiant skin as she begins to pray.

With closed eyes and an open heart, she allows the beautiful light to penetrate her soul. And from a special and sacred place, deep inside of her love-filled heart, She hears a familiar and angelic voice speaking to her, in all of its beauty and glory; And it says, "finally, I have arrived."

I hope this poem speaks to your heart, dear friends. If you have accepted Jesus as your Lord and Savior, He lives in your heart—you are saved. He has truly arrived! And He is walking with you on your journey, now and always.

God wants to make you into His treasure in an earthen vessel—broken, flowing through.

- "⁷ But we have this treasure in jars of clay to show that this all-surpassing power is from God and not from us. ⁸ We are hard pressed on every side, but not crushed; perplexed, but not in despair; ⁹ persecuted, but not abandoned; struck down, but not destroyed. ¹⁰ We always carry around in our body the death of Jesus, so that the life of Jesus may also be revealed in our body. ¹¹ For we who are alive are always being given over to death for Jesus's sake, so that his life may also be revealed in our mortal body. ¹² So then, death is at work in us, but life is at work in you." (2 Corinthians 4:7–12)

God wants to remake you from the inside out. He wants to take your shame and marry it to His beauty. He wants to take your darkness and envelop it with His light and life. He wants to take your doubt and give you hope. He wants to take your anxiety and give you peace. He wants to take your brokenness and give you healing and wholeness. Let His Spirit do a good work in and through you. He will. When we let go, we grow.

———•———

Not everything that happens to us is good. However, not everything that happens to us is necessarily God's will. We must believe that He will use evil for good. "And we know that in all things God works for the good of those who love him, who have been called according to his purpose. [29] For those God foreknew he also predestined to be conformed to the image of his Son, that he might be the firstborn among many brothers and sisters. [30] And those he predestined, he also called; those he called, he also justified; those he justified, he also glorified." (Romans 8:28–30) Say it with me: God works ALL THINGS together for good!

God's faithfulness is assured. He encourages us, in that our latter days will be more blessed than our former (see Job 42:12; Haggai 2:9). We must take heart, and press on,

———•———————————•———————————•———

- "¹² Not that I have already obtained all this, or have already arrived at my goal, but I press on to take hold of that for which Christ Jesus took hold of me. ¹³ Brothers and sisters, I do not consider myself yet to have taken hold of it. But one thing I do: Forgetting what is behind and straining toward what is ahead, ¹⁴ I press on toward the goal to win the prize for which God has called me heavenward in Christ Jesus." (Philippians 3:12–14)

———•———————————•———————————•———

- "¹⁴ Therefore, since we have a great high priest who has ascended into heaven, Jesus the Son of God, let us hold firmly to the faith we profess. ¹⁵ For we do not have a high priest who is unable to empathize with our weaknesses, but we have one who has been tempted in every way, just as we are—yet he did not sin. ¹⁶ Let us then approach God's throne of grace with confidence, so that we may receive mercy and find grace to help us in our time of need." (Hebrews 4:14–16)

- "Therefore, since we are surrounded by such a great cloud of witnesses, let us throw off everything that hinders and the sin that so easily entangles. And let us run with perseverance the race marked out for us, [2] fixing our eyes on Jesus, the pioneer and perfecter of faith. For the joy set before him he endured the cross, scorning its shame, and sat down at the right hand of the throne of God. [3] Consider him who endured such opposition from sinners, so that you will not grow weary and lose heart." (Hebrews 12:1–3)

On March 15, 2015, I received the following prophetic Word from the LORD. If you read it and it speaks to you, in your soul or in your spirit, it is for you, dear friends. Claim it.

———•——————————⬤——————————•———

"I have set you on a rock—on a high place—and I am watching over you, preparing you for what is to come. I have seen your struggles, and I have walked with you, in and through them. You have never been alone. My angels have kept watch over you. I have created you for a purpose. You belong to Me.

When the winds of change blow over you, My wind—the breath of Holy Spirit—also blows over you, guiding and directing your path. Yield to Me—this means to humble yourself before Me. Allow Me to set you on a new path, one that has been prepared for you. Do not become distracted by the voices around you that are not in alignment with Me—they don't know Me and My best for you. But listen to Me and the ones I have sent to walk with you, who will speak life and purpose into you. Get into my Word and allow IT to penetrate the deepest parts of your soul—your mind, your will, your emotions—because My Word is Truth, and IT is a lamp unto your feet and a light unto your path. I will never lead you astray.

I am sending you a new infilling of Holy Spirit and the fruit of the Spirit. Right now, as you read this prophetic word over you and your life, you are experiencing renewal from the inside out, from the depths of your being I am making you new. So, step out in faith, as you are lifted high upon the rock. Your latter days will be better than your former days—the best is yet to come! Keep your eye on Me. Walk in My ways. Hear my Voice. Heed my direction. I am taking you up, and I am taking you out of what you have walked in previously. Do not look back—I am taking you in a new direction. I will continue to go with you, to go before you, to follow behind you. Rise up. Go forth.

A new day, time, and call is upon you. Answer this call. Allow it to penetrate your heart and conscience. There is purpose in you. Let it come forth. Yes, let it come forth. Do not be afraid. Do not retreat. Stand firm in your real identity—who you are in Me. Know that I love you and I am for you. You can do all things through Me because I am your strength. Breathe in Holy Spirit. Breathe out anything that is not of Me. Stand firm. Rise up. Come into your new place, which I have prepared for you. Rise up!"

Say it with me, dear friends: The night is over, and morning is upon us. Our weeping may endure for a night, but our joy comes in the morning (see again, Psalm 30:5). Father

God is singing over us. We believe we are who He says we are, now and forever. This is our real identity in Christ. He restores our soul. We are children of the Living God. We are survivors. In and through Christ, we have overcome, by the blood of the Lamb and the word of our testimony (see Revelation 12:11).

If you know where I have been and you see where I am now, then you know what the power of God can do. Let go and let God. He will do a good work, in and through you, when you allow Him to do so. "Now to him who is able to do immeasurably more than all we ask or imagine, according to his power that is at work within us." (Ephesians 3:20) To God be the glory, for ever and ever. Amen!

Dear friends, what the LORD God had done for me, He can and will do for you. Believe!

CONNECTION

We invite you to join Chantel and Hope for the Soul Ministries on the Mission of Hope!

To learn more about the work of this ministry, or to contact Chantel for speaking, preaching, ministry, counseling, etc., please go to:

Email: hope4thesoulmin@att.net
Web Address: www.hope4thesoulmin.com
Facebook/Instagram/Twitter: @hope4thesoulmin

To support the work of this ministry, please send your financial love gifts to the following address:

Hope for the Soul Ministries
PO Box 83716
Lincoln, NE 68501

To give online:

www.paypal.me/hope4thesoulmin

"We have this hope as an anchor for the soul, firm and secure." (Hebrews 6:19)

AUTHOR BIO

Chantel D. Plautz is the Founder and President of Hope for the Soul Ministries (H4tS). She is an Abolitionist missionary, a Christian counselor and an advocate for victims of human sex trafficking, sexual assault, and child sexual abuse. She is a trained Stephen Minister and Stephen Ministry leader, a strategic-level intercessor, and an intercessory prayer warrior. She holds a certificate in Christian (Biblical) Counseling from Light University Online, a certificate in Victim Advocacy from Creighton University, and she is a trained Forensic Experiential Trauma Interviewer (FETI). She is also a member of American Association of Christian Counselors and Women Speakers Association. Chantel is a compassionate, dynamic, and inspiring survivor of multiple-instance rape, sexual assault, and child sexual abuse—she is an overcomer in Christ! Chantel serves on a mission field across the United States and throughout the continent of Asia. *My Joy Comes in the Morning* is Chantel's first book. It chronicles her healing journey from over 20 years of sexual violence and provides practical tools and resources to those taking a similar healing journey in their own lives. It also encourages those who may be in need of receiving the hope and healing that can only come from a saving relationship with the Lord Jesus Christ.

www.ingramcontent.com/pod-product-compliance
Lightning Source LLC
Chambersburg PA
CBHW070859030426
42336CB00014BA/2250